TO.
Chris.
Happy reading!
Len Foot
7th November 1997

FOOTSTEPS

THE LIFE STORY OF A DORSETSHIRE FOOT

By Leonard G Foot

Copyright.

© *Leonard G. Foot*

The right of Leonard G. Foot to be identified as Author of this Work has been asserted in accordance with the Copyright, Design and Patents Act 1988.

All rights reserved. No part of this publication may be reproduced, stored in a retrieval system, or transmitted in any form or by any means, electronic, mechanical, photocopying, recording or otherwise, without the prior permission in writing of the publisher.

Published by:

L G FOOT Esq.
15 Westborn Road
FAREHAM
Hants
PO16 7DH

First Published October 1997

ISBN 0 9530468 0 X

Printed and bound by:
Itchen Printers Limited, Southampton

PART ONE

THE HISTORY OF MY BRANCH OF THE FOOT FAMILY AND AN ACCOUNT OF MY CHILDHOOD IN THE COUNTIES OF DORSET AND WILTSHIRE

****

PART TWO

AN ACCOUNT OF MY LIFE IN THE ROYAL NAVY

****

PART THREE

RETIREMENT AND REFLECTIONS

****

BY
LEONARD G FOOT

ACKNOWLEDGEMENTS

I am greatly indebted to the following, without whose assistance and co-operation I would have not been able to put this work together.

My own dear wife, Audrey and my children Linda and David who have reminded me of details of events which we have shared over the past forty or so years.

My sisters Phyllis and Doris who have helped me to recall memories of my parents and childhood events.

Ann Foot, widow of Peter Foot my first cousin, who has enthusiastically provided me with many anecdotes of my uncles' and aunts' lives and most importantly, put me in touch with my second cousin Samuel Foote in Aurora.

Richard Bruce Foot, my first cousin, once removed, who has provided me with details of my Uncle Bruce and his family, thereby enabling me to confirm connectivity of the family relationships.

Samuel D. Foote, my second cousin in Aurora, Ontario, Canada, who sent me much detail of the 'Canadian Connections' and steered me towards solving many unknowns in my grandparents' and great grandparents' lives. He was also most kind to host me at a gathering of the Canadian Footes during my visit in May 1997.

My second cousin Mrs Mary Bertram, (nee Bennett), who has confirmed details of my grandparents of which I had been unclear and in addition provided me with much background on both the Foot and Bennett families.

Everett Edward Peters Cain of Ontario, a second cousin, for supplying me with the result of research he had done into the Foot/Foote family history in 1986.

Grace Foote-Powell deceased, late of Stouffeville, Ontario, a second cousin who did much work on the family history and who started a family scrap book in 1962 of which her brother Samuel is now the custodian.

My first cousin Pamela Spark (nee Foot) who helped me to get a clearer picture of my grandparents and of my Uncle Bruce and his family.

The Dorset County Records Office Staff who have been most helpful in assisting me to research my Family Tree.

My good friend and ex colleague Commander Les Orchard Royal Navy (Rtd) who gave me considerable assistance with the proof reading of my drafts. (Just as he did with my Staff Papers when he was my boss many years ago).

CONTENTS

Title Page	i
Reverse of Title Page	ii
Contents of Parts	iii
Acknowledgements	iv
Contents	vi
Contents of Part One Chapters	vii
Contents of Part Two Chapters	viii
Contents of Part Three Chapters	xii
Index of Photographs	xiii
Foreword	xviii
APPENDIX 1	385

A Summary of Important Dates
"Through Ten Generations"

APPENDIX 2	396

Countries I have visited during my Naval Career

CONTENTS OF PART ONE

THE HISTORY OF MY BRANCH OF THE FOOT FAMILY AND AN ACCOUNT OF MY CHILDHOOD IN THE COUNTIES OF DORSET AND WILTSHIRE

CHAPTER 1	Introduction	1
	The Foot Family Tree	3
CHAPTER 2	My Parental Family History Paternal Antecedents	15
CHAPTER 3	My Parental Family History Maternal Antecedents	54
CHAPTER 4	The Bennett Connections	67
CHAPTER 5	The Canadian Connections	87
CHAPTER 6	My Childhood Years (Ages 5 to 7)	126
CHAPTER 7	My Childhood Years (Ages 7 to 12)	136
CHAPTER 8	My Childhood Years (Ages 12 to 16)	149
CHAPTER 9	The Closing Years of my Parents Lives. (1946 to 1979)	164

CONTENTS OF PART TWO

AN ACCOUNT OF MY LIFE IN THE ROYAL NAVY

CHAPTER 10	The Early Years. HMS GANGES (1946 to 1947)	181
CHAPTER 11	My First Ships HMS DUKE OF YORK, HMS CADIZ and HMS SCORPION (1947 to 1952)	193
CHAPTER 12	Ceylon West Wireless Receiving Station. HMS HIGHFLYER (1952 to 1954)	213
CHAPTER 13	Back to Sea HMS BOXER, HMS GLASGOW (1954 to 1956)	223
CHAPTER 14	New Entry Instructing HMS MERCURY (1956 to 1957)	229

CHAPTER 15	South Africa (Slangkop W/T) HMS AFRIKANDER (1957 to 1960)	232
CHAPTER 16	Finding a Home Back to Sea HMS WAKEFUL Wireless Instructor's and Officers' Promotion Courses HMS MERCURY (1960 to 1962)	243
CHAPTER 17	My First Ship as a Commissioned Officer HMS NUBIAN (1962 to 1964)	250
CHAPTER 18	Ashore and Instructing HMS MERCURY (1964 to 1967)	263
CHAPTER 19	Back to Sea HMS ARGONAUT (1967 to 1969)	267
CHAPTER 20	Singapore HMS FORTH (1969 to 1971)	276

CHAPTER 21	My Introduction to Royal Naval Research and Development. The User Requirements and Trials Section HMS MERCURY (1971 to 1973)	287
CHAPTER 22	On the Staff of the Commander-in-Chief Fleet and NATO HQ at Northwood HMS WARRIOR (1973 to 1974)	295
CHAPTER 23	Bermuda HMS MALABAR (1974 to 1976)	305
CHAPTER 24	Managing a Communications Training Department. HMS MERCURY (1976 to 1978)	323
CHAPTER 25	Back to the User Requirements and Trials Section HMS MERCURY (1978 to 1981)	328

CHAPTER 26　Much more of the same　　335
　　　　　　　but as a Retired Officer
　　　　　　　HMS MERCURY
　　　　　　　(1981 to 1995)

CONTENTS OF PART THREE

RETIREMENT AND REFLECTIONS

CHAPTER 27	Retirement At Home (1995 to Now)	361
CHAPTER 28	Reflections. The Effect of my Background on my Character and Actions Through Life.	371
CHAPTER 29	Conclusion	383

APPENDIX 1 — 385

A List of Important Dates

"Through Ten Generations"

APPENDIX 2 — 396

Countries I have Visited during my Naval Career.

INDEX OF PHOTOGRAPHS

Description	Page
My great grandfather John Bennett with my uncles, Garnet (age 9) and Bruce (age 6) and my Aunt Ciss (age 4). (c. 1889).	31
My grandfather George Leonard Foot (c. 1900)	36
Pallington Farm House at Clyffe, near Tincleton, Dorset. (Built in 1782).	39
My Uncle Wallace with two farm hands at Tincleton.- (c. 1912)	40
My mother and father, George Arthur Foot and Alice Foot (nee Thorne) (wedding day photo 1921)	43
John Garnet A. Foot (my Uncle Garnet) (1880 - 1951)	47
Grand uncle Walter James Foote; on his third visit to England in 1925 at the age of 80, with my first cousin (once removed), Reginald Bennett and his daughter, Mary (my second cousin).	49
My mother in my father's first and only car. (c. 1927)	52

My maternal grandfather and grandmother, Joseph and Emily Thorne - c. 1919   55

My grandmother, Emily Thorne, my mother Alice Foot, sisters Phyllis and Doris, me and cousin Joan Thorne. - 1931   58

Uncle George and Aunt Dora Thorne   60

My sisters Phyllis and Doris and me at East Luccombe Farm (c. 1933)   66

My father with Mary Bennett - 1922   86

The standard barn which the pioneers built, or had built, in the 1830s and 1840s to accommodate the fodder above and the cattle and other livestock below. (To keep them warm in winter). This one still stands on my great grandfather's farm.   107

My great grandparents Samuel and Elizabeth Foot (c. 1860s)   113

Tombstone of Samuel and Elizabeth Foote, my great grandparents, in Newmarket cemetery, Ontario.   121

My sister, Doris, cousin Jack (Thorne) ,Darling the mare, my father (hiding), my sister, Phyllis and me (just!) - 1935   130

East Luccombe Farm House. The walnut tree is still there in 1997.   135

The 1st Downton Scout Troop - 1944   158

My mother, Alice Foot, my Aunt Dora (Thorne) and my father   170
George A. Foot in Trafalgar Square - 1953

My mother Alice Foot, daughter Linda, wife, Audrey and father   171
George Arthur Foot - 1964

My mother Alice Foot with her grandson David 1966   174

My father -George Arthur Foot after losing his leg in 1967   175

Audrey, Mother, David and Linda - 1966   176

Son David, my mother, son in law, Martyn and daughter, Linda   179
and my wife Audrey in 1978

Boy 1st Class Leonard Foot at HMS GANGES 1946   185

HMS DUKE OF YORK - 1946   194

HMS CADIZ - 1949   197

The author as a *Jolly Jack* - 1947   198

My then fiancé, Audrey Oaten and me - 1950   209

Our Wedding day 2nd August 1951	211
HM Troopship EMPIRE WINDRUSH - 1952	215
HMS GLASGOW - Leaving Portsmouth harbour - 1955	227
HMS GLASGOW Communications Staff - 1956	228
Petty Officer Telegraphist L G Foot - HMS MERCURY 1957	232
UCMS ARUNDEL CASTLE - 1957	235
Sub Lieutenant L.G. Foot - HMS NUBIAN 1963	255
HMS NUBIAN at Cochin, India - 1963	259
HMS ARK ROYAL at 2 cables from HMS NUBIAN - Indian Ocean - 1963	260
Lieutenant L. G. Foot - HMS ARGONAUT - 1968	270
HMS FORTH - Singapore 1970 - showing Audrey, Linda and David on the walkway.	281
HMS FORTH - 'Mothering' her submarines - Singapore 1970	282

Leading my small band on Remberance Day - Hamilton Bermuda - 1975	312
URTS Staff HMS MERCURY 1979	329
URTS Staff HMS MERCURY - 1981	337
Our Ruby Wedding Anniversary - 1991	340
Audrey and me - 1991	341
CRTPS Staff HMS MERCURY 1994	344
Samuel David Foote meeting and greeting his second cousin Leonard George Foot in Aurora on 10th May 1997	364
The Foot/Foote/Cain family gathering of cousins in Aurora, Ontario in May 1997.	365
My son, David George Foot standing at the entrance to the barn similar to that on his great, great grandfather's farm. (This was at one of his great granduncles' farms). Note the wood on the supports and ladder was not machine turned but shaped with an adze.	367

FOREWORD

FOOTSTEPS is a most descriptive and interesting account of the family history of one branch of the Dorsetshire Foot family. It is followed by an account of the author's parent's lives and of his own childhood until 1946.

The author then goes on to describe events and incidents of his working life in the Royal Navy, of his promotions through the ranks to Lieutenant Commander and then on to his retirement. He concludes with a self analysis of his own character by reflecting on how his ancestors, family background and naval career may have helped to formulate his own character and opinions.

FOOTSTEPS will be of special interest to members and descendants of the Foot/Foote and Bennett families, both in Dorset and in Ontario, Canada, and also to those interested in the Dorsetshire countryside and the events in the farming communities of both Dorset and Ontario over the last two hundred years.

Additionally it contains much interesting information on life in the Royal Navy from 1946 through to 1995. There will be many hundreds, perhaps thousands, of naval officers and ratings who will recognise and identify with the events, places and situations described.

FOOTSTEPS will form a useful addition to those describing life in this century and will be a valuable record for succeeding generations.

CHAPTER ONE

INTRODUCTION

"No distance breaks the tie of blood; brothers are brothers evermore"

John Keble (1792 - 1866) English churchman and poet

During my working life I have always had in my mind that when I retired and had time to do so, I would set down, as accurately and truthfully as I could, all the information I could gather about myself and my family. The original aim was not necessarily to publish, but to attempt to bring to my mind all the influences which have shaped my own character and perhaps those of my family, and leave a record for my descendants.

This time has now come. I retired at the age of 65 on 23rd April 1995 after 49 years continuous service in the Royal Navy. It is now February 1996. The weather is cold and wet and, although I have considerable outside interests, I am bored today. I will therefore start this account. Perhaps it will never be completed, but I believe it will keep me occupied for some time to come.

The first thing I had to do was to establish the family genealogical chart, or as I prefer to call it, my Family Tree. This I started in May 1996 and within a few weeks I was hooked. I visited churches, inspected parish registers,

County Libraries and Records Offices and in a very short space of time I discovered many cousins and second cousins who I did not know I had.

The greatest surprise was the discovery that a major part of the family were Canadians. At no time did my father or mother ever mention the Canadian connections. I assume that my father must have known that his father was born in Canada and that his parents had lived there and that his eldest brother Garnet was born there, but he never mentioned it. Whether my mother knew I do not know but I very much doubt it or she would have told us.

As it will be seen, the Foot family is inextricably linked to the Bennett family through the successive generations of cousins marrying cousins, I have therefore included a brief chapter on the Bennett genealogy to help in clarifying these relationships.

After these many months of checking and re-checking facts I feel that I have become to know and understand my ancestors. To me they were brave and good people. They brought up large families in what we would today consider to be a most harsh and primitive environment. They bravely emigrated to the New World, most would appear to have been successful and their descendants, are now valued citizens in Canada.

THE FOOT FAMILY TREE - DORSETSHIRE (MAPPOWDER DISTRICT) BRANCH

William = Elizabeth
b. circa 1680   b. circa 1680
│
├── William = Ann b. circa 1720
│   b. Fifehead Neville 29 Oct 1713   d. 1786 or 1787 aged 66
│   buried 23 Nov 1788 age 74 At Mappowder   buried at Mappowder 1786
│
Children:

- **Mary** 13 Aug 1745
- **John** 17 Mar 1747
  - m. Repentence 1768
  - buried at Mappowder 22 Jun 1829 age 82
- **George** 1 Aug 1751
  - m. Sarah Caines 29 Jan 1778 (sic) (Buckland Newton)
- **Thomas** Nov 1755
  - m. Sarah Biles 5 Oct 1775 (Milbourne St Andrew)
- **James** 17 Nov 1756
- **Robert** 6 Feb 1759
  - m. Christiana Caines 21 Apr 1783 (Buckland Newton)
- **Ann** 26 Nov 1760
- **William** 12 Jan 1766

Children of John & Repentence:

- **Betty** b. 27 Nov 1769 buried 10 Apr 1833 at Mappowder age 64
- **John** 27 May 1770
- **William** b. 1771
- **Mary** 14 Jan 1774
  - m. Susannah Mullet 22 Mar 1790
  - b. 26 Jul 1817
- **Ann** 17 Nov 1774
- **Samuel** 4 Sep 1775
  - m. Sarah Ann Foot 16 May 1799 →
- **James** 3 Aug 1777 d. 22 Oct 1835 age 59
- **Richard** 26 Nov 1778
- **Repentence** 12 Oct 1780
  - m. Sarah Dampney of Haydon 30 Jun 1801 (sic)
- **Repentence** 2 Jul 1782

William b. 7 Dec 1742
m. Mary Stickland 1762 at Mappowder
d. 1776
→

James b. 1776 at Mappowder
m. Rebecca Shephard 7 Jun 1797 Stoke Wake
→ → → →

3

THE FOOT FAMILY TREE - DORSETSHIRE (MAPPOWDER DISTRICT) BRANCH
(Continued)

(cont) → James & Rebecca Foot (of Stoke Wake)

Ann	James	William	Horatio	Edward	Walter
b.1779	b.1800	b. 1803	b. 1807	b. 1809	b. 1810
		d. 18 May			d. 1895
		1866 (age 63)			m. Jane
		at Mappowder			Taylor

(cont) → George & Sarah Foot (cont)

Sarah Ann	Richard	George	Betty	Mary	James
b. 6 Aug 1778	b. 29 Dec 1779	b. 13 Aug 1781	b. 26 Dec 1783	b. 17 Jun 1785	b. 3 Dec 1786
m. Samuel Foot 16 May 1799	d. 1859 (in Canada)	d.27 May 1860 at Mappowder age 78	→		m. Susannah Chaldicot 22 May 1809

Eliza	Annabel	Samuel	Abraham
29 Mar 1801	4 Sept 1804	13 Jan 1803	b. 5 Jun 1807
Mappowder	Mappowder	Mappowder →	Mappowder or Hazelbury Briant
			(Was Abraham the son of Sam and Sarah or baseborn of Betty ?)

Samuel Foot, son of John-and Repentence, married his cousin Sarah Ann Foot, daughter of George and Sarah Foot. Richard, Walter, Samuel and Abraham Foot (brothers and cousins), all emigrated to Canada together with some Bennett cousins and other friends in the early 1830s. Betty Foot married Cave Bennett in 1801 - see Bennett Family Tree.

THE FOOT FAMILY TREE (Continued)

Samuel Foot = Elizabeth Bennett
b. 6 Nov 1803 at Stoke Wake   b. 2 Jun or Jul 1812 at Hilton Dorset
m. 9 Apr 1839 in Toronto Canada
d. 6 Feb 1879   d. 9 Feb 1884

ALL CHILDREN BORN IN ONTARIO, CANADA

William Benjamin	Edward	George Leonard	Cave Nelson	Walter James	Samuel Herbert	Georgina Sarah	Mary Jane	Rebecca Elizabeth	Septimus Albert
b. 5 Jan 1840	b. 24 Mar 1841	b. 5 Jul 1843	b. 23 Feb 1845	b. 22 Aug 1846	b. 25 Nov 1854	b. 17 Nov 1851	b. 17 Nov 1851	b. 11 Nov 1848	b.22 Sep 1857
d. 27 Sep 1929	d. 22 Nov 1884	d. 1 Jun 1902	d. 9 Mar 1902	d. 2 Oct 1928	d. 2 Oct 1937	d. 15 Aug 1902	d. 23 Jun 1878	d. 21 Oct 1907	d. 23 Jun 1878
m. Eleanor Cook	m. Margaret Weir		m. Annie Jane McKewon Shillinglaw	m. Grace	m. Margaret Lee	m. Joshua Hilborn	m. James Bingham	m. William Cain	
b. 1845	b. 1844		b. 1837	b. 2 Mar 1844	b. 1855				
d. 1909	d. 1923	⇒	d. 1916	d. 12 Nov 1920	d. 1928				

(George Leonard came to England in the mid 1870s. Married Emily Bennett, his cousin, 26 Jun 1877. Returned to Ontario. Returned to England about 1882. Took over the tenancy of Pallington Farm in 1884.   Emily (or Emma) was born in 1847 and died 28 May 1930).

Sarah Ann Cordelia (Cissie)	Garnet	Leonard Bruce	George Arthur	=	Alice Thorne	Richard Wallace
b. 5 Jan 1885 bapt. at Affpuddle	b. 1880 in Ontario Canada	b. 17 Feb 1883 at Affpuddle	b. 4 Sept 1887 at Affpuddle		b. 27 Jul 1892 bapt. 3 May 1889 at Cheselbourne	at Affpuddle
		m. Lillian Hobbs			m. Alice Thorne 23 Jan 1921	m. Mabel Eady in 1930
d. 27 Mar 1972	d. c. 1949 in Devon	d. 1952	d. 13 Jan 1969		d. 26 Jan 1979	d.1952
→		→			→	No children

5

THE FOOT FAMILY TREE (Continued)

Sarah Ann Cordelia (Ciss) — **Leonard Bruce & Lillian Hobbs** — **George Arthur & Alice Thorne**

Peter
b.

James
b. 1 May 1921 at Liverpool
m. Ann — m. Marguerite
d. Jan 1990

Children of James:
- **George Brian** m. Sue, bapt. 1 Oct 1911 at Affpuddle but born at Witchampton
- **Iris** b. 1913
- **Nora** b. 1919
- **Kathleen** b. 1916
- **Pamela** b. 1930

Richard Bruce
b. 3 Jun 1936

| Jacqueline | Susanne Janet | Michael b. 6 Mar 1952 |

David

| Gillian b. 23 Nov 46 No children | Mary b. 6 Oct 48 m. Peter Marchant |

- Peter b. 1968
- Sally b. 1969

Peter
b. 8 Mar 1950 at Jarrow

Richard John
b. 4 Apr 1953

| Ginette | Carol | Robert Mark b. 20 Jan 1981 |

Phyllis Margaret
b. 14 Sep 1923
m. Robert William Giblett at Cheselbourne

Alice
b. 27 May 1926

Doris
m. Frederick Wearn
No children
at Cheselbourne

Leonard George
b. 23 Apr 1930 at Farnham

m. 2 Aug 1951
Gladys Audrey Oaten

| Linda b. 3 May 55 at Templecombe m. 15 Oct 1977 Martyn Edwin Abery | David George b. 4 Oct 65 at Portsmouth |

Ruth b. 31 Mar 52 m. Brian Fowler

| Michael b. 1981 | Benjamin b. 1984 |

Charlotte Louise b. 8 Jan 1983

6

OTHER DORSETSHIRE FOOTS

During my researches I took notes of many details of other Foot and some Bennett records, some of which I have not been able to connect directly to my own family tree. These may or may not be closely linked to my branch of the family.

Elizabeth Sarah Foot Bennett   d. 17 Jun 1900 age 65 at Mappowder.
Annie Bennett Barwell   d. 24 Feb 1891 age 60 at Mappowder
Mary Repentence (wife of James Chaldicott) d. July 28 1878 at Mappowder
William Gillingham   d. 22 May 1908 aged 58 at Hazelbury Bryan.
Robert Gillingham   d. 1866 at Hazelbury Bryan.

OTHER MAPPOWDER BURIALS:

Year	Name	Date	Age
1813	James Foot	17 Dec	72
1815	John Foot	6 Jul	2
1817	William Foot	26 Jul	46
1829	John Foot	29 Jun	82
1829	Henry Foot	14 Mar	73

Year	Name	Date	Age	Notes
1833	Betty Foot	10 April	64	(May have been the unmarried daughter of John and Repentence)
1833	Charles Foot	14 April	32	
1834	Mary Foot	19 Oct	42	
1835	Eliza Foot	21 Apr	22	
1835	Sarah Ann Foot	21 Apr	10 months	
1835	James Foot	22 Oct	59	(son of John and Repentence)
1838	Isaac Foot	15 Apr	25	
1842	Simon Foot	9 Sept	19	
1844	Louisa Foot	9 Jan	11 weeks	
1846	Elizabeth Foot	30 Jul	90	
1848	Sarah Foot	13 May	72	
1853	George Foot	9 Sept	50	
1858	Sarah Ann Foot	25 Jul	14	
1862	Elizabeth Foot	29 Jan	69	
1866	William Foot	18 May	63	
1867	Jane Foot	31 Jan	37	
1868	Barbara Foot	6 Jan	76	
1875	Samuel Foot	19 Jan	68	

1882 Sarah Bennett	20 Oct	73 (The Register states "From Pallington". This was my great grandmother).
1890 Elizabeth Foot	5 Feb	82
1892 Jacob Foot	22 Jan	76
1899 George Samuel	5 May	64
1900 Elizabeth Sarah Foot Bennett	20 Jun	65 (As generations of my branch of the family married Bennett cousins this would have been a maternal great grandmother or grandaunt, or both!)
1922 Sarah Foot	30 May	69

Burials at Hazelbury Bryan

1881 3 Jan	Julius Foot	age 68
1982 14 May	Arthur Herbert Foot	age 76
1818 17 Dec	Anne (daughter of Cave and Elizabeth Bennett)	
1994 26 Aug	Lily May Foot	age 88
1821 21 Jul	William (son of Cave and Elizabeth Bennett)	
1824 21 Feb	Jane (daughter of Cave and Elizabeth Bennett)	
1982 15 Mar	Caroline Emma (daughter of Leonard Foot)	
1827 25 Mar	Cave Thomas (son of Cave and Elizabeth Bennett)	

Marriages at Mappowder

1844 Arabelle Foot
(daughter of
of Sam Foot),
(a dealer)
m. John Brown

THE FOLLOWING BURIALS TOOK PLACE AT THORNFORD, DORSET

(I do not know of any connectivity between these and the Mappowder Foots)

Mary Ann Foot	5 Nov	1928	age 67
Charles Foot	8 Aug	1920	age 60
George Foot	8 Sept	1961	age 62
William George Foot	29 Nov	1895	age 19
Alice Matilda Foot	25 Nov	1887	age 10 weeks
James Foot	11 Dec	1885	age 76
Eliza Foot (wife of James)	12 Aug	1885	age 65
Henry James Foot	23 Apr	1883	age 13 months
George Leonard Foot	d. ?? b.1844 at Yeovil		

BAPTISMS AT ST JOHNS CHURCH TINCLETON:

Francis Rebecca Foote
daughter of George and Marion Foote
26 May 1844

NOTES AND OTHER RELEVANT INFORMATION

George Leonard Foot came to England from Canada married Emily, daughter of his uncle, John and his wife, Sarah Bennett of Pallington Farm on 26 June 1877. He then returned to Ontario with his wife, had a son in 1880 (Garnet). They returned to England in 1882 when Emily's mother was ill. He then took over the tenancy of Pallington Farm at Clyffe near Tincleton in 1884. The farm had been tenanted by John Bennett since 1868.

TOMBSTONE AT TINCLETON
(St.Johns Church)

George Leonard Foot
b. 1843
d. 1 Jun 1902

TOMBSTONE AT YARLINGTON (SOMERSET)
(St. Mary the Virgin)

George Arthur Foot
b. 4 Sept 1887
d. 13 Jan 1969

Alice Foot
b. 27 Jul 1892
d. 26 Jan 1979

1881 AND 1891 CENSUS RECORDS

1881 CENSUS

The 1881 Census shows the following living at Pallington Farm:
John Bennett, Farmer, age 71.   Sarah Bennett, wife, age 71.   Annie, daughter, age 38.
Ada, granddaughter, age 13.   Gussie, granddaughter, age 11.
(Therefore George Leonard Foot and his wife Emily with their son Garnet must have returned from Canada after this census).

1891 CENSUS

The 1891 Census shows the following living at Pallington Farm:
George Leonard Foot, Farmer, b. Ontario, age 46.   Emily Foot, b Dorset, age 43.
Garnet, son, age 11.   Bruce, son, age 8.   Sarah, daughter age 6.
George Arthur, son age 3.   Willie (Wallace) son age 2.

Emily Bennett was the daughter of John and Sarah Bennett and who, married George Leonard Foot on 26 June 1877, went to Canada, had their first son, Garnet, in Ontario in 1880 and then came back to England in 1882 and took the tenancy of Pallington Farm on the death of Emily's parents. Sarah Bennett who was my great grandmother, was buried at Mappowder 20 October 1882. John Bennett, Elizabeth's brother as well as my great grandfather, died at Mappowder 17 Aug 1890.

TOMBSTONES AT THE CHURCH OF THE HOLY ROOD AT BUCKLAND NEWTON.

Eliza Agnes Foot   d. 9 Mar 1889   age 35 (wife of John G Foot)
John Caines Foot   d. 22 Jun 1906 age 72
Alice D Foot   d. 14 Feb 1955
Fannie Agnes,   d. 18 April 1907 (wife of H A D? Foot)
William Pearse Foot   d. 27 Feb 1907
Henry D. Foot   d. 21 Jan 1886
Henry Thomas Foot   d. 20 Mar 1875
William Foot   d. age 76
Jane Foot   d. 30 April 1801
Tabetha Biles   d.3 January 1891
Thomas Caines   d. age 66 July 1789
Priscilla Caines   d.16 Feb 1811
Mary Ruth   d.15 August 1912 (wife of John Churchill)

Plaque in the Church:
Henry Dunning Foot   d.30 May 1918 age 81 (Church Warden)
Edwin Henry Foot (5th Dorset's)   d. at Gallipoli 9 Aug 1915 age 20

TOMBSTONES IN THORNHILL, ONTARIO, CANADA

In memory of Abraham Foot
died 20 Jan 1887 age 80 years
Native of Dorsetshire England
Catherine Hooper, wife of the above
died 31 Dec 1857 age 53 years.
Native of Hazelbury Briant,
Dorsetshire England

In memory of Richard Foot
died 3 Feb 1859 age 80 years
Native of Dorsetshire England

CHAPTER TWO

MY PARENTAL FAMILY HISTORY

"The accent of one's birthplace lingers in the mind as well as in the heart as it does in one's speech"

Francois, Duc de la Rochefoucauld (1613 - 1680) French writer 'Maxims'

PATERNAL ANTECEDENTS

Until I started to research my family tree in the summer of 1996, the facts I had been able to ascertain were as follows:

My paternal grandfather George Leonard Foot was born 5th July 1843 and died 1st June 1902 at the age of 58, (I believe of pneumonia), when my father was only 14 years of age. He farmed at Pallington Farm, Clyffe, Tincleton, near Dorchester, Dorset and there is a record of him taking on the tenancy of the farm in 1884, when he would have been 41 years old. He had married his cousin Emily Bennett sometime in the late 1870s or early 1880s. He won a silver cup in 1895 given by the Winfrith Farmers Club presented by James Carter & Co., The Queen's Seedsmen for the best acreage of *Carters Prize Swedes*. I know this because I have this engraved trophy today and will one day pass it on to my son. I am also told that he rode on horseback and frequently went to the local Inns where he imbibed freely. The faithful horse would then take him home.

My paternal grandmother Emily or Emma (nee Bennett) was born in 1847 and died 28th May 1930, aged 83, one month after I was born. She was George Leonard Foot's cousin and came from another and well known Dorset farming family, the Bennetts'. She was of a strong character, a trait perhaps forced on her by the early death of her husband and the necessity to run the farm and bring up four unruly, and it would appear, quarrelsome, boys and one daughter.

A large tombstone in remembrance of both of my paternal grandparents still exists in the churchyard of St John the Evangelist at Tincleton.

The above details of my grandparents were the sum of my knowledge until the summer of 1996, when after visiting the Dorset County Records office in Dorchester and examining various parish records and census returns I began to gather together a comprehensive family tree.

With the assistance of a new found cousin, Mary Bertram (nee Bennett), Ann Foot the widow of my first cousin Peter, Richard Foot son of my first cousin Brian Foot and of a second cousin Samuel D Foote in Ontario Canada, and also with the results of research done by another second cousin Everett Edward Cain of Ontario, I have now pieced together a more accurate record of my family history dating back to about 1680. (See Family Tree). The big surprise to me was that my grandfather was born in Canada and therefore I suppose I can claim Canadian descent! Had I known this years ago I may have been tempted to ask for a naval posting to Canada and perhaps even consider claiming Canadian citizenship. Sam Foote tells me that they have a very generous state pension plan in Canada!

There are records of Foots in the Mappowder area in various documents dating back to the thirteenth, fourteenth, fifteenth and sixteenth centuries, some of them yeoman farmers, but I cannot connect them directly to my own proven ancestors so I will start at a point where I am certain there is a direct line of ancestry.

A difficulty I am sure that many researchers in family histories have is that birth dates and christening dates are often many months apart, in some cases years. Also when a child died in infancy it was not uncommon for the next child to be given the same name. To make things even more complicated, sometimes the second name given to a child is the surname of the mother. For example the Christian names of *Bennett Foot* and *Foot Bennett* sometimes occurs.

My great, great, great, great, great grandfather William Foot was born about 1680 and married Elizabeth who was probably born about that time. I know nothing else about them other that they were the parents of William who was to become my great, great, great, great grandfather and whom I regard as the patriarch of this branch of the Foot/Foote family.

My great, great, great, great grandfather William Foot was born 29th October 1713 in the village of Fifehead Neville in Dorset. He married Ann, maiden name unknown, in 1740 or 1741. Ann was born about 1720, and probably came from one of the surrounding parishes. The two settled in Mappowder where they raised a large family of nine or maybe ten children. William was a yeoman farmer which meant he owned his own land and may well have farmed at or very near to, Thirnwood (now called Thurnwood) farm at Mappowder.

William was also the Churchwarden of St. Peter and St. Paul Church in Mappowder. The first child of William and Ann Foot was a son, also named William, born December 7th 1742. This son married Mary Stickland at Mappowder in 1762 and had a son named James in 1776 in the same year that William died. The son James married Rebecca Shepherd on 7th June 1797. They then had one daughter, Ann, and five sons, James, William, Horatio, Edward and Walter. Edward and Walter emigrated to Canada. Walter who was born in 1810 married Jane Taylor in 1814, emigrated with his cousin Samuel in the 1830s and they were to become neighbours and life long friends. More of Walter in the Canadian Connection Chapter. Of the other sons it is believed that two emigrated to Australia in the early 1800s but I have not yet had time to pursue this sub branch of the family.

William and Ann's second child was a daughter Mary, christened on August 13th 1745. Their third and fourth children were John and George. John who was to become my great, great, great grandfather, was born in 1747 and was to marry a lady named Repentence in 1768. He also became Churchwarden of St. Peter and St. Paul Church in Mappowder. George was also to become my great, great, great grandfather not once but twice as he married Sarah Caines at Buckland Newton in 1778, had a daughter named Elizabeth (or Betty or Betsy) who married Cave Bennett and then became the parents of my great grandmother Elizabeth Bennett. Also George and Sarah's other daughter Sarah Ann Foot married her first cousin Samuel Foot, who was my great great grandfather, on 16th May 1799.

Thomas was their fifth child and fourth son. He was baptised in November 1755. On October 15th 1775 he married Sarah Biles from the parish of Milbourne St. Andrew, only a few miles south of Mappowder. Their sixth child was James, christened on November 17th 1756. I do not know who James married but he had a son John, who was still only a child when his father died. William Foot Sr. stated in his will - *"to sons John, George, Thomas and Robert, provision to be made for grandson John, son of my late son, James.."*. (See below). William and Ann's seventh child was Robert who was baptised on February 6th 1759. Robert married Christiana (or Caristian?) Caines of neighbouring Buckland Newton on April 21st 1783. It would appear that Christiana Caines and Sarah Cains who married my great, great, great grandfather George Foot, were sisters as both came from Buckland Newton and their marriages to the two brothers were only five years apart. The differences in name spelling meant nothing in those times.

Here is a copy of Robert Foot's Will which reflects thinking and relationships of that time:

This is the last will and testament of Robert Foot of Beaulywood in the Parish of Buckland Newton in the County of Dorset.
First I give and bequeath to my daughter Ann Foot of Glanvilles Wootton in the County of Dorset, the sum of sixty pounds of good and lawful money of Great Britain to be paid within one year next after my decease, also I give to my said daughter Ann, a chest of drawers now standing in the room in which my son William usually sleeps, with my best coloured quilt.
For my daughter Mary Foot now living with me, I give and bequeath the sum of One Hundred and Forty

pounds of like good and lawful money of Great Britain to be likewise paid within one year of my decease. Also I give to my said daughter Mary, my bed in the room I now usually sleep in with all the bedding, bed clothes and furniture belonging to the same, also a chest of drawers, dressing table, night stool, three chairs, a large chest, a sewing shape ?, also one other feather bed in the room my son William usually sleeps.

For my son John Foot of Glanvilles Wootton in the County of Dorset, I give and bequeath the sum of sixty pounds of like good and lawful money of Great Britain to be paid within one year of my decease.

For my son James Foot now living with me, I give the sum of One Hundred and Forty pounds to be vested in the lands of my executor, here-in-after named, the interest of which my said executor is to withhold so long as he shall keep and provide for him the said James Foot.

Also I give to my said son James Foot a feather bed, bedstead and furniture, quilt sheets and blankets thereto belonging and my will further is that in case my son James who is now ill should die, that then my said surviving children shalt divide the said sum of one hundred and forty pounds so bequeathed, between them, share and share alike.

And also I give and bequeath to my son William Foot, also now living with me, the sum of one hundred and forty pounds of like good and lawful money of Great Britain to be paid within one year of my decease.

All the rest, residing and the remainder of my money, stock, household goods and chattels of every description or denomination whatsoever, after the payment of the legacies herein before bequeathed, I give and bequeath unto my said son William Foot whom I make and appoint my sole executor to this my last will and testament.

In witness whereof I have this twenty ninth day of January, One Thousand Eight Hundred and Twenty Five put my hand and seal in the presence of:

Robert Young **Robert Foot**
Thos. Cains

William and Ann's eighth child, and second daughter, was Ann, christened on November 26th 1761 and their last child, another William, was christened on January 12th 1766 .It seems strange to name another son William when the first one was still alive. Perhaps this is how he was registered in the parish register but was then called by his second name.

In the book *"Shell Guide to Dorset"* it states that Mappowder's Church of St. Peter and St. Paul is *"brilliantly lighted by the well restored fifteenth century windows which are all clear glass and has the air of waiting for a large and lively congregation....* The cottage by the entrance to the churchyard was the home of the novelist, "T. F. Powys". In the gallery of the church, between the large oval piece of the wooden rails was the following:

"William Foot died 23rd November 1788 age 74
Anne Foot died 1787 age 66

The parish records state that Ann died on December 7th 1787. During the 1800s Mappowder Church was restored and partly rebuild, and the gallery with the plaques of William and Ann Foot have all been removed. There are several stones in the churchyard for William and Ann's children and presumably William and Ann lie there too. These two were the Patriarch and Matriarch of this very large branch of our Foot family.

I found a manuscript copy of William Foot's Last Will and Testament at the Dorchester County Records Office. It was written in June 1786. The following is the most I could make out of the faded and indistinct writing:

In the name of God Amen. I William Foot of Mappowder in the county of Dorset .... being of sound mind and sound memory and .... my last will and testament in .... and form .....
following is to say First I .. give unto ....Michael Miller ? and Robert Foot of this Parish in the county of
Dorset....Gentleman and Scholar of .... Robert Foot.......John Foot. My grandson John Foot the son of my late son. James Foot the sum of two hundred pounds allowing for him being age of twenty one years. After all my .... debt legacy and funeral expenses are...... and paid. I give and bequeath unto my sons John, George, Thomas and Robert to equally be divided c..... ...... share and I .... by nominate and appoint my said sons John, George, Thomas and Robert joint.... Esq.... of this my last will and testament.
Hereby and hereunto set my hand and seal the eleventh day of June in the year of our Lord one thousand seven hundred and eighty eight.

William Foot

One day I will try again to decipher this will which is in the Dorset County Records office in Microfiche pack No. MIC/R/224. There are a considerable number of additional words where the blanks are shown.

My great, great, great grandfather John Foot was christened on St. Patrick's Day 1747, and like so many of his relations before and after, the locale for that christening was the little church of St. Peter and St. Paul in Mappowder. In Britain at that time George II was on the throne, the Young Pretender, Bonnie Prince Charlie had just finished waging his losing battle for George's crown at Culloden Moor in Scotland. John was the third son of William and Ann Foot who already had a son, William, and a daughter, Mary, Their ages were five and two at the time of John's birth. During the next nineteen years his parents presented him with five more brothers and one, probably two, sisters making a total of ten children.

John married Repentence in 1768 when he was twenty one years old. Their first child Betty, was christened March 27th 1769. Their second child and first son John was baptised on May 27th 1770, then William was next on November 26th 1771. Three years elapsed before their second daughter, Mary was christened on January 4th 1774. Just eleven months later, on November 17th 1774 their third daughter Ann joined the family circle. Just a year later my great, great grandfather Samuel's arrival was recorded in the baptisms record at the Church of St. Peter and St Paul as September 4th 1775.

Two more sons, James and Richard, were christened on August 3rd 1777 and November 26th 1778 respectively. On October 12th 1880, John and Repentence had their latest daughter baptised. She was named Repentence after her mother. However it seems that she must have died in infancy because less than two years later on July 2nd 1782 their last child, another daughter, was also christened Repentence.

There was a monument in Mappowder Church on the south aisle in the gallery *"To the memory of John Foot, Churchwarden 1796"*, but it was removed during restorations and not replaced. I assume that John took over the position from his father William when he died.

My great, great grandfather Samuel Foot was born to John and Repentance and baptised September 4th 1775. He was one of ten children as stated above and he grew up with many aunts, uncles and cousins who all lived in the Mappowder area. It was not surprising therefore, that when Samuel was twenty four years old he married his first cousin, Sarah Anne Foot, the daughter of his Uncle George. They were married on May 16th 1799 in Mappowder's little church. Samuel and Sarah had four children. The eldest was a daughter named Eliza, christened on March 29th 1801, and the next was my great grandfather Samuel, Jr. born on November 6th 1803 in Stoke Wake. Their third child was Annabelle, just one year younger than Samuel and christened on September 4th 1804 in Mappowder. Their fourth child was another son, Abraham, and he was christened on June 5th 1807. About thirty years later, if my great, great grandfather was still alive at the age of sixty, he would have seen his two sons, Samuel and Abraham, take leave of their home and loved ones and set sail for a new life in Canada. I have looked carefully for any record of Samuel Sr.'s burial details but can find none. He is probably buried at Mappowder or nearby Kingston where he lived in his later years, but many of the stones are now unreadable due to the ravages of time. I do know that both he and his wife were alive and well in 1836 as one of the Bennett letters in a later chapter refers to him and his wife 'returning from Guernsey and living in Kingston'.

My great great grandmother, Sarah Anne Foot was christened on August 6th 1778 in Mappowder. Her parents were George Foot (son of William Sr.) and Sarah Cains. Sarah was their first child. She was just over a year old when her parents presented her with a baby brother, Richard. (Many years later, probably in 1835, this brother emigrated to Canada at the age of 58. This was a good age to be starting a new life as a pioneer in the New World but he appears to have been successful and reached the age of eighty years, he lies buried in the Old Holy Trinity Anglican Churchyard in Thornhill, Ontario).

Two years elapsed before Sarah Anne's second brother George arrived. Her first sister was Betty, who was born in 1783 when Sarah Anne was just five years old. She was followed in two years time by another sister, Mary. Her youngest brother was Thomas, and his birth in 1786 completed the family. As with her husband Samuel, I cannot find any trace of Sarah Anne's death but she is most likely to be buried at Mappowder with her husband.

My great grandfather Samuel Foot was born to Samuel and Sarah Anne Foot November 6th 1803 at Stoke Wake in Dorset. He is regarded as the Patriarch of the Canadian branch of the Foot/Foote family and I have therefore included a full description of his life in a later chapter on 'Canadian Connections'.

Similarly **my great grandmother, Elizabeth Bennett**, who was born at Hilton, Dorset Jul 2nd 1812, and was the daughter of Cave (pronounced *Keeve*) Bennett and Elizabeth (Betty) Foot and who married Samuel in Ontario in 1839, is also fully described in that chapter.

Samuel, together with several cousins and friends, of both the Foot and Bennett families, emigrated to Canada about, or shortly after, 1830. The nearest I can get to this date is that Susannah Hooper, who was married to George Bennett, who was one of the cousins who emigrated, died in Ontario in 1833.

This was about the time of much agricultural unrest in England due to the rich landowners ganging together to increase the rents to their tenant farmers and also to reduce the agricultural labourers' wages. The Tolpuddle Martyrs were prosecuted and deported to Australia in 1834 for daring to attempt to resist these oppressive measures.

Perhaps this was the reason they left England. Canada was seen as a land *"free of the convention and prejudices of English country life"*. It is interesting to note that the Tolpuddle Martyrs George Loveless, John Standfield and James Brine who had been deported to Australia in 1834 and who returned to England after being pardoned in 1836, also emigrated to Canada. George Loveless lived at Fanshawe, London, Ontario and is buried at Siloam, London, Ontario. John Standfield had a store at Bryanston, London, Ontario and James Brine lived at Clinton, Ontario.

An interesting historical fact about Mappowder which will be of particular interest to the Canadian branch of the family is that King John, (1199 - 1216), declared Mappowder and surrounding villages as part of the Royal Forest and an important royal lodge was built at Mappowder. He banned hunting by the local inhabitants and even ordered that all dogs claws should be removed to prevent them chasing the game, which at that time comprised deer, bear, wolves and boar. At this time the name of the parish was MAPELDRE which was a Middle English form of the Anglo Saxon MAPULDOR or MAPLE TREE. Under the influence of the French language the 'L' was lost and the word came to be spelt MAPOUDRE in 1303 and MAPOWDRE in 1447. I do not know if this has any significance to the maple leaf emblem of Canada, nor of the significance of the maple tree in the Mappowder area. Could it be that the Foot family introduced the maple leaf emblem to Canada? (Just my wishful thinking!).

Whatever their motives in emigrating, one can but admire them all for their courage in leaving their Dorsetshire villages of Mappowder, Hazelbury Bryan, Stoke Wake, Hilton and neighbouring hamlets and taking what must have been a tortuous journey in a sailing ship to Canada and then moving inland via the Great Lakes to the province of Ontario. Then I assume they got in their wagons and moved inland, with or without the consent of the indigenous Indians, and settled on homesteads allocated to settlers by the Government. Their first task, after building a house and barns for the animals, and an equally onerous one, must have been to clear the forests to make farmland as I am told the whole area was then heavily forested. Our families were, of course, but few among the 800,000 immigrants from Britain who went to Canada between 1815 and 1850.

The following article published in *The Times* in 1854 gives this first hand account of just what it was like to take passage in an emigrant ship.

"The immigrant is shown a berth, a shelf of coarse pinewood in a noisesome dungeon, airless and lightless, in which several hundred persons of both sexes and all ages are stowed away on shelves stacked two feet apart. Each shelf is three feet wide and six feet long. Each immigrant believes that the

shelf is his own and only finds when the anchor is up that he must share his space with a bedfellow.

He finds that cleanliness is impossible, among hundreds of men, women and children, dressing and undressing, washing, quarrelling, fighting, cooking and drinking, one often hears the groans and screams of a fellow passenger in the last agonies of the plague (cholera). The passage took six weeks"

I wonder who supplied the food. Did they take their own?. How did they cook it in those conditions?

We are indeed the descendants of 'survivors'.

These good people, my great grandparents, then had ten children of whom my grandfather, George Leonard Foot was one.

I have not had time to research the emigration of my ancestors to South Africa and Australia but this extract from emigration papers dated 25th October 1849 gives an insight to the happenings of that time:

Buckland Newton Emigration Papers.
From Plymouth.
*Sums to be paid to emigrants when they leave the depot to join the "**ANGLIA**".*
Mary Foot £14 - 1 - 0d.
Chest marked Mary Foot contains:
1 Woollen gown, 1 cotton gown, 1 Flannel petticoat, 1 cotton petticoat, 1 shawl, 1 bonnet, 1 brush, 1 comb.

For Amelia Foot; 2 pair shoes 1 woollen gown, 1 cotton gown, 1 flannel petticoat, 1 bonnet, 1 shawl.

Aggregate expenses for outfits for emigrants August 1849:
Mary Foot   age 14   £2 - 7 - 6d.
Jane Foot   age 12   £1 - 16 - 7d.
Amelia Foot   age 9 £1 - 11 - 3d.
This money to be paid to..??? Buckland Newton in Dorsetshire on their landing in Sydney in cash ....

The above is a starting point should I ever try to trace the "Australian Connection"!

My grandfather George Leonard Foot was born on 5th July 1843 near the Township of Whitchurch, Ontario. Whereas all the other children of Samuel and Elizabeth apparently stayed, lived, wed and died in Canada, my grandfather did what was not uncommon for an adventurous young man to do in those days. Sometime in the mid 1870s he came to England on a cattle boat, probably working his passage. The conditions on this vessel were probably much worse that on the emigrant ships. There is a story of the filth and stench and of how they had a problem with a cow stuck head first down a hatch with the hind quarters firmly wedged and of the cursing and beating of the poor animal.

On arrival in England I believe he went to stay with his mother Elizabeth's brother, his Uncle John and his wife Sarah at Pallington Farm at Tincleton. John Bennett had moved from Mappowder and taken the tenancy of Pallington farm in 1868. Whilst there, George Leonard fell in love with and married their daughter, his cousin, Emily (sometimes called Emma), Bennett. This marriage took place at Affpuddle on 26th June 1877. I had much difficulty in finding the date of this marriage and only found it in July 1997, just before going to print. It is recorded in the marriages register which is held by the rector of the

Affpuddle parish who is now based at and lives at Bere Regis.

Once married, George Leonard took his new wife back to Ontario with him, probably later in 1877. He stayed at the farmstead home of his parents in Whitchurch parish, some thirty miles north of Toronto. His father Samuel died in 1879, I do not know whether he arrived back home in time to see him, but assume he did. In 1880 their first son, John Garnet A Foot was born. I do not know what the 'A' stands for but it could have been Arthur. Although his first Christian name was John, he was forever after called Garnet to which I will refer to him from now on.

From stories told me by my Canadian cousins, Emily did not like it in Ontario. She hated the long cold winters, she was homesick and to make matters worse, her mother Sarah was seriously ill home at Pallington. I am told that she had many letters from her mother imploring her to return home. She was remembered as to be always crying and wiping her eyes. George Leonard, his wife Emily and son Garnet therefore packed up and returned to England.

Emily's mother died in 1882, I do not know whether she got home in time to see her. I hope so. She was buried at Mappowder on 20th October 1882. Emily then stayed at Pallington farm to look after her father John Bennett and had a second son, Leonard Bruce in 1883. In 1884 my grandfather, George Leonard, assumed the tenancy of Pallington farm and in 1885 their only daughter Sarah Ann Cordelia, or Cissy as she was to be called, was born. In 1887 my father George Arthur was born and in 1889 another son, Richard Wallace (hereafter called Wallace) was born. John Bennett died in 1890.

My great grandfather, John Bennett with my uncles, Garnet (age 9), Bruce (age 6) and my Aunt Ciss (age 4). Photograph taken about 1889. John Bennett died in 1890.

It is interesting for me to surmise that had Emily acted as firmly as her aunt Elizabeth had done in 1836, she would have stayed in Canada with her husband and my father would then have been born there and I suppose I would also have been a third generation Canadian.

My grandfather, George Leonard Foot died on 1st June 1902 at the age of fifty eight, I believe of pneumonia but am not certain, it could have been of a stroke like his brother Cave Nelson of whom he was much alike, and who died only a few months before him. My father was then only 14 years old.

My paternal grandmother Emily or Emma (nee Bennett) was born in 1847 and died 28th May 1930, aged 83, one month after I was born. She was George Leonard Foot's cousin and came from another and well known Dorset farming family, the Bennetts, as will be seen in the chapter on the Foot/Bennett Connections. In her later years she appeared to be of a strong character, a trait perhaps forced on her by the early death of her husband and the necessity to run the farm and bring up four unruly, and it would appear, quarrelsome, boys and one daughter. She was remembered by her daughter-in-laws, Mabel, wife of Wallace, and Lillian, wife of Bruce, as a *'sweet and kindly lady and a very fine woman'*. The strange thing is that I cannot recall my own mother, who was also her daughter-in-law, ever saying much about her.

A large tombstone in remembrance of both of my paternal grandparents still exists in the churchyard of St John the Evangelist at Tincleton.

The marriage of George Leonard and Emily made four successive generations of my own branch of the Foot family marrying first cousins:

Samuel Foot and Sarah Foot in 1779
Sarah Foot and John Bennett about 1830
Samuel Foot and Elizabeth Bennett in 1839
George Leonard Foot and Emily Bennett in 1877.
(There are even more instances of Foots marrying Bennett cousins as will be seen in later chapters.)

My grandmother's elder sister Elizabeth who was born in 1835, left this will which is also of interest:

Will of Elizabeth Sarah Foot Bennett (spinster) of Sea Hurst Dorchester

Brother Richard Cave Bennett and brother in law Leonard Foot executors.

To brother Richard Cave Bennett; pictures and green velvet easy chair, old oak chest, wool mattress and feather bolster.

Sister Mary Jane Burch wife of Arthur Burch; china stand, oak sideboard, feather bed.

Sister Emily Foot wife of George Leonard Foot; dinner service, pictures, 8 day clock, feather bed, large deal base with cushion cover.

Nephew Cuthbert Harry Vivian ? Scott in South Africa: bedstead, feather mattress and bolster, marble clock, mahogany dressing table and washstand also £100.

(I wonder if these items ever got to him?)

All the rest of my household furniture to niece Aphelia Bessie Alberta Bennett and £100.

Also all my freehold cottages and land at Buckland Newton, let to Mr Salpen, 2 fields and land at Brockhampton, Buckland Newton.

For each of the children of my sister Mary Jane Burch and Emily Foot and brother Richard Cave Bennett £100.

£100 each to my nieces Ada Bennett and Gussie Bennett, children of my brother John Bennett residing in America.

Signed 30th May 1900   Probate granted July 26th 1900.

Once again I have a starting point if I decide to pursue research into the "South African Connection"!

My father, George Arthur Foot was born on 4th September 1887. He was one of a family of four sons and one daughter born to George Leonard Foot and Emily Foot (nee Bennett). They lived at Pallington Farm at Tincleton near to Dorchester in the county of Dorset. My father would never speak of his family, for reasons which never become clear to me, other than that he did not communicate freely with anyone and therefore, until recently, I had been unable to discover very much about them or of his early years. Why, oh why, do we not pay more attention to our parental details when they are alive as I am sure that if I had, I could have obtained a much clearer picture of their way of life and the early influences on my father and mother.

My father, as did all the boys, left school at the age of 14 and went to work on the farm. From notes left by my granduncle Walter James Foote who came over from Canada and visited Pallington in the spring of 1902, it appears that my father and his brother Wallace were then away at boarding school at that time. I take this to mean that they probably boarded at Dorchester or Wareham during the week near the site of the senior school as without transport it was not possible to commute daily from Pallington farm at Tincleton which was very much out in the country.

After the death of her husband I believe that it was grandmother Emily who ran the farm and was the power in the family. I am told that she was very strict and correct, a regular churchgoer and instilled in the children the need to obey the Sabbath. Only essential farm work was done on Sundays. She ran a clean tidy home, had nice things and took afternoon tea with friends. None of the boys was called up during the Great War of 1914 - 1918 as farming was a reserved occupation. All therefore survived the war which was unusual for most families during that dreadful time.

The daughter, Sarah Ann Cordelia or Aunt Ciss, as we knew her, went into service as a companion or children's nurse (nanny), I am not quite sure which, and during the Great War become a Red Cross nurse working in Liverpool. She had 2 children (boys) out of wedlock by a man with whom she lived and who had promised to marry her, but who I understand was already married and also that he mistreated her. Her sister-in-law Lillian who was her brother Bruce's wife visited her in Liverpool and took her home to Pallington Farm. When her ex partner came after her, her brother Wallace threatened him with a shotgun and sent him packing.

Aunt Ciss looked after her mother at Pallington Farm until she died and then her brother Wallace, with money left by her mother, helped to place her in a thatched cottage at Highcliffe, and she brought up the boys on her own. I recall

*My grandfather, George Leonard Foot
(1843 - 1902)*

visiting her at Highcliffe together with my mother and sister Doris on one occasion, when I was about five years old. My father would never speak about her but my mother was fond of her and tried to keep in touch. I recall that her sons used to come to stay with us on the farm during their summer holidays when we lived at Chapel Farm and also at East Luccumbe Farm.

Aunt Ciss died in 1972. I met one of her sons, my first cousin Peter, very briefly, in 1948, soon after I had joined my first ship in the Royal Navy. It was in a ship at Portsmouth in which he was serving at that time as a Leading Electrical Mechanic, we spoke for only a few minutes. I have since heard from Peter's wife Ann that he died in January 1990.

Their son, also called Peter Foot, and who is my first cousin once removed, now lives in the same house, which still has a thatched roof and is a most delightful cottage with a large garden. I have now visited Ann Foot and the cottage, to gain more information of this side of my family. She has given me much interesting information which I have included in this narrative. The other son Jim or James is still alive and I visited him and met his wife Marguerite when I visited Ann, the widow of Peter in July 1996.

Of my father's brothers, the youngest was Wallace, (I note from the 1891 Census return that he was called 'Willie' when he was 2 years old), he remained at the home farm (Pallington) and ran it with his wife Mabel after his mother died in 1930. The mother, Emily or Emma, helped to place the oldest son, Bruce, who married a Lillian Hobbs, in a farm at Witchampton where they were living when they had their first son George Brian in 1911. At some later time, probably in 1922, they moved to a farm, I believe it was Egbury Farm, at St. Mary Bourne near Andover, where he prospered, had more family and later moved to a farm at Sherborne St. John near Basingstoke. I understand that during the depression he was enabled to take on the tenancy of much extra land at a very cheap rent of about £1 an acre, *'just to keep the weeds down'* and that this land then remained in his tenancy. I believe Uncle Bruce died in 1952. I never met him and I do not think he ever visited us after the late 1920s or early 1930s and I assume this was because my father and he had quarrelled, or at least did not get on. I recall my mother once saying that Bruce was annoyed with my father for his stubbornness in not listening to good advice from others. This not only included advice from his brothers Bruce and Wallace but also from his cousin Reginald Bennett. This also probably applied to his relations with his oldest brother Garnet.

A story told to me by Richard Bruce Foot, Bruce's grandson, and my first cousin once removed, is that in the 1930s Uncle Bruce used to go out in his car late at night and shoot rabbits out of the car window, hang them on the fences or bushes and then send his farm foreman round in the mornings to collect them.

Bruce's youngest daughter, Pamela, now lives near Honiton and she remembers her father as a very quiet man who never communicated readily to anyone (just like my own father) and that he was always very placid and very kind, polite and correct with his employees and that he never lost his temper (not at all like my own father!). Bruce had a son, George Brian, who was born in 1911 and who would have been my first cousin, he is now dead and his son Richard now runs the farms. I understand that cousin Brian didn't like farming and originally joined the Palestine Police Force, but after a four year tour he came home and

*Pallington Farm House at Clyffe, near Tincleton Dorset.
Built in 1782 - (Photograph taken June 1997)*

(centre)
*Richard Wallace Foot (Uncle Wallace)
with two farm hands at Pallington Farm Tincleton.
(c.1912)*

his father gave him 100 acres of his land on which he ran a poultry farm. He eventually took over the rest of the farm from his father when he died in 1952. I made my first contact with Richard Bruce Foot in December 1996 and he has given me these snippets of information and has promised to give me more details in due course.

I recall we used to receive a Christmas card and a tin of toffees from Uncle Bruce and Aunt Lillian every Christmas. This was during the 1930s.

At that time many arable farms were so plagued by rabbits that they lost up to half their crops. The introduction of myxymatosis in the late 1940s and early 1950s was a life saver to many struggling farmers.

Uncle Wallace remained at Pallington farm until he retired in 1954, the farm was then sold. I am told by Ann Foot that Wallace offered to turn over the farm to his nephew Peter Foot in the early 1950s in order to keep it in the family. Peter and his wife were not keen to live in the country and farm so the farm was sold to a neighbouring farmer. I could speculate that had my father remained friends with and kept in touch with his brother Wallace, perhaps he would have offered it to me as I was then in my early twenties. This would have very considerably changed my life and that of my parents.

This extract from the *Western Gazette* in 1954 is of interest:

£10,000 for Dorset Farm

Messrs. Rumsey & Rumsey, of Bournemouth, offered at auction at Dorchester, Pallington Farm, Clyffe, which has been in the same ownership - that of the Frampton family - since the days of the Reformation, and has been tenanted by the same family for nearly a century. It has become vacant owing to the retirement of Mr. R. W Foot, who had succeeded his father and grandfather. The farm embraces 212 acres and has a period farmhouse built in 1782, four cottages and well arranged farm buildings. The property was sold at £10,150 to Mr. E. R. Chilcott of Clyffe Farm, adjoining.

Initially I had a problem with the above extract as I knew that my Uncle Wallace's paternal grandfather had been born in Canada. I then realised that the above referred to his maternal grandfather who would have been a Bennett. Everything then fell into place as I discovered that Pallington farm had been tenanted by my great grandfather, John Bennett from 1868 until 1884 when George Leonard (my grandfather) took on the farm. The present (1996) owner of Pallington farm is a Brigadier Michael Webb who has about 20 acres of the original farm which he runs as a small holding. I have visited him and the house in which my grandfather and great grandfather lived and where my father and uncles, except Uncle Garnet, and aunt were born.

*George Arthur Foot and Alice Foot (nee Thorne) on their
wedding day 23 January 1921
(My mother and father)*

It was Squire Frampton, the owner of Pallington Farm and many other farms in the area, who employed the Tolpuddle Martyrs and as a magistrate he had a hand in sentencing and deporting them in 1834.

I am told by my sisters Phyllis and Doris that I was taken to Pallington when I was about 2 or 3 years old but I cannot remember. They can both just remember visiting in the late 1920s and early 1930s. A second cousin, with whom I have made contact and who was then named Mary Bennett, recalls visiting the farm in the late 1920s to see her 'Granny Foot' and tells of how she as a little girl hated these visits, and that she didn't like the bead curtains in the kitchen and that she was afraid of Aunt Ciss. (As a little girl she thought Aunt Ciss was a witch!).

Mary also tells me that as she was an only daughter from such an old and well established farming family, she was brought up by her father, Reginald Bennett, to take over his farm. She was sent to agricultural college and worked in the Dairying industry for a while but she married in 1947 and went to live in South Africa, where she lived for many years before returning home to Dorchester where she now paints portraits of people, pets and landscapes on commission.

My father, George, was placed in a farm, North Field Farm, at Cheselbourne near Dorchester in 1921 and lived there on his own for some months. He married my mother, a local girl, Alice, on 23rd January 1922, I suspect because he needed someone to look after him. This farm was of about 120 acres and was mixed dairy on the chalky Dorset downland. My father did not make a success of this farm for reasons I am not wholly sure but one of the reasons for his moving in 1926 was lack of mains water for the cattle. Additionally, very few farmers were making money in those days of low prices for their produce and before mechanisation enabled them to work the hilly landscapes and chalky soil. In 1926 he went into partnership with his eldest brother Garnet, and took the lease of a 450 acre farm, called Chapel Farm at Farnham near Sixpenny Handley. This partnership lasted only a few years, or maybe even less, maybe only months, when the brothers quarrelled and Garnet pulled out of the partnership and went to farm in Canada.

Garnet never married and farmed in Canada, somewhere in Manitoba and also, I believe, in Sasketchewan Province, until he sold up and retired in the late 1940s and returned to England where he lived either in the St. Austell area of Cornwall or near Newton Abbot, Devon until his death a very short time later. He died either late in 1949 or early in 1950. I found a letter from a solicitor dated May 1950 which states that my father was left £28.2.9d from his estate. I have no memory of him but my second cousin Mary Bertram (nee Bennett) believes she remembers him from the mid 1920s as having a ginger beard. My cousin Richard from Basingstoke also remembers stories of Garnet with a large ginger beard so I assume this must be true, but why has no one else in the family got ginger hair or beards ? Sam Foote tells me that shortly after Garnet sold his farm in Canada, oil was found there and if only he had held on to it another year or so he would have been a very rich man. This is also confirmed in letters written by Grace Foote-Powell which are reproduced in a later chapter. Such is life.

Another anecdote of Garnet told to me by my second cousin Sam from Aurora was that in 1948/9 when Garnet was on his way from Manitoba, or Sasketchewan, to England he called to see Sam's parents and Sam remembers him sitting by the fire and peeling an apple with a knife and of another occasion of Garnet saying " *No matter what happens I will not stay in England*". Poor Garnet, as mentioned above, he took lodgings in or near Newton Abbott, Devon or St Austell, Cornwall and died a couple of years later. I believe he found a lady friend during this period as he left what other monies he had to her.

Here is an extract of a letter sent to Garnet by one of his cousins in Ontario in 1937. It is only one half of an A5 size sheet of writing paper and I believe it was in Garnet's belongings when he died. My father travelled to Devon to his funeral in about 1949 or 1950 and brought back a few old items, including, I recall, a silver pocket watch but it did not work and it, together with the other items are all gone now.

1251 Gerrard ST -E
19 Dec 1937
Dear Garnet,
We often speak of you and wonder how you are. Did you meet that very beautiful wealthy girl you were looking .... (missing)...
.....They had splendid crops in our part of Ontario. Food stuffs is very high in price, almost war time prices - butter is 35 cents lb. eggs 35 cents dozen up. Milk has gone up to 13 cents quart - bread 11 cents loaf - meat and .....

I wondered if any of my new found Canadian cousins would recognise the address and identify the writer ?

John Garnet A. Foot (my Uncle Garnet)
(1880 - 1951)

They certainly did!. cousin Sam tells me that the address is of his Aunt Stella and Uncle Bill. Garnet stayed there overnight on his final trip home. Sam was also there that night and remembers that he was in poor shape.

Sam tells me that the incident with the apple was in 1928/9 when Garnet was on his was out to farm in Manitoba, and the statement that *'No matter what happens, he would never stay in England'* was made in 1948 when he was broke and on his way back to England

Although Garnet had a beard, from the photograph it does not look a very imposing one. I believe the bearded gentleman remembered by Mary Bennett and Brian Foot could have been that of my granduncle Walter James Foote J.P. on his third and last visit to England in 1925. Walter James was the brother of my grandfather George Leonard and the grandfather of my second cousin Samuel David Foote in Aurora. More of Walter James in the 'Canadian Connections'.

My father continued on his own at Chapel Farm, Farnham, near Sixpenny Handley, throughout those years of the depression but was barely solvent and in 1932, he moved, as a tenant farmer, to East Luccombe Farm near Milton Abbas. This was again a mixed dairy and arable farm of about 150 acres and he worked extremely hard for the next four years, when, in 1937 the landowner sold the farm over his head, without giving him the option, as a sitting tenant, to buy and he was served notice to quit. This broke his heart, as he was just beginning to see his fortunes on the upturn after four years of very hard work in putting a neglected farm into shape, and coming at the depressed time it did, it ended his life as a tenant farmer for ever.

My grand uncle Walter James Foote J.P. on his third visit to England in 1925 with my cousin Reginald Bennett and his daughter Mary.

Had he only remained there for a few more years until the Second World War broke out, his and all our lives may have been much changed as farmers were then much in demand to produce food and most prospered very considerably.

Of my father's youthful years, I recall he told me that he and his brothers and others often walked to Dorchester and to Wareham. They drank quite a lot of cider and beer and frequently played cards till the early hours, sometimes all night, in the barn or hayloft. He continued to drink fairly heavily after his marriage in 1922, especially on Market days in Dorchester and Blandford where he was well known for his generosity in treating his companions. His farming worries probably aggravated his drinking habits.

My cousin Pamela told me of the story she had heard that in about 1928 or 1929 all the family went to Pallington Farm for Christmas day and that it snowed very heavily. My father, who had to return to Chapel Farm to milk the cows at 4.30 a.m. the next day, then walked throughout the night in the snow to get home.

Such was my father's dedication to his animals. The distance is at least thirty-five miles. My sister Phyllis, who was there, also recalled this incident when reminded of it.

The normal means of conveyance was by pony and trap, of which the family had several, and I have heard that it was not unusual for his friends to pile him into his pony trap after a heavy session at the pub on a Saturday night and rely on the pony to get him home - just like his father before him!

He bought a car - I think it was a Morris or such like, in 1929/30 period and I remember once finding a newspaper clipping with a heading of *"Dorset farmer fined for driving under the influence of drink"*. This happened at the top of Blandford hill on what is now the A354 Blandford to Salisbury road as he was returning from Blandford to Chapel Farm on Market day! Another story told to me by Richard Foot is that he recalls that when as a boy he used to drive down the A354, the Salisbury to Blandford road, with his father, as they passed the Cashmoor Inn at Farnham, his father used to say:

"I have an uncle who farmed near here and who drank and gambled all his profits away in that pub".

Father was not, however, an alcoholic, but he obviously over indulged and behaved very foolishly during this period. He worked very hard and rose to do the milking by hand at 4.30 a.m. seven days a week. I never knew my father to lie in bed or take any holiday during his working life. The mention of gambling was new to me but I know my father liked to play cards, even in later years he always liked to go to the village whist drives. He had to give these outings up when his sight and hearing became worse in the mid to late 1950s.

Neither did he ever visit a doctor until much later in life, when it was too late to help him. He never visited a dentist and pulled all his bad teeth out by hand, either using pliers or a string tied round it and jerking with his hand. Pain and discomfort were not senses which he acknowledged. Nor was weather; he had been brought up to go out and work in all weathers and this he did to the end of his days.

My mother in my father's first and only car. (c. 1927)

In fact, on the day of his funeral in January 1969 it was cold windy and pouring with rain and as we stood round the grave with mud all over our shoes, someone remarked *"George would have been happy out in this weather"*.

I will cease this largely hearsay account of my father's life at this stage, as by 1937, I was then 7 years old and the remainder of his life story will be combined with my own memories.

CHAPTER THREE

MY PARENTAL FAMILY HISTORY

"We never know the love of a parent until we become parents ourselves"

Henry Ward Beecher. *Proverbs from a Plymouth pulpit.*

MATERNAL ANTECEDENTS

My mother, Alice Foot (nee Thorne), was born on 27th July 1892 in the village of Cheselbourne near Dorchester. Her father, Joseph Thorne was born 25th December 1857 and died of pneumonia on 2nd December 1921. He was a shepherd and by all accounts a quiet and kindly man but not of a strong constitution.

My maternal grandmother, Emily Thorne (nee Parks), was born 14th November 1857, married Joseph Thorne on 21st August 1879 and died of old age at our home in January 1951. She is buried in the church cemetery at Yarlington, only a few yards from my mother and father. She was the eldest of 13 children, at least four of her brothers were killed in the World War I trenches. I recall her telling me that she had been told that *'brother Tom's head was rolling about on the ground like a football'*.

My maternal grandmother Emily Thorne (1857 - 1950)

My maternal grandfather Joseph Thorne (1857 - 1921)

My maternal grandmother was of a very strong character and constitution. She had never been to school but had self taught herself to read from the Bible and had a sharp brain. From the age of 12 she was "in service" as a housemaid at various places in the Dorchester area. She told me many tales of walking 7 miles to Dorchester to the market, of having to walk 5 miles to get to work by 6 am seven days a week and walking home again after 6 p.m. I believe that her family, the Parks, had lived in the Powerstock area to the west of Dorchester. Throughout her entire life she seldom travelled more than 10 miles from Dorchester and indeed only left Dorset on two occasions: once when she visited her son Uncle George, at Barnet in the 1930s and when she was living with us at Wincanton and Yarlington in Somerset just before her death.

On the death of her husband in 1921 she lived in a thatched cottage across the road from North Field Farm which my father took over in 1921 and she turned the living room into a general store. Customers came in, sat on her old settee and bought crisps, tea, biscuits, sweets etc. whilst Gran made them tea. I can just remember visiting her when I was five or six and sitting by a huge open fire with chains hanging for the cooking pots. One bedroom was her store room but I wasn't allowed to run up the stairs as they were very creaky and unsafe. I also recall that the bedroom floors swayed dangerously and we were all exhorted to tread very lightly. In fact the thatched roof fell in on her in 1938 whilst she was in bed and she then came to live with us. My father had, long before that time, moved from the Northfields Farm opposite and the new owner had kept turkeys which I remember used to fly up onto the thatched roof and Gran always said that it was the turkeys which caused her house to fall down. I did indeed meet the daughter of that farmer very recently as she is a friend of my sister Phyllis and during conversation she mentioned that Gran has always blamed her father's turkeys for destroying her house.

There was of course no electricity or running water. I remember the *'Privvy'* at the bottom of the garden and the well very clearly. When she was older she used to ask visitors to her shop to draw up a bucket of water from the well for her, in return she repaid them with goods. Going down the very long garden path to the toilet with a candle at night was quite an adventure. She made just enough money to supplement her ten shillings a week pension to live on. I believe the children who visited her shop stole far more than they ever bought. I very recently discovered that Gran was known by the villagers of Cheselbourne and by many in surrounding villages as *'Granny Joe'*, it is strange that this snippet of information should become known to me for the first time in 1997. When I discussed this with my sister Phyllis she said *"Oh Yes. I knew that!"*.

Gran was a very independent person and at the age of 73/4 she lost an eye through a wood splinter whilst she was chopping wood for the fire. The eye was removed at the Weymouth Eye Hospital, this being the only time she ever went into hospital in her life and I recall her telling me about this great event many times. I may even recall the often repeated name of the surgeon who took out the eye before I complete this story. (I think it was Dr. McCall).

My sister Phyllis has a family portrait of my grandmother with her eye bandaged holding me when I was about 1 year old, together with the rest of the family.

From left to right: My sister Phyllis, sister Doris, my mother (Alice Foot), grandmother, Emily Thorne (holding me in her arms), and cousin Joan Thorne. Photograph taken 1931.

I remember seeing, when I was about 9 years old, a copy of the Picture Post or Holborn's Weekly, printed in 1938 or 1939 which had a large centre fold spread of my Grandma in her shop/living room together with an account of her life. I aim to try to get a copy of this in due time and will try to include it with other photos in this story.

My maternal grandmother had four children, one son and three daughters, of whom my mother Alice was the youngest.

The son George Albert Thorne, joined the Royal Navy at the age of 14 or 15 in 1906 or thereabouts. As a country boy who went away and visited foreign parts he was much respected by everyone and as her elder brother my mother adored him and they remained very close throughout their lives. Uncle George did well in the RN, he went through the Great War, fought at the Battle of Jutland and spent at least two three-year commissions on the China Station. He told me many tales of *'coaling ship'* and being attacked by Chinese gangsters with knives. We have many old postcards of his ships and of places he visited over the period 1906 to 1930, some of these may be included in this story. Uncle George retired on pension at the age of 40 as a Petty Officer Gunnery Instructor.

He went to live in Barnet which was the home of his wife's family and took the job of a milkman. As a country boy he had no problems with the horse drawn milk float. He was called up, or as is more likely, volunteered for service, for World War II, at the age of 51, in 1940 and served in HMS VERNON a shore base in Portsmouth. He was wounded in the bombing in 1942/3 and lost a leg.

*Uncle George Thorne and Aunt Dora
Photograph taken in the early 1920s*

He was kept on in the navy as President of the Petty Officers Mess in HMS VERNON until near the end of the war when he was invalided out of the service.

I am expanding on the life of Uncle George as he was much admired and looked up to by my mother and father, he visited us from far off Barnet in north London every year with his wife Dora and children, Jack, Joan and Doreen. Joan died of kidney problems in 1963 at the age of only 41 years, Doreen now lives in the Milton Keynes area and Jack lives at St Leonards/Hastings and with whom I am still in touch.

It was because of Uncle George's 'success' in life of breaking out of the dull and onerous country life, travelling the world and getting a pension from the navy at the end of it, which influenced my father to urge me to join the Royal Navy. The only alternative in those days was to work on a farm, as lack of transport largely precluded any thought of getting other work near to a town.

Of my other maternal aunts, Amelia was the eldest and was born 2nd May 1880, married and became Amelia New on 22 April 1903 and died of consumption on 6th July 1908. That is the sum of my knowledge of Aunt Millie.

The shock of her father's death is said to have been the trigger which caused the next eldest daughter, my Aunt Annie, who was born in 1887 and was then aged 33, to have some kind of nervous breakdown and she became 'funny' inasmuch that she talked to herself aloud, didn't listen to what one said to her and was wholly forgetful. She could not be relied on to do any cooking as she would put on the kettle or stove and then go out. An endearing habit I will always remember was that she often wore two or even three hats, one on top of the other. She would then go out wandering and talking to herself. She was strong, she ate well and could do housework well if pushed and supervised. One problem was that she would not get up in the mornings, this used to infuriate my father when she lived with us. She was always well spoken and polite but virtually impossible to hold any sustained conversation with as she would quickly wander off the subject. When she later went to live in Barnet with her brother, George, she loved to wander round the shops, complete with hats, and talk loudly to herself. She was once accused of shoplifting in Woolworth's and she was highly indignant and got very excited at such an accusation as she was scrupulously honest and would never dream of taking anything which was not hers.

It is often said that all sons think their mother to be the perfect woman. In my case this is very largely true. She went into service on leaving school at the age of 14 and eventually moved to the Bournemouth area where she was parlour maid and then housekeeper to various gentlefolk. There she learned about the gentry and etiquette, which remained important to her throughout her life. During the Great War she worked in a munitions factory in Poole, she enjoyed the conviviality of working with lots of other girls and was, I suspect, often the life and soul of the party. She was very hard working, intelligent and compassionate. This was shown by the way in which she made many friends and kept them throughout her life. She was always prepared to put herself out for others and of course we children were the centre of her life. She put up with my father's drinking bouts and with the lack of money and near homeless situations she was to find herself in with a selfless pride and cheerfulness which makes my memories of her so endearing.

My mother Alice, married father on 23rd January 1922, shortly after her father's death and moved in to North Field Farm at Cheselbourne, where on 13th September 1923, my eldest sister Phyllis Margaret was born. As Grandmother Emily lived across the road it was natural for Phyllis to be very close to her and after my sister Doris Alice was born on 27th May 1926 and my parents moved away from Cheselbourne to Chapel Farm, near Farnham, Phyllis, who was by then 3 years old, stayed behind with her grandmother. This took some strain off my mother who was often not well, as she suffered from headaches and was, I believe, at that time anaemic, perhaps caused by both overwork and worry over my father's money and drinking problems.

At Chapel Farm on 23rd April 1930, I was born as one of a twin. My twin sister was named Grace but sadly lived only ten days and died on 2nd May 1930. I have only one personal memory of Chapel Farm but I know my mother was very happy there. There was a Chapel in the grounds of the farmhouse and my mother was a regular churchgoer, a member of the local Mothers Union and cleaned and decorated the Chapel twice weekly. I have a framed photograph of the Chapel taken about 1930/1 which I intend to return to the Custodian when I can find it open. It is still in use and services are still held weekly (or fortnightly)? My Godparents were a Mr and Mrs Hayter who lived at nearby Gussage St Michael.

I am told that as a two and three year old, I used to ride on the back of one of the sows in the farmyard. Also that the dairyman used to lead the big bull by the ring in its nose and take him right to the kitchen door with its head inside, just to tease us children. The one hazy memory I have was that, probably at the age of 4, I walked with my mother and sister Doris about a mile or so up the road towards Farnham where we visited and took tea with a Mr and Miss Humby, a genteel brother and sister couple with whom my mother had made friends. My sister Doris was tossed by a cow whilst at Chapel Farm, probably at about the time I was born so she must have been about 3 or 4 years old at the time.

My father spent too much time in the local public house, The Cashmoor Inn, which is on the main Blandford to Salisbury road, and according to my mother neglected the farm at a time when changes in agricultural practices were essential for the survival of tenant farmers. The dairyman was a man named Arthur Stickland and the head Carter was a man named George Bazell or Basell, he was very loyal to my father and when we moved to East Luccombe Farm near Milton Abbas in 1933/4, he and his family came with us.

To sum up the character of my parents at this time, (1934), I believe the following is accurate:

George Arthur Foot was then 47 years old, he had very fair, flaxen hair which never changed colour to the end of his life. He was quite a handsome man of sturdy build about 5 feet 7 inches in height. He was a scrupulously honest and a very hard working man. He had a very short temper but attracted respect for his farming expertise, albeit of a fast becoming outdated kind, and made many friends. Perhaps this was due to his fun loving and generous nature, particularly when it came to treating his cronies to a round of drinks.

Unbeknown to himself, or his family, I believe my father already suffered from diabetes. Both his sight and hearing were already very poor and I have been told that even then the farm hands used to play tricks on him by taking advantage of his poor eyesight, such as passing him a sack with an open bottom so that the contents fell out.

He was also a very stubborn man and never visited a doctor or admitted to any ailment or pain and he always believed himself to be right in farming matters, and indeed all other matters, and this was to prove to be his downfall when the time came for him to work for others. Although I am sure he loved my mother and we three children most dearly, he made life very difficult for my mother by his stubbornness and drinking bouts and who I believe suffered far more than I can now assess.

Alice Foot was then 43 years old, who as a young girl had been very attractive, if not beautiful. Although still retaining her basic attractiveness, she was by then thin and drawn, beginning to go grey, overworked and not in the best of health. She remained loyal to my father and her cheerful and brightly intelligent personality sustained her and the whole family. Her greatest asset was a cheerful disposition, a strength of character and a love of nice people and nice things.

*My sisters, Phyllis, Doris and me at East Luccombe farm.
(Photograph taken 1933)*

CHAPTER FOUR

THE BENNETT CONNECTIONS

"Study the past if you would divine the future"

Confucius (551 - 479 BC

As I researched the Foot family history, the connections with the Bennetts became increasingly important. I had first thought that there were only two generations of Foots marrying Bennett cousins but as I researched, I found that the two families were inextricably connected to a greater extent and even further back than I realised. This chapter is intended to reflect the Bennett connections as far as I can ascertain. I am indebted to Mary Bertram (nee Bennett) for the details of the Bennett Family Tree and for the letters quoted. Although the original custodian of these letters was my second cousin Grace Foote-Powell, now dead, of the Township of Stouffeville, Ontario.

The following is a copy of a letter written in 1836 by John Bennett to his sister Elizabeth. I believe the Foots and Bennetts emigrated to Canada about 1832/3. This letter was written well before Elizabeth married Samuel Foote in Toronto in 1839.

Thirnwood Farm
Mappowder

Dear Sister,
I am desired by Father and Mother to send for you to come home. You say that you are thinking of going into the States but instead of going into the States you must come home, as none of us is coming out and then if you like to come back again some of us will go with you and if you have not got enough money to bring you we will send you some at any time.

But if you have got money enough you come home immediately and then it shall not be no loss to you if you like to go back again but you never will want to go there no more if you was to come home as you must if please God as we want to see you once more if please God and George had better sell what he has there and come with you so he shall have my farm so soon as he do come home, as I have got aplenty of work at my trade as he can live and do well upon the farm.

Edward have took a farm at Morton under Esq. Frampton called Snellings Farm about 230 acres of land and he goes with Betty Hounsell at Aimsell.

Dear Sister you say that you are not in want of anything but to be with your dear parents and that is all they want - to be with you and then their trouble would be no more as for you and George to be in your own country and now make up your mind to come home and put your trust in the Lord God and he will bring you safe to your native land. Dear

Sister, you say that you are better off there than here but you never wanted for anything here nor never will nor not for that happiness which you do now for if you bide there this fifty years you never will be any better off than if you was to come home now.

Now you write to me as soon as possible and let me know when you are coming home and how George is getting on and if my nephew do come home I will show him the trade for I am his Godfather.

Please to give my kind love and Sarah's to Mr & Mrs Hooper, Mr & Mrs Foot and to all friends not forgetting Edward Cave.

I am dear Brother and Sister,
   Yours truly,

J. Bennett

The following is a copy of a letter also written in 1836 by Mary Bennett in England to her sister Elizabeth in Canada.

Dear Sister,

I have the pleasure of writing these few lines to you hoping we shall see you home by next Christmas.

Joseph Dibben came home in nineteen days from the States to Portsmouth. Give my kind love to Samuel Foot and to Mr & Mrs Hooper and to Joe Foot and how glad I should be to see Harriet Hooper and we have not heard a word about her not since she has been in that country and we should like to hear where she is must have got married.

My dear George, Mother take it very unkind not writing a few lines to her and we should like to hear what state of health Edward Cave is enjoyed of and Sister Sarah and her two children came home at Christmas and she said she should not come home no more not till you were at home. Uncle Richard and all the family send their kind love to you all and Uncle court Barbara Foot and Eliza Foot is very well and Uncle Thomas and Aunt Mary send their love to you all and she is almost dark and Sarah said how glad she should be to see you and Jane have three sons and they live very happy and doing very well. Uncle Geo. is living with Mrs Mollett at Sharnell Green. He has lived with her this twelve months.

Eliza Mitchell have five children and they live down there still. Mary Simmonds have a son. She and her mother they had four children christened this Christmas. Mr and Mrs Lemon are very well and they have answered that letter Joseph brought home with him. George is to be sure to take care of poor Susannah's clothes 'tis Mother's wish to let her have it but you must do what you think proper and if sister Elizabeth do come home without George you must bring Mother a keepsake of dear Susannah Bennett's.

(The above indicates to me that Susannah Bennett nee Hooper died shortly after arriving in Ontario and giving birth to a son. I believe this was in 1833).

We join all in love with you both from the oldest to the youngest. Barwell is very much like his brother George. That is what people do say. You are more in our minds than ever. Uncle and Aunt Samuel send their kind love to you all and Annabella is very well.

Now I remain your Affectionate and your loving Sister Mary Bennett and if you do come home this summer and any wish to go back again I will go back with you

These letters very much reflect the thinking of those Dorset country people who stayed home and could not understand why the young people emigrated to Canada.

The following is a copy of a letter written in 1836 by Edward Bennett, in England, to his oldest brother George Foot Bennett, and his sister Elizabeth, in Canada. George's wife, Susannah Hooper, died in Canada in 1833, he remarried in 1836.

Elizabeth married Samuel Foot and never returned to England. Mary Bennett, her sister, later married Joseph Dibben. A grandson of theirs, Robert George Dibben, known as 'Ross' Dibben, went to Canada in 1907 at the age of 21.

Thirnwood
9th March 1836

Dear Brother and Sister,

I take this opportunity of writing to you these lines hoping it will find you in good health as it leaves us all at present thanks be to God for it. I am now going to inform you a little how our country folk is and how they are going on.

William Foot and sister Sarah is living at Nottingham and are doing very well. They have only two children. Father, Mother and all remember to you and all acquaintances in that country and hope to see you both home again as they don't think anything about coming out in that country.

Joseph Dibben came home in the fall and never brought any letter but he told us George was going to get married again in a day or two after he left but as for the truth we don't know as we have not received any letter from him, not this two years but we received a letter from Elizabeth in February that was directed Toronto January 5th 1836 and she did not say anything about George and we should thank him for writing home a little oftener, as we are very happy to hear from any of you. We have had a cold winter and a great deal of snow this winter.

Samuel Foot's father and mother is come back from Guernsey and took a house at Kingston of Andrew Rubens and is going to live there.

Richard Foot is not out of Ihehaster ?(Dorchester? or Ilchester?) *gaol yet but he expects to come out Lady Day.*

James Crop is dead and his son Michael Crop is gone off and we expect he is gone to his uncle in America and they have had a sale at Kingston.

John Bennett is living at Sharnell Green (now called Sharnhill Green) *and doing very well as he has got the land of Godwins and has a midling share of work at his trade.*

Elizabeth talked of going to the United States to live but we rather she did come home as Mary don't think anything about coming out.

Dear brother do you let us know how you are getting on, Hooper, Foot and all.
I remain yours truly,
Edward Bennett

Here is a copy of a letter, perhaps it was an advertising circular, written in 1873;

CORN, SEED BRAN AND MEAL STORE,
Trinity Road, North Quay, Weymouth.

Sir, I beg to inform you that I have opened a Store as above, and shall be pleased to supply you with a superior article at a moderate price. Soliciting the favour of your commands,

I beg to remain,
Yours faithfully,

R.C.G. BENNETT
Pallington, Dorchester, May 7, 1873.

I have an envelope of a registered letter posted in 1898 and addressed to:

Miss E. Bennett
Thirnwood Farm (now called Thurnwood)
Mappowder
Blandford
Dorset

Who was this Miss E. Bennett? I expect it was Elizabeth born 1835 to John and Sarah Foot and the sister of my grandmother Emily. Was this farm, "Thirnwood", the original farm owned by my great, great, great, great grandfather William Foot? I believe this to be so and it then passed into the hands of Cave Bennett when he married Elizabeth (Betty) Foot in 1801. This was the first of the Foot/Bennett marriages as Cave Bennett and his parents had been born in Leicestershire.

Also a pre formatted letter card written to my Uncle Bruce at the time of the Boer War:

Dear Bruce,

We have raised the Royal Standard in the capitals of the late Free State and Transvaal and the whole Empire rejoices. Military Bands have played "God Save the Queen" and on the Market Place in Bloemfontein and Pretoria, and gallant "Bobs" has been cheered to the echo.

So in memory of these glorious days, I am sending you a card from
Yours,

Arthur

Who was Arthur? I assume that "Bobs" was General Lord Robert Baden-Powell.

The above indicates that some of my ancestors, were in the army, I also have a pre-formatted postcard addressed to Mrs Foot at Pallington stating that *"I have been admitted to hospital and am going on well"* This was signed by "Tom" ?? and dated 2nd November 1914.

These two items taken from the "SWANAGE SPIDER" dated Wednesday 30th July 1873, reflect the thinking of Dorset men of those times. The "Swanage Spider" was an army paper printed within the lines of the Dorset Volunteer Encampment and was aimed to provide *"A glimpse of Camp Life of the Dorset Rifle Volunteers".* Price one penny.

Hurrah for Dorset
Tune: *Life let us Cherish*

Where is the Dorset Man
Who is not ready when danger comes
To do his best whene'er he can
For his bonny Dorset home?
He is not of true Dorset breed
Who will not for his country bleed,
And help her in the time of need
To defend his home.
    Chorus:
Hurrah for Dorset
We're all ready whenever they come.
To strike a blow for Dorset
Our bonny English home.

Where is the Dorset man,
Who when Victoria summons her sons,
Cowers and hides where'er he can,
And from the danger runs?
Such men old Dorset never knew,
On this old soil they never grew;
For here they are all staunch and true
Towards their English home.

You may search old Dorset through,

But cowards their you'll never find;
For there they are all staunch and true
Towards their English home.

The Zoldier's Death

You ax me why I veel so zad,
And why my tears do fall,
I'm thinking of me darling lad,
Me vust born an' my all.
An' yet I glory how 'e died,
Though 'e was me jay and pride,
Vighten bravely zide be zide
His comrades in the vield.

My buoy, the last time that 'e wrote,
Avore the fight was on,
An' oh ! 'twas such a purty note,
I think o't now 'e's gone
He zaid 'e'd fight for his own hea'th,
Zoo long as 'e'd got life or breath;
An vreely meet a zoldier's death,
Vor me and vor his whuome.

"Gie my love to Meary dear,
An' zay I still be true,
I ha'nt vorgot her tho' I'm here,
Wi' dangers to go droo;
I ha'nt vorgot the vow I meade,
A zitten downe below the sheade,
O' thik girt woak that's in the gleade,
Where we did often goo."

"Farewell I hear the bugle zound,
The foe they be a come,

75

Foemen may dare us,
And bring their hosts into the field,
And seek with stern defiance
To make our soldiers yield;
Perdition then shall mark their track,
With shame they shall be driven back,
When Dorset men lead the attack,
To defend their homes

Dorset men before us,
Havrer bravely for their freedom bled,
Then let us strive to emulate
Their deeds though long since dead;
May each respond to honour's call,
And be prepared to fight or fall,
And yield ther lives up one and all
Tod defend their homes.

Ye gallant men of Dorset,
Long may you maintain her fame,
Matrons then, who bore you,
Will proudly own your name.
Be ready when in time of need,
And bravely for your country bleed,
And blessing will fall on your head,
From many a Dorset home.
By:
Private Charles Powell 1st Dorset Reserve Volunteers.

When vighting where the shots abound,
I'll think of all at home;
An' if in vighten I should die,
There I wool in honour lie,
Back to vield and face to sky,
An' veet towards the foe."

An' zoo he rushed into the vight,
An' then got shot they zay,
He lay a bleeden all the night,
Till the mornen ray
Light up all the vield wi' light,
An' shewed the horrors of the vight;
They zaid that 'twas a shocken zight
To zee zoo many dead.

Thye buried 'en bezide a stream,
They had no coffins there -
The waters zinged his fune'l hymn,
As they vlow'd on zo clear,
They buried 'en az 'e was dres't,
They put no stone wher he da rest,
The grass da grow above his breast
An' daisies o'er his head.

By:
Private Charles Powell
1st Dorset Reserve Volunteers

Although the above words may not be classic writings nor even wholly pertinent to my story, they help me, and I hope, the reader, to get an insight into the minds of the Dorset people who were my forebears.

THE BENNETT FAMILY TREE

William Bennett Living in N. Kilworth Leics in 1749 m. Hannah ?

William Bennett   m. Elizabeth Russell
b. 1749 at N. Kilworth   at S. Kilworth Leics 28 Nov 1774

Children of William Bennett and Elizabeth Russell:

- **Hannah** b. 29 Sep 1776
- **Cave** b. 2 Feb 1777
- **Elizabeth** b. 13 Jan 1780
  - or b. 2 Dec 1777 at S. Kilworth
  - m. at Mappowder 21 Aug 1801
  - d. 22 Aug 1867 at Mappowder
- **Anne** b. 15 Jul 1781
- **Mary** b.18 Dec 1782
- **Penelope** b.24 Jul 1785
- **Charlotte** b. 6 Feb 1788
  - m. Elizabeth (Betty) Foot daughter of George Foot
  - b. 26 Dec 1783 and baptised in 1784
  - d. 25 May 1876 at Mappowder
- **Sarah** b.9 Dec 1789
- **William** b.1 Jul 1782
- **Rebekah** b.20 Jul 1784
- **Dinah** b.27 Mar 1796
- **Edward Russell** b. 21 Jul 1799

Children of William Bennett (b.1 Jul 1782) and Elizabeth (Betty) Foot:

- **George Foot** b. 1802
  - m. 12 Oct 1828 to Susannah Hooper (1851 Census)
  - Geo. said to be of Alton Pancras (emigrated to Canada)
- **Sarah** b. 1803
- **Edward Russell** b. 1806
  - at Stoke Wake
  - b. Hilton)
  - m. Elizabeth Mary Hounsell
  - 20 Apr 1837 at Mappowder
- **John** b. 8 Apr 1810 at Stoke Wake
  - d. 17 Aug 1890
  - m. Sarah
  - d. 9 Oct 1882
  - at Mappowder
  - lived at Brockhampton Farm
- **Elizabeth** b.1812 →
- **Mary** b. 1815
  - m. Joseph Dibben ?
- **Ann** b. 1818
  - (By 1841 Census a straw hat maker at Wonston)
  - (1851 Census a Housekeeper to Bro. William)
  - d.4 Sept 1876
- **Jane** b. 1824
  - m. 25 Dec 1856 at Brockhampton to Edmund Strange a cattle dealer of Hazelbury
  - d. 23 Feb 1880
- **William** b. 1826
  - m. Lavinia
- **Cave** b. 1828 d. Plush Nov 1899 age 73
- **Barwell** b. 1830
  - d. 2 Feb 1890 at Mappowder age 60 years
  - (From 1871 census) a Farmer at Thirnwood 325 acres. Employing 6 men, 2 women
  - Br. John's daughter Elizabeth then with him)

Children of William and Lavinia:

- **Mary** b. 1858
- **Walter** b. 1859
- **Lavinia** b.1861

Add to the above: Elizabeth b.2 Jun 1812 m. Samuel Foot in Toronto 9 Apr 1839 d. 9 Feb 1884. They had 10 children - see Foot Family Tree and the Canadian Connections.

THE FOOT/BENNETT FAMILY TREE (Continued)

John Bennett = Sarah

Edward Russell Bennett = Elizabeth Mary Hounsell

- **Elizabeth** b. 1843, m. George Wallbridge
- **Kate Amelia** (Wallbridge?), m. Samuel Churchill
- **Mildred Elizabeth**, m. Charles Marsh
- **Eileen**, m. John Moore
  - Christine Moore

Children:
- **Charles** b. 1833
- **Elizabeth** b. 1835
- **William** b. 1837
- **Candine** b. 1839
- **John** b. 1840
- **Mary** b. 1842, m. Arthur Birch 16 Jun 1870
- **Ann** b. 1846
- **Emily** b.1847, m. George Leonard Foot at Affpuddle 16 Jun 1877
- **Richard Cave** b. 1850
  - **Jack** b. 1879
  - **Regirald** b. 1880
  - **Winifred** b. 188?
  - **Mary** b.1920 (now Mrs M Bertram)

George Foot of Mappowder

married at Buckland Newton 29 Jan 1778 by licence

Sarah Caines of Buckland Newton

Children:
- **Sarah Ann** bapt. 6 Aug 1778, m. Samuel Foot 16 May 1799
- **Richard** bapt. 29 Dec 1779
- **George** bapt. Aug 1781
- **Elizabeth (Betty)** bapt. 26 Dec 1783, d. 1860, m. Cave Bennett 1777 b.1876 →
- **Mary** bapt. June 1785
- **Thomas** bapt. 3 Dec 1786

THE FOOT/BENNETT FAMILY TREE (Continued)

Elizabeth (Betty) Foot married Cave Bennett

Children:
- George Foot Bennett b. 1805 →
- Sarah
- Edward Russell b. 1807
- John m. Sarah Foot
- Elizabeth b. 1812 d. 1884 Samuel Foot (b. 1803. d. 1879)
- Mary b. 1814 m. Joseph Dibben (Had 7 sons, lived at Sharnell (now Sharnhill) Green, Buckland Newton)
- Ann m. Kingman
- William b. 1826
- Jane b. 1826
- Cave Thomas b. 1828
- Barwell b. 1830

Children of Elizabeth and Samuel Foot:
George, Joseph Shepherd, John Cave, Barwell Bennett, Herbert, Edwin, Alan.
(Mother Mary died early leaving Joseph to bring up the boys)

Children of George Foot Bennett:
- William Benjamin
- Edward
- George Leonard
- Cave Nelson
- Walter James
- Samuel Herbert
- Georgina Sarah
- Mary Jane
- Rebecca Elizabeth
- Septimus Albert

(Then as in the Foot and Canadian Connections)

THE FOOT/BENNETT FAMILY TREE (Continued)

George Foot Bennett m. Susannah Hooper
b. 1802   b. 1801
at Mappowder   at Mappowder
d. circa. 1862   d. 1833 (in Ontario)

Both emigrated to Canada about 1832. Susannah died after giving birth to a son, Edward Cave.
George married again in 1836 probably to a Hammel

Edward Cave
b. 1832/3
d. 1 Apr 1901 (age 73)
m. Mary Ann Lee in Ontario
b. 1842
d. 8 Mar 1913 (age 71)

George	William	James	Barwell	Francis	Libbie	Ester	Septimus
m. Annie Mann	m. Mary Ann Hammel		m. Bella Scutt	m. Melinda?	m. Albert Lee	m. Geo. Cook	m. Sadie Middleton
Connie	Wellington Edith			3 girls, 1 boy (Edward)	Annabel	Norman	William

THE BENNETT FAMILY TREE (Continued)

NARRATIVE.

The children of Cave Bennett
b. 2 Dec 1777 d. 22 Aug 1867 m. Elizabeth (Betty) Foote   d. 27 May 1860 (on WhitSunday age 76)

(Canada) George Foot Bennett   b. 1805   m. Susannah Hooper who died in Canada 1833 age 31 leaving a baby boy (Edward Cave) who was born in 1832. George married again in Ontario in 1836

(Canada) Sarah Bennett   b. 1 Nov 1803 d. 28 Sep 1857 age 53. m. William Foote - (Letter of 1836 says William Foote and sister Sarah living at Nottingham, have only two children).

Edward Russell Bennett   b. 9 Mar 1806 m. Mary Elizabeth Hounsell who died 1872 aged 59. Buried at Mappowder. Had 3 children: Amelia, Mary and George. He farmed the home farm. Their own - Chaston at Buckland Newton.

John Bennett   b. 12 Feb 1810   m. Sarah Foote. These are the parents of Aunt Emma (Emily) who married grandfather's brother George Leonard, grandparents of Garnet etc.

(Canada) Elizabeth Bennett   b. 2 Jul 1812 d. 1884 Married Samuel Foot - parents of Walter James and George Leonard etc.

Mary Bennett   bapt. 21 Jul 1815   m. Joseph Dibben. Died early leaving her husband to bring up their seven sons: George, Joseph, Sheppard, John Cave, Barwell Bennett, Herbert, Edwin and Alan Charles.

Ann Bennett   bapt. 7 Dec 1818   d. 1856. buried at Mappowder. m. Thomas Kingman who died 1863

81

THE BENNETT FAMILY TREE - NARRATIVE (Continued)

(USA) William E Bennett	b. 18 Nov 1820	d. In Chicago 23 Dec 1864 age 44 years 1 month 5 days. Buried at Newmarket, Ontario (near the graves of Elizabeth and Samuel).
Jane Bennett	bapt. 21 Feb 1824	d. 1880 age 56. buried at Mappowder. m. Edmund Strange
Cave Thomas Bennett	bapt. 25 Mar 1827	Farm Bailiff - was bailiff for Squire Miller. He married the housekeeper (Ann Travers a widow) in 1878 who died in 1906 aged 81. A fine couple. Given a cottage and a plot of land to end their days. Buried at Plush 1899 age 83. (This tombstone is still there in June 1997).
Barwell Bennett	bapt. 5 Jul 1830	d. 24 Feb 1891. Buried at Mappowder. Left money to nephews and nieces all over the world. Granduncle (William James Foote) and Edward Cave Bennett, his first cousin went to England in 1892 to bring back the share for the Canadian nephews and nieces.

BENNETT FAMILY DETAILS FROM THE MAPPOWDER PARISH REGISTER

Robert Foot   m. Ann Strange 1810

Richard Foot, widower, m. Barbara Foot 1838.   (The letter of 1836 says; "Uncle Richard court Barbara Foot").

From an old prayer book cover printed 1772. Children of Henry Foot:
    Simon   b. 1781
    Mary   b. 1783
    Ann   b. 1785
    Samuel b. 1789
    Barbara b. 1791

The Children of Richard Cave Bennett b. 1850   Jack b. 1879   Reginald Ernest b. 1880   Winifred b. 188?
    |
    Mary
(now Mrs Mary Bertram and living in Dorchester)

My great, great, great, great grandfather **William Bennett**, living in North Kilworth Leicestershire in 1749 married Hannah. They had a son, **my great, great, great, grandfather William Bennett Jr.** who was born in 1749 also at North Kilworth and who married Elizabeth Russell at South Kilworth on 28th November 1774. William and Elizabeth had twelve children as shown on the family tree.

Their first son, **my great, great grandfather, Cave** (pronounced *Keeve*) was born 2nd February 1777 at South Kilworth. He married Elizabeth (Betty) Foot (who again was not unrelated as she was the daughter of George Foot and Sarah Caines and who was born in 1783), at Mappowder on 21st August 1801. Cave was then twenty one years old and Betty was only sixteen. There is a story of how Cave rode on horseback down from Leicestershire to Mappowder to court and wed his bride. They appear to have settled in Mappowder and this is where their first son, George was christened on January 25th 1802. Sadly the Mappowder Register records that George died less than four months later on May 20th 1802. They had another son in 1805 who they christened George Foot Bennett. It was often the case that if a baby did not survive childhood its parents named a subsequent child after the one they had lost. Their next child was another boy, Edward Russell christened at Stoke Wake on January 14th 1807. The next son John was born on 8th April 1810. He was to marry Sarah at Mappowder in about 1830 and become the father of my grandmother. He then lived at Brockhampton Farm.

Cave and Elizabeth's first daughter arrived in 1812, she was named Elizabeth and was christened at Hilton, a nearby parish and was to emigrate to Ontario and marry my great grandfather Samuel in 1839. If ever there was to be a prize for a set of complicated family relationships this must be the winner!

To recap. **My great grandmother Elizabeth Bennett** was born June 2nd 1812. She was born in the parish of Hilton, in Dorset, England, just south of Stoke Wake, and was baptised on August 9th 1812. Elizabeth was fourteen years old when her mother gave birth to twins, William and Jane. The year was 1826. In 1827 brother Thomas arrived and a year later, in 1828, her brother Cave arrived and finally, in 1830, her youngest brother Barwell was born, by then his mother, Elizabeth or Betty or Betsy Bennett (nee Foot), was forty four years old.

In addition to the above they also had daughters Mary, date of birth unknown, and Ann who was born in 1818. There is a possibility that there was another daughter, Ann, a twin sister to Barwell born in 1830. Cave and Elizabeth (Betty) Bennett probably had thirteen children if one includes the first son George who died at four months.

Their oldest son, George Foot Bennett married Susannah Hooper in the parish of Hazelbury Bryan on October 12th 1828. They emigrated to Canada and I believe Susannah died shortly after their arrival whilst giving birth to a son, in about 1833 whom they named Edward Cave. George Foot Bennett married again in 1836.

Although George Foot Bennett may have had more sons after he remarried in Ontario 1836 and his own son Edward Cave married and had four sons in Ontario, cousin Sam can find no trace of these Bennett descendants in that area today. (see page 80).

My father, George Arthur Foot holding Mary Bennett at North Farm, Cheselbourne. (c. 1922)

CHAPTER FIVE

THE CANADIAN CONNECTIONS

"Happy he who like Ulysses has made a great Journey.

Joachim du Bellay (1522 - 1560) French poet.

I am much indebted to Samuel D Foote of Aurora, Ontario for many of the following details, although I understand that the original compiler of the Canadian Genealogical chart was Clifford Vickery. I do hope that I have interpreted these details correctly. I will happily amend any errors or mis-interpretation which may be found.

As shown on the Family Tree, my great grandfather, Samuel Foot emigrated to Canada in the early 1830s, married his cousin Emily Bennett from Hilton in Dorset in 1839 in Toronto and then had ten children between 1840 and 1857. The best accuracy I can determine on these dates is that it was probably about 1833 that they sailed to Canada, it is probable that Elizabeth Bennett emigrated separately in about 1835. At some time the name of Foot became Foote and it would appear that all descendants from then on continued with the 'e' on the name.

One explanation for the Foot/Foote difference was that in the early 1900s, one of the Foot families in Ontario quarrelled with a neighbouring cousin Foot family over the building of stables at a church. Apparently Walter James, my granduncle, built stables and the neighbour regarded this as an anachronism as the motor car was just then being introduced and becoming popular. They quarrelled and Walter James added an *'e'* to his name in pique! After later discussions with Samuel Foot it is not possible to confirm this story. It is more likely that, in the 1890s or early 1900s, as Walter James became more important in the township of Whitchurch and was made a Justice of the Peace he added the 'e' to his name to give it more substance. I cannot even really be sure of this and it could have been that Samuel himself added the *'e'* way back in the 1840s.

So far I have only scant information about these granduncles and grandaunts and their descendants who are now my second or third cousins. I hope to gather more information when I visit Ontario in May 1997.

The information I have at present is that Samuel D. Foote, who is a second cousin, lives in Aurora, Ontario and is a retired engineer. He is the present 'keeper' of the Foote family records and has written to me and asked me to visit him which I will do in May 1997.

Another second cousin, Grace Foote Powell was a school teacher, (as I also understand were several other of my cousins and second cousins), she came to England in about 1961 and stayed with Peter Foot, my cousin and his wife Ann. She also met and stayed with Mary Bertram (nee Bennett) another cousin. She was married to a vicar, the Rev. Percy Powell and thus changed her name to Foote-Powell. Grace is, unhappily, now dead and I regret very much that I did not meet her as the following narrative was written by her in 1982. This was when my cousin Peter Foot and his wife Ann were about to fly to Toronto to visit her. It indicates to me she had a fine mind and a good sense of humour and would have been a most interesting person to know.

HELLO, PETER !

Peter and Ann were due to arrive at the airport at five o'clock. Twenty one years ago I enjoyed their hospitality in England; now they were coming to Canada for the first time to visit me. The only definite arrangements we have made were that they would telephone me from the airport when they arrived.

At thirty minutes past five the telephone rang.

"Hello Peter !" *I said, my voice reflecting the excitement I felt.*
"Hello Grace", *said the voice.* "This is Doug".
"Doug?" *I asked, my voice betraying my sudden surprise.*
"Yes, Doug from Hamilton."
"Oh! yes I know. ! You are Douglas my cousin, I *replied. (I always gave him his full name).*
"Will you be home next Sunday ? If it is convenient for you, mother, Claudette and I would like to visit you next Sunday"
"Come for lunch, Douglas. You will meet Peter and Ann; and you will want as much time as possible".
"Who is Peter ?" *inquired Doug.*
"Peter is a cousin of yours and mine. I met him twenty-one years ago in England. He is coming to Toronto this afternoon: I am waiting for his telephone call from the airport when he arrives."

When our short conversation came to an end and I had no more than put the receiver in place, the telephone rang again.
"Hello Peter !" I said into the mouthpiece, my excitement rising high as I waited for his voice in the receiver.
"Hello Grace!" said the voice. "This is Sam. I phoned to see if Peter and Ann had arrived. I will come over for a short time, if you let me know when they telephone."
"How typical of Sam " I said as I once more put the receiver in place.
My hand was still on the receiver when the telephone rang for the third time.
"Hello Peter" I called into the mouthpiece.
"Hello Grace !" the voice was Mildred's.
"Oh Hello Mildred !" I said, my voice suddenly quite flat. Mildred was laughing, and in a split second I was laughing too. Mildred laughed and I laughed and we couldn't say a word. Never had anything any funnier happened to me - or so it seemed - but before I had time to think about it, the telephone rang for the fourth time.
"Hello Peter!" I said, placing the emphasis on Peter.
"Hello Grace ! How did you know it was I ? I couldn't get through for a long time: the line was busy."
"It's a long story Peter; I'll tell you when I see you. The whole family is waiting to welcome you".

Grace Foote Powell
June 1982.

Here is another letter written by Grace in 1964 to Mrs Mary Bertram (nee Bennett) which gives a very considerable insight to her character, and also solves many questions I had with regard to the Foot/Foote/Bennett relationships:

Yarrow Manor
R.R.2 Stouffeville
Ontario
Canada

18th September 1964

Dear Mary,

I was thrilled to get your letter. I read and reread it three or four times. "I am the child in the photographs". I could hardly believe what I read. It's like the characters in a story book suddenly springing to life.

I have been to England twice. In the summer of 1928 I travelled with the University Travel Club to Scotland, England, Holland, Belgium and France. Incidentally, the whole trip for six weeks only cost me between three and four hundred dollars. I had completed two years of teaching and was twenty one years old. You were a little girl of eight, younger than your own two daughters now.

My grandfather Walter James Foot, passed away at our place in the fall of that year. I am anticipating another visit some day. I am all in love with England, Dorset is beautiful. I felt so completely at home with my new found relations. There is a decided family resemblance and what a similarity of names - Mary, Richard, Elizabeth, Samuel !

I am sending what I have found out about the family of Cave Bennett and Betty Foot, his wife, also a genealogical chart showing where I fit in, and three old letters of 1836. I cannot guess who your grandfather, R.C. was. He may have been the son of Cave Thomas Bennett, if he were married twice or John Bennett who married Sarah Foote or he may have been the son of one of Cave Bennett's brothers.

My great grandparents; Elizabeth Bennett 1812 - 1884 and Samuel Foote, 1803 - 1879 were first cousins. I don't know how. I do not know who Samuel Foot's parents were or what occupation they followed. They are mentioned in one of the old letters. Two of his brothers went to Australia, two came to Canada, Samuel and Walter, and two remained in England, and I always understood that because of their size and strength and great loyalty they were in the Queen's bodyguard. I wonder if they were in any way connected with Samuel Foote (1720 - 1777), the writer and dramatist. There were Footes in Cornwall at the time of Charles II.

Elsie Dibben sent me some names with dates found in an old Mappowder Register. I copied that for you also. Who was Sarah Foote that John Bennett married and who were their two children.

I am so glad that you are interested in old family history. Little by little the story unfolds. I have found the grave of dear Susannah Bennett, the wife of George, she was a Hooper - George Bennett did marry again but as yet I don't know who. Edward Cave was his only son. He died April 1904 at the age of 72. I have also found the graves of Mr & Mrs Hooper, Mr & Mrs Lemon, Abraham Foote 1807 -1887, Richard Foote 1779 - 1859, William

Foote 1829 - 1874 and another William Foote 1812 - 1887.

I, too, remember Garnet, I think Garnet experienced a number of crop failures in the west (Manitoba) and finally gave up. Had he stayed and lived he might have been a wealthy man. They discovered oil there. Lillian said that he came to a sad end. I don't know how, I didn't like to ask. Perhaps you can tell me.

You will be interested in a story I have been told about my grandfather, Walter James Foot. He always wore a beard. At the time of the Boer War, a neighbour, by the name of Seneca Baker, who also wore a beard, drove down the road waving the Boer flag. Grandfather immediately drove into town and had his beard shaved off.

My brother Sam, is a civil engineer. He spent a month in England the year I was married there, 1961. He met Mabel (Foot) and visited Pallington Farm but missed seeing Lillian because he was through Basingstoke before he realised it, and didn't turn back. He smiled at your remarks about the business. He has had the same experience.

I have one sister Mildred, a teacher who married a teacher who is the principal of a public school. They have three boys; the youngest attends his father's school; the oldest is entering university in the fall. Walter, my oldest brother, also the principal of a public school, retired in June and is running our home farm. My youngest brother Joe, is a veterinary surgeon.

My parents were farmers but originally both teachers. They are living with me. We keep a nurse for *mother. She had a stroke nearly six years ago and is now a bed patient.*

I have as delightful bit of property - five acres of good land, a creek crossing it through the middle and a pond which I had made. The house is over one hundred years old. I added to it and remodelled it slightly and had the whole thing covered with white stucco. The roof is a coral colour. I made my own concrete blocks for a patio from material left over from the building using cement colouring powder to tint them. I am doing my own landscaping. In fine weather I spend all my spare time in the garden.

When your letter came, I was managing alone as my little nurse who is in her eightieth year had just had an emergency operation for acute appendicitis. She came through gallantly and is back with us trying to help all she can.

I do all my own writing at night after my dear ones are settled down. My eyes sometimes begin to go blurry before I have gone very far. I notice that I wrote grandfather for godfather. I hope that I haven't made many mistakes like that.

I feel quite sure that we shall meet sometime. The day is coming when I shall be left all alone. Then, I think, for comfort, I shall fly to England. Who knows, maybe when your business begins to prosper you will come to Canada. How welcome you will be ! Do come.

Yours sincerely

Grace

P.S. Do you know the history of Pallington Farm and Thirnwood ?
Are you interested, as I am, in old photographs. The old one which you think is your grandmother says on the back, Libbie Bennett. It was made by Gosney, Sherborne. The Richard Foot mentioned in Edward's letter could be a brother of Samuel. If there is any way of finding out why he was in gaol - in debt or on guard ? I am anxious to hear the truth - good or bad. Grandfather had a brother Cave , he was known as Uncle Keeve. Do you know the origin of the name ?
G.

I visited Yarrow Manor during my trip to Canada in May 1997, it is truly a lovely spot and still much as she described it. I also met my second cousin Mildred who is now widowed and is a delightful lady and extremely fit and active at the age of 86.

Here is yet another example of Grace Foote-Powell's talents:

There Cannot Be Another You

Children play 'neath skies of blue,
And babies sleep in their cradles new.
Flowers bloom in the morning dew,
And apples grow red for me and you.
Bluebirds fly where daisies grew,
And people sit in a Sunday pew.
Mothers homely tasks pursue,
And fathers stand for things right and true.
Grandmas make cookies and candy and stew,

Grandpas hoe cabbages all the day through.
People or bluebirds or meadow-rue -
No two are alike whether many or few.
There cannot be another you;
No one on earth can fill your shoe.
        Grace Foote-Powell

    I believe this lovely little poem was written in the 1970s.

THE FOOT FAMILY TREE - THE CANADIAN CONNECTIONS

Samuel Foot = **Elizabeth Bennett**
b. 6 Nov 1803 at Stoke Wake or b.13 Jan 1807 at Mappowder   b. 2 Jun or Jul 1812 at Hilton Dorset
m. 9 Apr 1839 in Toronto Canada
d. 6 Feb 1879   d. 9 Feb 1884

ALL CHILDREN BORN IN ONTARIO CANADA

Children of Samuel Foot and Elizabeth Bennett:

William Benjamin
b. 5 Jan 1840
d. 27 Sep 1929
m. Eleanor Cook
b. 1845
d. 1909

Edward
b. 24 Mar 1841
d. 22 Nov 1884
m. Margaret Weir
b. 1844
d. 1923

George Leonard
b. 5 Jul 1843
d. 1 Jun 1902

Cave Nelson
b. 23 Feb 1845
d. 9 Mar 1902
m. Annie Jane McKewon Shillinglaw
b. 1837
d. 1916

Walter James
b. 22 Aug 1846
d. 2 Oct 1928
m. Grace
b. 2 Mar 1844
d. 12 Nov 1920

Samuel Herbert
b. 25 Nov 1854
d. 2 Oct 1937
m. Margaret Lee
b. 1855
d. 1928

Georgina Sarah
b. 17 Nov 1851
d. 15 Aug 1902
m. Joshua Hilborn

Mary Jane
b. 17 Nov 1851
d. 23 Jun 1878
m. James Bingham

Rebecca Elizabeth
b. 11 Nov 1848
d. 21 Oct 1907
m. William Cain

Septimus Albert
b. 22 Sep 1857
d. 23 Jun 1878

Next generation (children of William Benjamin and Eleanor Cook):

Alberta
m. William Marshall

Elizabeth
m. Peter Cane

Alfretta
m. Alfred Sharples

May
m. Joseph Mitchel

Benjamin
m. Phoebe Madill

Eva Caroline
m. Moston ?

Herbert
m. Margaret Annan

Frank
m. Jessie Humphey

Vera
m. Russell Flumerfelt

Laura
m. William Sheppherd

Lila
m. Kenneth Turner

Velma

Douglas
m. Mary Vessey

Ruby   Jack   Lyman

97

THE CANADIAN CONNECTIONS (Continued)

Samuel Foot = Elizabeth Bennett

b. 6 Nov 1803 at Stoke Wake or b.13 Jan 1807 at Mappowder   b. 2 Jun or Jul 1812 at Hilton Dorset

m. 9 Apr 1839 in Toronto Canada

d. 6 Feb 1879   d. 9 Feb 1884

William Benjamin	Edward	George Leonard	Cave Nelson	Walter James	Samuel Herbert	Georgina Sarah	Mary Jane	Rebecca Elizabeth	Septimus Albert
b. 5 Jan 1840	b. 24 Mar 1841	b. 5 Jul 1843	b. 23 Feb 1845	b. 22 Aug 1846	b. 25 Nov 1854	b. 17 Nov 1851	b. 17 Nov 1851	b. 11 Nov 1848	b.22 Sep 1857
d. 27 Sep 1929	d. 22 Nov 1884	d. 1 Jun 1902	d. 9 Mar 1902	d. 2 Oct 1928	d. 2 Oct 1937	d. 15 Aug 1902	d. 23 Jun 1878	d. 21 Oct 1907	d. 23 Jun 1878
m. Eleanor Cook	m. Margaret Weir		m. Annie Jane McKewon	m. Grace Shillinglaw	m. Margaret Lee / m. Joshua Hilborn		m. James Bingham	m. William Cain	
b. 1845	b. 1844		b. 1837	b. 2 Mar 1844	b. 1855				
d. 1909	d. 1923		d. 1916	d. 12 Nov 1920	d. 1928				

Children of William Benjamin & Eleanor Cook:

| Alberta m. William Marshall Humphrey | Elizabeth m. Peter Cane | Alfretta m. Alfred Sharples | Florence m. George Parkinson | Kenneth m. Gertrude Treloar | Jack | Doris | Leonard Russell | May m. Joseph Mitchel | Benjamin m. Phoebe Madill | Eva Caroline m. Moston? | Herbert m. Margaret Annan | Frank m. Jessie Humphey |

Children of Herbert & Margaret Annan: Bruce, Cecil, Muriel, Helen, Jack, William, Harold, Gordon, Audry

Children of Alberta & William Marshall Humphrey:

| Rosella Mary m. Wesley Thompson | Helen | Leonard | Clifford | Rae | Lucille | Yvonne m. Ray Upson | Loraine | Eugene | Lloyd | Dianne |

THE CANADIAN CONNECTIONS (Continued)

Samuel Foot = Elizabeth Bennett
b. 6 Nov 1803 at Stoke Wake or b. 13 Jan 1807 at Mappowder   b 2 Jun or Jul 1812 at Hilton Dorset
m. 9 Apr 1839 in Toronto Canada
d. 6 Feb 1879   d. 9 Feb 1884
ALL CHILDREN BORN IN ONTARIO CANADA

William Benjamin	Edward	George Leonard	Cave Nelson	Walter James	Samuel Herbert	Georgina Sarah	Mary Jane	Rebecca Elizabeth	Septimus Albert
b. 5 Jan 1840	b. 24 Mar 1841	b. 5 Jul 1843	b. 23 Feb 1845	b. 22 Aug 1846	b. 25 Nov 1854	b. 17 Nov 1851	b.17 Nov	b. 11 Nov 1848	b. 22 Sept 1857
d.27 Sep 1929	d.22 Nov 1884	d.1 Jun 1902	d. 9 Mar 1902	d. 2 Oct 1928	d.2 Oct 1937	d.15 Aug 1902	d.23/6/78	d. 21 Oct 1907	d. 23 Jun 1878
m. Eleanor Cook	m.Margaret Weir		m. Annie Jane McKewon	m. Grace Shillinglaw	m. Margaret Lee	m. Joshua Hilborn	m. James Bingham	m. William Cain	
b. 1845	b. 1844		b. 1837	b. 2 Mar 1844	b. 1855				
d. 1909	d. 1923		d. 1916	d. 12 Nov 1920	d. 1928				

| Alberta m. William Marshall | Elizabeth m. Peter Cane | Alfretta m. Alfred Sharples | | May m. Joseph Mitchel | Benjamin m. Phoebe Madill | Eva Caroline m. Moston ? | Herbert m. Margaret Annan | | Frank m. Jessie Humphrey |

Ross m. Irene Bellanger   Robert m. Lavinia Wilmott   Nora m. Lorne Alcorn   Cora m. Roy Richardson

Robert

William   Beverley

THE CANADIAN CONNECTIONS (Continued)

Samuel Foot = Elizabeth Bennett
b.6 Nov 1803 at Stoke Wake or b. 13 Jan 1807 at Mappowder   b 2 Jun or Jul 1812 at Hilton Dorset
m. 9 Apr 1839 in Toronto Canada
d. 6 Feb 1879   d. 9 Feb 1884
ALL CHILDREN BORN IN ONTARIO CANADA

William Benjamin	Edward	George Leonard	Cave Nelson	Walter James	Samuel Herbert	Georgina Sarah	Mary Jane	Rebecca Elizabeth	Septimus Albert
b. 5 Jan 1840	b. 24 Mar 1841	b. 5 Jul 1843	b. 23 Feb 1845	b. 22 Aug 1846	25 Nov 1854	b. 17 Nov 1851	b. 17 Nov 1851	b. 11 Nov 1848	b. 22 Sept 1857
d. 27 Sep 1929	d. 22 Nov 1884	d. 1 Jun 1902	d. 9 Mar 1902	d. 2 Oct 1928	d. 2 Oct 1937	d. 15 Aug 1902	d. 23 Jun 1878	d. 21 Oct 1907	d. 23 Jun 1878
m. Eleanor Cook	m. Margaret Weir	m. Emily Bennett		m. Annie McKewon	m. Grace Shillinglaw	m. Joshua Hilborn	m. James Bingham	m. William Cain	
b. 1845	b. 1844	b. 1847			b. 2 Mar 1844				
d. 1909	d. 1923	d. 1930			d. 12 Nov 1920 b. 1855 d. 1928				

Ernest   Freda   Wolfe   Arthur
                        m. Ruby Ford

Lillian
m. Samuel Larmon

William   Clarence   Minetta   Grace

100

THE CANADIAN CONNECTIONS (Continued)

Samuel Foot = Elizabeth Bennett
b. 6 Nov 1803 at Stoke Wake or b. 13 Jan 1807 at Mappowder   b 2 Jun or Jul 1812 at Hilton Dorset
m. 9 Apr 1839 in Toronto Canada
d. 6 Feb 1879   d. 9 Feb 1884

Children:

William Benjamin
b. 5 Jan 1840
d. 27 Sep 1929
m. Eleanor Cook
b. 1845
d. 1909

Edward
b. 24 Mar 1841
d. 22 Nov 1884
m. Margaret Weir
b. 1844
d. 1923

George Leonard
b. 5 Jul 1843
d. 1 Jun 1902
m. Emily Bennett
b. 1847
d. 1930

Cave Nelson
b. 23 Feb 1845
d. 9 Mar...d. 2 Oct 1902   1928
m. Annie McKewon
b. 1837
d. 1916

Walter James
b. 22 Aug 1846
d. 2 Oct 1928
m. Grace Shillinglaw Lee
b. 2 Mar 1844
d. 12 Nov 1920

Samuel Herbert
25 Nov 1854
d. 2 Oct 1937
m. Margaret
b. 1855
d. 1928

Georgina Sarah
b. 17 Nov 1851
d. 15 Aug 1902
m. Joshua Hilborn

Mary Jane
b. 17 Nov 1851
d. 23 Jun 1878

Rebecca Elizabeth
b. 11 Nov 1848
d. 21 Oct 1907
m. William Bingham Cain

Septimus Albert
b. 22 Sept 1857
d. 23 Jun 1878

Descendants:

Septimus — Elizabeth

Pearl
m. Frederick Whittlesea

Jean
m. R W Warren

Nancy   Linda   Frederick

Everett
b. 1882
m. Mary Peters

William   Everett Edward Peters   Noreen

Victor

Florence
m. Jack Wagg

William
m Catherine Brown

Evelyn Mildred Stanley Gordon Doris Don Lorna

Victor   Lucille
m. Jim Reilly

Loraine   Glenna   Leila

Horace

101

THE CANADIAN CONNECTIONS (Continued)

Samuel Foot = Elizabeth Bennett
b.6 Nov 1803 at Stoke Wake or b. 13 Jan 1807 at Mappowder   b 2 Jun or Jul 1812 at Hilton Dorset
m. 9 Apr 1839 in Toronto Canada
d. 6 Feb 1879   d. 9 Feb 1884

Children:

William Benjamin
b. 5 Jan 1840
d. 27 Sep 1929
m. Eleanor Cook
b. 1845
d. 1909

Edward
b. 24 Mar 1841
d. 22 Nov 1884
m. Margaret Weir
b. 1844
d. 1923

George Leonard
b. 5 Jul 1843
d. 1 Jun 1902
m. Emily Bennett
b. 1847
d. 1930

Cave Nelson
b. 23 Feb 1845
d. 9 Mar...d. 2 Oct 1902
m. Annie McKewon Shillinglaw
b. 1837
d. 1916

Walter James
b. 22 Aug 1846
d. 2 Oct 1928
m. Grace Margaret Lee
b. 2 Mar 1844
d. 12 Nov 1920 b. 1855 d. 1928

Samuel Herbert
25 Nov 1854
d. 2 Oct 1937
m. Margaret

Georgina Sarah
b. 17 Nov 1851
d. 15 Aug 1902
m. Joshua Hilborn

Mary Jane
b. 17 Nov 1851
d. 23 Jun 1878
m. James Bingham

Rebecca Elizabeth
b. 11 Nov 1848
d. 21 Oct 1907
m. William Cain

Septimus Albert
b. 22 Sept 1857
d. 23 Jun 1878

Descendants of William Benjamin line:

Samuel David Newton 1871-1887
Annie Victoria b. 1872 m. Jessie Brown
Horatio Nelson
Gertrude m. Daniel Hall

George   Laura   Bruce   Victor   Ruby m. Walter Pearson   Roy
m. Marie Cowie

Joan   David   Philip

Descendants of Walter James line:

George Wellington
m. Mrs Edith Buley 1876-1964

Septimus Herbert m. Cora Young

Estella Jane b 1880 m. William Jackson

Daisy Grace b. 1906
Walter James b.1908
Mildred Emma Louise b.1911 m. Lorne Wideman
Samuel David b.1914 m. Mary. Weir
Joseph Richard b.1919
Edythe Nuttall
Rodney

m.Rev. Percy George Powell
m.Hazell Watts

Descendants of Samuel Herbert line:

Richard James ?? -- 1960
m. Elffeda Forsyth

Doris m. Bert Johnston

Carol Douglas   Robert m. Anita   James
                                  Lydia

THE CANADIAN CONNECTIONS (Continued)

Samuel Foot = Elizabeth Bennett
b.6 Nov 1803 at Stoke Wake or b. 13 Jan 1807 at Mappowder b 2 Jun or Jul 1812 at Hilton Dorset
m. 9 Apr 1839 in Toronto Canada
d. 6 Feb 1879   d. 9 Feb 1884

Children:

William Benjamin
b. 5 Jan 1840
d. 27 Sep 1929
m. Margaret Weir
b. 1845
d. 1909

Edward
b. 24 Mar 1841
d. 22 Nov 1884
m. Eleanor Cook

George Leonard
b. 5 Jul 1843
d. 1 Jun 1902
m. Emily Bennett
b. 1847
d. 1930

Cave Nelson
b. 23 Feb 1845
d. 9 Mar...d. 2 Oct 1902

Walter James
b. 22 Aug 1846
1928
m. Annie McKewon Shillinglaw
b. 1837
d. 1916

Samuel Herbert
25 Nov 1854
d. 2 Oct 1937
m. Grace
m. Margaret Lee
b. 2 Mar 1844 b. 1855
d. 12 Nov 1920 d. 1928

Georgina Sarah
b. 17 Nov 1851
d. 15 Aug 1902
m. Joshua Hilborn

Mary Jane
b. 17 Nov 1851
d. 23 Jun 1878
m. James Bingham

Rebecca Elizabeth
b. 11 Nov 1848
d. 21 Oct 1907
m. William Cain

Septimus Albert
b. 22 Sept 1857
d. 23 Jun 1878

Descendants of Septimus Herbert = Cora Young:

Daisy Grace
b. 1906
m. Rev. Percy George Powell

Walter James
b.1908
m. Hazell Watts

Mildred Emma Louise
b. 1911
m.Lorne Wideman

Samuel David
b.1914
m. Mary Weir

Joseph Richard
1919
m. Edythe Nuttall

Children of Walter James b.1908:
- **Mary Elizabeth** b.1946

Children of Mildred Emma Louise:
- **Ronald David** b.1946
- **Lorne Mark** b.1951
- **Larry Stephen** b.1956

Children of Samuel David:
- **Mary Ellen** b.1942
- **Donald Joseph** b.1945
- **Keith Weir** b.1948

Children of Joseph Richard:
- **Joseph Rodney** 1948
- **Jo-Ann Cora** 1949
- **Susan Edythe** 1951
- **Janis Naomi** 1956

Walter James b.1944

Margaret — Grace Ann Mildred 1962

Matthew — Sarah

103

THE CANADIAN CONNECTIONS (Continued)

Samuel Foot = Elizabeth Bennett
b. 6 Nov 1803 at Stoke Wake or b. 13 Jan 1807 at Mappowder   b 2 Jun or Jul 1812 at Hilton Dorset
m. 9 Apr 1839 in Toronto Canada
d. 6 Feb 1879   d. 9 Feb 1884

Edward	George Leonard	Cave Nelson	Walter James	Samuel Herbert	Georgina Sarah	Mary Jane	Rebecca Elizabeth	Septimus Albert
b. 24 Mar 1841	b. 5 Jul 1843	b. 23 Feb 1845	b. 22 Aug 1846	25 Nov 1854	b. 17 Nov 1851	b. 17 Nov 1851	b. 11 Nov 1848	b. 22 Sept 1857
d. 22 Nov 1884	d. 1 Jun 1902	d. 9 Mar 1902	d. 2 Oct 1928	d. 2 Oct 1937	d. 15 Aug 1902	d. 23 Jun 1878	d. 21 Oct 1907	d. 23 Jun 1878
m. Margaret Weir	m. Emily Bennett	m. Annie McKewon	m. Grace Shillinglaw Lee	m. Margaret	m. Joshua Hilborn	m. James Bingham	m. William Cain	

William Benjamin
b. 5 Jan 1840
d. 27 Sep 1929
m. Eleanor Cook
b. 1845
d. 1909

Walter James line:
b. 2 Mar 1844
d. 12 Nov 1920

b. 1837
d. 1916

b. 1855
d. 1928

George = Mrs Edith Buley

George m. Mary Pilkey	Claude	Betty	Clarence m. Irene Pattenden
Jimmy Larry			Sheila Douglas

104

THE CANADIAN CONNECTIONS (Continued)

Samuel Foot = Elizabeth Bennett
b. 6 Nov 1803 at Stoke Wake or b. 13 Jan 1807 at Mappowder   b. 2 Jun or Jul 1812 at Hilton Dorset
m. 9 Apr 1839 in Toronto Canada
d. 6 Feb 1879   d. 9 Feb 1884

William Benjamin	Edward	George Leonard	Cave Nelson	Walter James	Samuel Herbert	Georgina Sarah	Mary Jane	Rebecca Elizabeth		Septimus Albert
b. 5 Jan 1840	b. 24 Mar 1841	b. 5 Jul 1843	b. 23 Feb 1845	b. 22 Aug 1846	25 Nov 1854	b. 17 Nov 1851	b. 17 Nov 1851	b. 11 Nov 1848		b. 22 Sept 1857
d. 27 Sep 1929	d. 22 Nov 1884	d. 1 Jun 1902	d. 9 Mar 1902	d. 2 Oct 1928	d. 2 Oct 1937	d. 15 Aug 1902	d. 23 Jun 1878	d. 21 Oct 1907		d. 23 Jun 1878
m. Eleanor Cook	m. Margaret Weir	m. Emily Bennett	m. Annie McKewon	m. Grace Shillinglaw	m. Margaret Lee	m. Joshua Hilborn		m. James Bingham	m. William Cain	
b. 1845	b. 1844	b. 1847	b. 1837	b. 2 Mar 1844	b. 1855					
d. 1909	d. 1923	d. 1930	d. 1916	d. 12 Nov 1920	d. 1928					

Minetta Vivian	Joseph Arthur m. Amelia Soules	Charles Edwin m. Mary Wright	Herbert m. Ethel W. McCormack		Lillian Maude m. Joseph Burrows	
Hazel Dean m. Ernest Franks	Dorothy Hope m. Douglas Ross	Edith May	Jean Vivian m. Joseph Getty	John Nelson	Ruth Marguerite	Robert Hugh
Ernest James	Joseph Edwin	Douglas	Ramsay	Sarah Ann		

105

THE CANADIAN CONNECTIONS (Continued)

Samuel Foot = Elizabeth Bennett
b. 6 Nov 1803 at Stoke Wake or b. 13 Jan 1807 at Mappowder b 2 Jun or Jul 1812 at Hilton Dorset
m. 9 Apr 1839 in Toronto Canada
d. 6 Feb 1879   d. 9 Feb 1884

Children:

William Benjamin
b. 5 Jan 1840
d. 27 Sep 1929
m. Eleanor Cook
b. 1845
d. 1909

Edward
b. 24 Mar 1841
d. 22 Nov 1884
m. Margaret Weir
b. 1847
d. 1923

George Leonard
b. 5 Jul 1843
d. 1 Jun 1902
m. Emily Bennett

Cave Nelson
b. 23 Feb 1845

Walter James
b. 22 Aug 1846
  - m. Annie McKewon
    b. 1837
    d. 1916
    - **Samuel** m. Elizabeth Rae
      - **Elizabeth** m. Alfred Sanson
        - Milton
        - Stanley
        - Cecil m. Marguerite Stewart McDonald
          - Allen
          - Jean
        - Helen
        - Mary
      - **George** m. Ella Einarson
        - Walter m. Estelle Neff
          - Douglas
          - Howard
        - Verna
        - Jean
        - Jack
      - **Clarence** m. Norma McQuaig
        - Betty Ann
  - b. 9 Mar 1902
    d. 2 Oct 1928
    m. Grace Shillinglaw
    b. 2 Mar 1844 b. 1855
    d. 12 Nov 1920 d. 1928

Samuel Herbert
25 Nov 1854
d. 2 Oct 1937
m. Margaret Lee
  - **Barwell** m. Florence
    - Emma m. Nelson Baker
    - Edward
    - Samuel
    - Rae m. Sarah Grenki
      - Rena
      - Robert
    - Bruce m. May Boyd
      - Allan

Georgina Sarah
b. 17 Nov 1851
d. 15 Aug 1902
m. Joshua Hilborn

Mary Jane
b. 17 Nov 1851
d. 23 Jun 1878
m. James Bingham
  - Ada m. Claude Vickery
    - Clifford m. Florence Harrison
      - Charles
    - Beatrice
    - Florence
  - George m. Parret ?

Rebecca Elizabeth
b. 11 Nov 1848
d. 21 Oct 1907
m. William Cain
  - John
  - Marion
  - George
  - Helen m. Richard Casson
    - Peter
    - Gail
  - Melville

Septimus Albert
b. 22 Sept 1857
d. 23 Jun 1878

106

A typical farmstead barn as was built and used by my great grandfather in Ontario in 1835 and still in use to this day. The animal fodder was stored by taking it up the earthen ramp to the higher floor and this helped to keep the cattle warm on the lower floor below during the severe winters.

The details of the Canadian Connection given in the preceding part of this chapter were as I understood them up until my visit to Ontario in May 1997. As they are still substantially correct I will not change them but will now add the very considerable additional detail given me by my second cousin Sam during my visit to Ontario in May 1997.

The following extracts from Grace and Sam's '*book*' are particularly interesting and give background to the Canadian dynasty of the Foot and Foote families.

"*In the year 1800 the families of the Foot's and Bennett's both resided in the County of Dorset in the South of England. Samuel Foot Jr. was born in 1803. His cousin Walter was born August 8th 1810. These two cousins emigrated to Canada in 1835, together with several other cousins and neighbours, and settled in the Township of Whitchurch where both raised families*".

"*Samuel had another brother named Abraham and Walter had four other brothers and at least one sister. Two of the brothers went to Australia and two stayed in England. The latter two were in the "King's" body guard (William IV) because of their height and size and their great loyalty to the Crown. Samuel also applied but was turned down as he was just under the required height and weight. This was an extreme disappointment to Samuel, as the families were committed to serving the Crown*".

My great grandfather Samuel Foot was the son of Samuel and Sarah Foot and Walter was the son of James and Rebecca Foot. This is reflected clearly in the Foot family tree in Chapter One.

108

The records indicate that one of the brothers of Walter who remained in England was named William and he married his first cousin Sarah Bennett who was Elizabeth's sister.

The parents of **my great grandmother Elizabeth Bennett** were Elizabeth (or Betty or Betsy) Foot and Cave Bennett, they too were first cousins. Betty and Cave strongly opposed the marriage of Elizabeth and Samuel as they wanted the practice of first cousin marriages to stop. However, Samuel and a number of relatives and friends sailed off to Canada, Elizabeth was either with them or followed soon after.

Prior to marrying Samuel in 1839, Elizabeth resided with a family named Denison who lived in Toronto on Lot Street. While at the Denisons, during the time of the 1837 Rebellion, Elizabeth was entrusted for safekeeping with important documents and valuable jewellery which belonged to the governor of Upper Canada, Sir Francis Bond Head.

Members of the Foote family are familiar with a story handed down about the two cousins and their loyalty to one another. It seems that in the year 1837 when the election in Upper Canada was taking place that it was common for fights to break out in the taverns. Samuel was unfortunately present during one free-for-all. Luckily Walter happened to ride up to the tavern on horseback as the brawl was unfolding and was greeted by the hostler who commented *"They're going to kill your brother"*.

(It was generally thought that these two were brothers because they had the same name, lived on adjoining farms and were such firm friends).

Walter being of a larger and heavier size than Samuel, was very capable of using his fists. It wasn't long before the tavern was empty, except for the two cousins each enjoying a glass of the best ale. These two men had a reputation for *"their high regard for truth and fair play"* and their loyalty to God, to the Queen (Victoria) and to their country (Canada)."

Samuel married Elizabeth in Toronto in 1839 despite the pleas from Elizabeth's parents and her brother and sister back home at Thirnwood Farm near Mappowder, (as recounted earlier), for her to return home. They then raised ten children on their farm. William Benjamin was the eldest and was born in 1840. The youngest was Septimus who was the seventh son and was also said to be named after the Denison's youngest son born a few months earlier.

My grandfather, George Leonard Foot was born on this farm in 1843 and the story of his life has already been detailed.

When Samuel and Elizabeth were expecting their seventh child , Samuel rode off on horseback to fetch the midwife. Upon returning to the house with the midwife both were surprised to see Elizabeth in a rocking chair by the stove, with an infant in each arm. Twins had been born which she had had unaided. They were named Georgina Sarah Ann and Mary Jane Eliza. The date was 17th November 1851.

Walter Foot married Jane Taylor in 1847. Jane was of Quaker descent. Their family consisted of four children, James Walter, John H., Ann Rebecca and Jane Elizabeth. All are buried in the Newmarket cemetery, except Ann who rests in Mount Pleasant Cemetery, Toronto. I have now visited and seen and photographed all of these gravestones.

Samuel and Elizabeth at first bought a farm on the fourth Concession of Whitchurch Ontario. At this farm their first three sons, William Benjamin, Edward B, and my grandfather George Leonard were born. I have now visited this farm and seen the old building and remains of the barn built so many years ago.

In 1845, Samuel sold this farm and moved to a farm on the sixth concession of Whitchurch. Here is a copy of the sale inventory.

CREDIT SALE
to be
sold by Auction
on Thursday October 16^{6th} 1845
on the Premises of

Samuel Foote
No. 28 4th Concession of

WHITCHURCH

The following property consisting of:

35   Sheep
5   Colts (each rising 3 years old)
3   Yolk of Oxen
1   Sow and litter of Pigs
2   Ploughs

1   gang of Harrows
1   Fanningmill
    and a Churn

TERMS: *Fifteen months credit for Sums above One Pound upon furnishing approved Client Notes.*
Sums of One Pound and under - Cash down.

SALE *to commence at ELEVEN O'CLOCK October 6th 1845.*

_____Auctioneer
Porter, Printer Newmarket

Samuel purchased his next farm side by side with his cousin Walter on the sixth concession of Whitchurch. Their houses were not far apart and they shared a laneway.

I cannot determine whether the fourth son Cave Nelson was born on the first or the second of Samuel's farms.

In amplification of details given above, the following contains many extracts from narratives of my great grandparents lives, which were compiled by Everett Edward Peters Cain in 1986 are of interest. The great similarity between the results of our completely independent researches tends to confirm that between us we have just about got it right.

*My great grandparents, Samuel and Elizabeth Foot.
Photograph probably taken at their farm near
Whitchurch Ontario in the 1860s or 1870s.*

My great grandfather, Samuel Foot was born on November 6, 1803 in a pretty village called Stoke Wake which is in Dorset, a very beautiful county in Southern England. I think there were just four children in Samuel's family and he was the second one. His older sister, Eliza was born on March 29, 1801 and his younger sister, Annabelle was christened in the nearby village of Mappowder on September 4th 1804. His younger brother Abraham completed the family and was christened in Mappowder June 5th 1807. Mappowder is only a couple of miles to the west of Stoke Wake, and the parish registers of these two places abound with Foots, as do the registers of a great number of the surrounding villages, all of which are only a few miles from each other.

Samuel's parents were Samuel Foot and Sarah Ann Foot who were first cousins, and he and his sisters and brother had at least twelve aunts and uncles and many many cousins who all grew up in one or the other of these picturesque small villages.

As well as the Foots, another family living in that area, particularly around Buckland Newton, were the Cains. (sometimes spelt Cain, Cane, Kaynes, Caines or Canes). When a family decided to emigrate and go to a new land like North America they often set out as a large family group - brothers and sisters, aunts, uncles, cousins, parents and very often neighbours as well. They would settle in the new world near each other and often marry into each other's families as their ancestors had done in the past.

As early as the middle 1830s many members of the Foot clan from Dorset had made that long and perilous journey across the Atlantic to Canada, settling in the general area just North of Toronto. One of those who made the voyage was my great grandfather Samuel Foot. One of the families whose names kept cropping up with the Foots was the Bennett family of Stoke Wake who came to the same area just north of Toronto at the same time as the Foots. On April 9th 1939 my great grandfather Samuel Foot married Elizabeth Bennett. The ceremony took place at Holy Trinity Anglican Church, Thornhill, Ontario.

Samuel and Elizabeth settled on a farm in Whitchurch township, a few miles north of Thornhill where they began their married life. Their first child was William Bennett (or was it Benjamin?) Foote, who was born on January 5th 1840 in Whitchurch. He was followed, on March 24th 1841 by another son, Edward. Their third son George Leonard, was born July 5th 1843 (my grandfather), their fourth son was Cave (pronounced '*Keeve*') Nelson born February 23rd 1845 followed by a fifth son, Walter James on August 22nd 1846. In 1848 their first daughter, Rebecca Elizabeth was born on November 11th, she was followed on November 17th 1851 by twins Georgina Sarah and Mary Jane. A sixth son Samuel Herbert was born November 25th 1854. Finally on September 22nd 1857 their seventh son Septimus Albert was born. I cannot be sure whether he was named Septimus because he was the seventh son or was named after another relation, perhaps both.

Samuel and Elizabeth spent all their married life in Whitchurch, Samuel's second cousin Walter Foot lived on the next farm. Down in Markham township, immediately south of Whitchurch, lived Abraham Foot, Samuel's brother. Abraham and his family are buried in Holy Trinity Anglican Church in Thornhill. The old wooden church itself, where Samuel and Elizabeth were married, has been moved to another location, and a red brick Baptist Church now stands on the original Yonge Street site. The old

Anglican churchyard is still there however. Samuel though is not buried in Thornhill. He lies in Newmarket Cemetery, Whitchurch township, only a few feet away from the grave of his second cousin Walter who had been his friend and neighbour for so many years. My great grandfather died on February 6th 1879 at the age of seventy five years and three months, and was laid to rest beside the grave of his youngest son, Septimus Albert, who died just eight months before his father.

It is recounted that during the funeral service someone missed Ernest and Arthur, the two little sons of Samuel and Elizabeth's daughter Georgina Sarah. Several people searched quietly everywhere for them. When the doors of the hearse were opened to receive the coffin, they were found sitting inside the hearse. They said they wanted to go to Newmarket!

My great grandmother Elizabeth Bennett was born June 2nd 1812. She was born in the parish of Hilton, in Dorset, England, just south of Stoke Wake, and was baptised on August 9th 1812. Her parents, Cave and Elizabeth (Betty) Bennett (nee Foot), already had one son, George who was born in 1802 or perhaps a year earlier, but had only lived for three months. As stated earlier, it was common practice in those days to give a later child the same name as the deceased child. I do not know if this is what happened here but it seems a good possibility. Their second son was named George Foot Bennett and was born in 1805, a third son Edward Russell, who had been born in 1806 and christened on January 14th 1807, and a fourth son John was born April 8th 1810. Elizabeth was fourteen years old when her mother gave birth to twins, William and Jane. The year was 1826. In 1827 brother Thomas arrived and a year later, in 1828, her brother Cave arrived and finally, in 1830, her youngest brother Barwell was born.

In addition to the above they also had daughters Mary, date of birth unknown, and Ann who was born in 1818. There is a possibility that there was another daughter, twin sister to Barwell born in 1830. To recap, Cave and Elizabeth (Betty) Bennett (nee Foot) probably had thirteen children.

George Foot Bennett married Susannah Hooper on October 12th 1828. They appear to have emigrated to Canada in about 1832 as Susannah died in the Toronto area in 1833 leaving a baby son. I believe he was named Edward Cave.

The Foots, Bennetts and Hoopers arrived in the Toronto area between 1832 and 1836 and most took farms to the north of the city. There is some evidence to believe that Elizabeth came out on her own in 1835.

The Toronto areas in the middle 1830s was a seething political turmoil culminating with William Lyon Mackenzie's ill fated rebellion of 1837. It must have been a rather difficult transition for a twenty three year old girl who had grown up in a quiet country village in Dorset to find herself in a fast growing, restless pioneer town that was Toronto at that time. However, just a year and a half after the Rebellion, Elizabeth Bennett *'of Toronto'*, according to the marriage register, was married in Holy Trinity Church, Thornhill to Samuel Foot *'of Whitchurch'* whose home village in Dorset, England was only a few miles from her own. One of the witnesses at the wedding was George Foot Bennett whose wife had been Susannah Hooper who died a few years previously.

Elizabeth and her husband, Samuel, began their married life on a farm in Whitchurch Township, not far north of Thornhill, the community where Samuel's brother Abraham Foot and his wife Catherine Hooper, had their farm. Abraham and Catherine had been married in Hazelbury Bryan where George Foot Bennett and Susannah Hooper had also been married. Catherine Hooper had been a witness to George and Susannah's marriage and we can be reasonably sure that Susannah and Catherine were sisters.

Life could not have been easy for any of our great grandparents trying to make a home in the forestland of Ontario in the 1830s and 1840s. The main road, Yonge Street, that ran north from Toronto was not much more than a trail hacked through the woods. In any case, my great grandparents and all their fellow pioneers were not daunted, but worked very hard clearing the land and making homes for themselves and their families.

For the information of the non Canadian reader, Yonge Street starts at the Toronto waterfront on Lake Ontario and runs north for 1900 Kilometres. It is indeed the longest street in the world and certainly for the first twenty or so Kilometres which I drove along during my visit, also one of the busiest!

Elizabeth and Samuel Foot's first four children were all boys, William, George, Cave and Walter, then their first daughter Elizabeth Rebecca was born, followed by their fifth son, Samuel Jr. Their second and third daughters were twins, Georgina and Mary. Twins run in families and as narrated earlier I myself am also one of a twin. After the twins birth two years elapsed before Elizabeth gave birth to her last child, a son, Septimus Albert.

My Foot great grandparents raised all their nine children in Whitchurch Township. They knew the sorrow of losing their youngest son, Septimus, who died in June 1878. He had not yet reached his twenty-first birthday. Seven months later my great grandfather Samuel died just two months before he and Elizabeth would have celebrated their fortieth wedding anniversary. My great grandmother was a widow for five years. In 1882 her daughter, Elizabeth Foote Cain had given birth to Everett Thomas Cain. He was just two years old when Elizabeth Bennett Foot died on February 19th 1884. She was laid to rest in Newmarket Cemetery beside her husband and son. She was in her seventy first year.

I cannot conclude this chapter on the Canadian Connections without making some reference to my grandfather's brother and my granduncle, Walter James Foote, if for no other reason he was the grandfather of my second cousin Samuel in Aurora, and also of several other cousins who I met on my visit to Ontario.

Walter James Foote was born August 22nd 1846, married Grace Shillinglaw and was the father of five sons and three daughters. He died October 2nd 1928.

The following extracts from the obituary notices of his death describe him well.

PIONEER OF WHITCHURCH
WALTER J. FOOTE
IS DEAD.

Stouffeville October 2nd 1928.

Death today claimed one of the pioneers of Whitchurch, Walter James Foote, J.P., 83 years old, who expired on the farm of his son, Septimus H. Foote,

Concession 6, where he latterly made his residence, which is within six miles of his birthplace.

Walter J. Foote was one of the best known figures in the district having farmed all his life until retirement some years ago in Whitchurch, Vaughan and Uxbridge. He was appointed Justice of the Peace by the late Sir James Whitney more than fifteen years ago, was a veteran of the Fenian Raid, a member of the Orange Order, and a Conservative.

Some three years ago, he attracted attention by his feat of travelling unaccompanied to Great Britain at the age of 80, which he had visited three times in his life. Mr Foote made the journey without mishap, visiting the Wembley Exhibition and touring extensively in the course of his three months in the Old Country.

During the Fenian Raid he enlisted under Captain Carthew of Newmarket. He has been a life long member of the Anglican Church and has served Uxbridge Township as school trustee for many years.

Walter James had first visited England in 1892 to collect monies left by Barwell Bennett in his will for his Canadian nephews and nieces. He also visited in 1902, only months before his brother George Leonard died. During his final trip in 1925, he was photographed with his cousin Reginald Bennett who was holding his then four year old daughter Mary on his knee.

My granduncle Walter James is buried in the Uxbridge cemetery where his son Septimus Herbert is also buried and where my dear second cousin Sam also hopes to be laid to rest one day.

The tombstone of Samuel and Elizabeth Foote, my great grandparents, in Newmarket cemetery.

The considerable amount of material given to me by my Canadian cousins referring to my other granduncles and grandaunts, I must of necessity omit from this narrative as *FOOTSTEPS* is already getting too long!

Before concluding this Chapter I feel I must also record some detail of the Cain family, particularly as it was my second cousin Everett Edward Peters Cain who had research carried out on our family genealogy in the mid 1980s and whom I met in May 1997. He has passed much of the result of his own work on to me.

My great, great, great, grandparents, George Foot and Sarah Cain.

George Foot was the brother of John Foot, my other great great, great grandfather. George like his brother was born and raised in Mappowder, Dorset. He was four years younger than John and was the third son in a family of seven sons and two daughters.

The parish registers of St. Peter and St. Paul show that George Foot was christened there on August 1st 1751. When he was twenty-seven years old he married a girl from the neighbouring parish of Buckland Newton, a few miles west of Mappowder. Her name was Sarah Cain and their wedding took place on January 29 th 1778 in the Church of the Holy Rood, Buckland Newton. I visited this lovely church a few months ago and it is situated in a most peaceful spot and would be the perfect place for a wedding today and it seems that it has changed very little since that wedding over two hundred years ago.

George and Sarah settled in Mappowder where they raised six children. The oldest was a daughter, Sarah Anne, my great, great grandmother, who has already been described earlier in this book. Their second child was a son, Richard, christened in Mappowder on December 29th 1779. He lived a long life of eighty years, and now lies buried in Thornhill Ontario, over three thousand miles from his native soil. Their third child was another son, George, who was christened on August 13th 1781, followed by a daughter Betty, whose christening date was the day after Christmas in 1783. Two years later they had another daughter, Mary who was baptised on June 17th 1785, and finally, a year and a half later their last child, a son, Thomas was born on December 3rd 1786.

George Foot died in 1791 at the young age of forty years, there is no trace of when my great, great, great grandmother Sarah died but it is likely they are both buried at Mappowder with a great many of their family members from generations before and after buried around them.

My grandaunt, Elizabeth Rebecca Foote was born to Samuel and Elizabeth Bennett in September 1848 and, (I believe), christened on 11th November 1848. She was their first daughter. The Foots were good friends of the Cain family who also lived in Whitchurch, Ontario but moved away in about 1855 to Sandford, Ontario. The families kept in touch and sometime around 1880, Elizabeth Rebecca married William Cain, son of Thomas Cain. They settled on a farm in the community of Sandford where they raised five children, Everett Thomas being the oldest, he was followed by two brothers, Victor, Samuel and William Herbert, then by his only sister, Florence Elizabeth. Their last child was a son, Horace Milton.

Elizabeth Rebecca Foote Cain lived all her married life in Sandford. She died at the age of fifty nine on October 21st 1907 and is buried in Sandford Cemetery.

Everett Thomas Cain married Mary Peters and they had three children, William, Everett Edward Peters and Noreen.

As stated above, I met Everett Edward Peters Cain on my visit to Ontario in May 1997 and am much indebted to him for much of the information given in this Chapter.

I have not yet found any evidence of when a male member of the Buckland Newton Cain family emigrated to Canada but must assume that the parents of Thomas Cain emigrated from the Buckland Newton area sometime in the 1830s or 1840s. Perhaps he was a brother or nephew, of the two sisters, Sarah and Caristian (or Christiana?) Cain who had both married into the Foot family at Mappowder. I will try to resolve this question one day.

The consequence of the tangled relationships caused by the inter marrying of my ancestors produced interesting results when I fed them into a computer programme called the *'Family Tree Maker'*.

This informs me that I am not only myself but also my own 3rd, 4th and 5th cousin. My son and daughter are therefore shown as my 3^{rd,} 4th and 5th cousins once removed and my own father is also my 2nd, 3rd and 4th cousin.

From the Family Tree schematics shown in Chapter One it will also be seen William Foot was my great, great, great, great grandfather, not once but four times over. Once through his son John and three times through his son George. I think I, or rather we, as this will apply to all of us, must have had more great, great, great grandfathers and great, great grandfathers and mothers than anyone!

CHAPTER SIX

MY CHILDHOOD YEARS

(AGE 5 TO 7)

"Wait, thou child of hope, for time shall teach thee all things"

Martin Farquhar Tupper (1810 - 1889) English writer.

This account begins in 1935 when I was 5 years old. We had moved to East Luccombe Farm which my father leased from the Hambros Estates, in 1932. He worked very hard during the difficult years of farming depression and was beginning to make a success. His former heavy drinking was much reduced, limited now only to Market days in Blandford and Saturday night at the Hambro Arms at Milton Abbas. He remained, however, a most stubborn man with a strong will. He was not seeing, or maybe not accepting, the changes in agriculture which were then beginning to be implemented by others. My mother was very happy there, we had a nice house with running water but no electricity. Mother again joined the Mothers Union and made many friends. My eldest sister Phyllis remained with Grandmother Emily at Cheselbourne so I only had my sister Doris for company.

I have very fond memories of East Luccumbe. I went to school at Milton Abbas for the first time at the age of 5. We, that is my sister Doris and I, had to walk about a mile and a half, part of the way being a short cut across a field and I recall us being chased by an angry cow which had recently being deprived of her calf. It was one of father's cows. There was a beautiful walnut tree in the front garden of our house, I revisited it recently and 60 years later that tree is still there, but looks in poor condition now.

My sister tells me that one Christmas Dad took a churn of milk to the school for the children's Christmas party but a German girl who worked at the school shut the door on him and said she didn't want it. She thought he was trying to sell it to her. Dad said, or rather, shouted: *"I'm bloody well giving it to you"*. Also that whilst at East Luccombe Dad had a young woman agricultural student to work with him for a short while. She loved it there and thought Dad was a superb and most dedicated farmer.

I recall one summer when I was about 5 years old that we were having tea on the lawn with visitors and mother opened a tin of salmon (a luxury for us), the salmon was for the grown ups and I cried because I couldn't have any and hid under the table. I suffered under the nickname of *'I want some salmon'* for many years. I used to visit another boy of my own age named Kenneth who lived in a new bungalow on the road to Milton Abbas. I was close to my sister Doris but didn't really know my eldest sister Phyllis as she was still living with her grandmother at Cheselbourne.

Other memories. Riding on the back of the sow. The butcher coming and slaughtering one of the pigs; of it being gutted and the hairs scraped off in a bath of boiling water, of blood everywhere which the dogs licked up. We had a sheep dog named Jack which was given to mother and father by his mother as a wedding present. Jack would cross three fields and providing the gates were open, bring the cows in for milking and take them back to the right field afterwards. He seldom left father's side and when father went to market at Blandford on the bus which ran past the top of the lane, Jack would wait all day at the bus stop for him to come home. The other dog was a small terrier named 'Spot'.

Of Aunt Cissy's boys, Peter and James (Jim) coming to stay and of them and I hammering old horseshoes on the anvil in the barn on a Sunday afternoon and my father being roused from his nap and chasing us down the lane, with his stick. Although I suppose I was too young to know better. Of these boys who were about 13 and 14 years old, egging me to ask father for his shotgun. That didn't go down very well either!

I remember the cart horses, father loved his horses and they were never overworked and were well looked after by father and the Carter, George Basell. There was "Captain", "Major", "Sergeant", "Darling" and one other whose name I forget. Of course, all of us children could sit on the back of any one of them with room to spare. Darling was sired with a thoroughbred hunter and had a foal called Primrose, Dad had ideas of rearing and training this foal and riding to hunt on it one day. Alas this was never to be.

I have said that father had a short temper, he often threatened me with the 'strap' or 'a clip round the ear' when I was naughty, but although he shouted a lot, I do not ever remember him actually hitting me or my sisters when we were naughty. On one occasion when I had got hold of a box of matches and was burning some cardboard, it was the cardboard carton from a box of lemonade crystals which mother used to make up for us, he chased me round the house and I hid in the attic for what seemed like hours until Mum had calmed him down.

Also in the summer, Uncle George, Aunt Dora and their three children, Joan, Jack and Doreen always came to stay. Jack was 12/13 and had an air gun. I used to follow him slavishly as we stalked the hedgerows and shot every bird in sight. There used to be a coloured snapshot of Jack and I holding about twenty dead birds threaded on a string. There were robins, blue tits, yellow hammers, finches, blackbirds, and every species of bird which were then so abundant in the Dorset countryside. In those days, before the conservationists put us right, we thought nothing of it, neither did the adults admonish us. When Uncle George and family were with us we usually went on the only holiday we ever had each year and it was always a day trip to Weymouth, where we played on the sands for a few hours. Once at Weymouth, probably in 1937, we went on board HMS Royal Oak which was anchored in Weymouth Bay (or at Portland), I cannot remember for sure, Uncle George, by then having retired from the Royal Navy helped show us round and we were all impressed by the big 15 or 16 inch guns and by the Galley where they were making chocolate. This beautiful ship was lost with great loss of life, eight hundred and thirty three, at Scapa Flow in October 1939. It was probably this experience, together with my fathers urgings which led me to first consider joining the Royal Navy.

My sister, Doris, cousin, Jack Thorne, Darling, the mare, my father (hiding), my sister Phyllis and me (just!) in 1935.

I remember mother going off to Southampton for the day with the Women's Institute or Mothers Union and visiting RMS Queen Mary the new liner. She came back with marvellous tales of this fine ship and brought me back a small metal model of RMS Queen Mary which I kept for years and of which I was very fond and made me ever more keen to go to sea.

During this period my mother had a baby girl which she had planned to call Hazel Emily but unfortunately she died at birth. My mother was not well, being 'run down' and anaemic, my sister Doris went to stay with sister Phyllis at her grandmother's cottage at Cheselbourne for some months during this period in 1934 or 1935 in order to give her a break. She must have returned home by September 1935 as I remember her accompanying me to school when I started in September 1935.

My father was, by this time, in his late forties. His eyesight was not good , neither was his hearing, he never visited a doctor and did nothing to remedy these failings. In retrospect we believe that he was by then a diabetic. This probably accounted for his short temper, stubbornness and his sight and hearing difficulties. An incident I recall which highlighted his problem was that he had sent a cow to market with an ingrown horn, for this he was served with a summons. When the Police Constable came on his bicycle to deliver the summons (or warning?), I remember father swearing at him and threatening him with his walking stick.

Another similar situation arose during harvesting when Uncle George, who had father's twelve bore shotgun and was shooting the rabbits which ran out of the wheat field in large numbers as the binder reduced their hiding places, shot into the corn and unwittingly killed a hare.

Hare was '*game*' and belong to the estate. The estate gamekeeper who was also there to help shoot the rabbits then remonstrated with Uncle George for his 'crime'. Father seeing the row, jumped off the horse drawn binder which he was operating, rushed over in his bull-headed fashion and set about the gamekeeper with his stick. Perhaps these incidents explain why, in late 1937, we were served notice to quit this lovely farm.

Another early memory is that of myself as a 6 year old helping to stack the sheaves of corn into hiles (or stooks) to dry and then father and his men coming along with the horse and wagon to pick them up to put into the stack where they dried even more and then, at the end of October or early November the big traction engine with the threshing machine arriving. It had written on it in big letters *'Robert Thorne of Verwood'*. The corn was then threshed and this operation was very dusty and everyone finished the day black with the dust of the husks. I remember thousands of mice, and I do mean thousands, running out from under the straw stack as they neared the bottom and of the sheep dog, "Jack" and also our little terrier, "Spot", chasing and killing the mice and of me helping with a stick. We killed hundreds but thousands got away. Of "Spot" catching the occasional rat, and of one instance of a rat with its teeth clamped firmly on to the dogs jaw as he shook his head to free it.

All this was to come to an end. I remember the day of the sale and as a 7 year old it was most exciting for me to see so many people and so much activity. My mother produced ham sandwiches and lots of bread and cheese and there was also beer and cider laid out on a long trestle tables. I have a copy of the Farm sale of implements and cattle when father sold up on Friday 1st October 1937.

Here are some extracts:

SALE BY AUCTION
Friday, October 1st 1937
East Luccombe Farm, Milton Abbas, Dorset
by Thos. Ensor & Son

Farm Implements:

Iron pig trough	2/-
Wheelbarrow	12/-
32 round ladder	22/-
"Ransome's" Double furrow Plough	£7 .. 15 .. 0d
Grindstone	12/-
Portable fowl house	15/-
Hen coops	2/-
3 Nosebags (new)	13/-
Plough	3/-
Horse rake	25/-
"Deering" 6 - ft, self Binder	£19 .. 0 .. 0d
Two-horse farm wagon and laders	£ 5 .. 15 .. 0d
Folding elevator and horse gear	£13 .. ..0 .. 0d
Scotch cart and laders	£3 ... 10 .. 0d
Carpenter's bench and vice	11/-
2 milking buckets	4/-
Dung Putt	7/-
"Harrison McGregor" Corn Grinding Mill	£4 .. 10 .. 0d

Cart Horses:

Bay Horse	"Captain"	7 Guineas
Bay Horse	"Sergeant"	5 Guineas
Bay Filly	(3 years old)	40 Guineas
Bay mare	"Darling" (with foal)	40 Guineas

Cattle:

"Topsy" and calf	£21 .. 0 .. 0d
"Lee" and calf	£26 .. 10 .. 0d
"Pansy" and calf	£38 .. 10 .. 0d
"Phyllis" and calf	£15 .. 0 .. 0d
"Rose" and calf	£37 .. 10 .. 0d
Pure Bred Guernsey Bull (2 years old)	£13 .. 4 .. 0d
"Daisy" (barren)	£11 .. 15 .. 0d
"Doris" (in calf)	£19 .. 10 .. 0d
etc. etc.	

Although the above is only an extract, it can be seen from the very low prices, even for those days, that the proceeds from this sale were in no way sufficient for my father to start again by himself in the only profession which he knew.

The timing of my father losing his farm was most unfortunate as I am told that it was in 1936, with stirrings of war on the horizon, that farming started to come out of the doldrums and farmers actually started to make money. This trend of course continued and most farmers did very well during the war, and even better since.

East Luccumbe Farm House.
The walnut tree is still there in 1997

CHAPTER SEVEN

MY CHILDHOOD YEARS (AGE 7 TO 12)

"Ah! Happy years! once more who would not be a boy!"

George Gordon, Lord Byron (1788 - 1824)

We moved from East Luccombe Farm in October 1937 to a three bed terraced house at Winterbourne Whitechurch, a village about four miles from Milton Abbas and on the main Blandford to Salisbury road, now called the A354. I remember little of this period, except that the house seemed very small. My sister Doris and I went to the local school which was only about 200 yards from home. I recall that we both caught measles or German measles and of lying in bed all day reading comics.

My father worked on a nearby farm. One of his tasks was to look after some heifers in a field about a mile down a country lane and he borrowed mother's old high stepping bicycle. Whether he could ride a bicycle when he was younger I do not know, but I remember him trying to ride it and steering himself straight into the ditch amongst the stinging nettles. Poor father, his sight, hearing and balance were getting progressively worse. I do not know why we left Winterbourne Whitchurch, but we did in the spring of 1938, it must have been about May as I do remember receiving my 8th birthday cards whilst we were there. Whilst at Winterbourne Whitechurch my sister Phyllis became 14, left school and her grandmother and came to live with us for a short while but she was taken on as a children's nurse by a family living in London. She tells me she was picked up from home and driven to London in a black and yellow Rolls Royce in June 1938.

We moved to Charlton, a hamlet near to Ludwell and about 3 miles from Shaftesbury, our house was called Holly Bush House and it was a very pleasant place to live. We could look up over the chalk downs to see 'Wyngreen', a local beauty spot and landmark at the top of Zig-Zag hill. I went to the nearby Infant's School and my sister Doris who by this time was 12, went to the big school for over 11's at Donhead St Andrew.

We only stayed at Charlton about 6 months, my father quarrelled with his boss. This was the first of many such occurrences where I suspect my father either didn't hear his instructions properly or decided to do things his own way, *'because he knew better'*, or didn't do the job properly because of his poor eyesight. Some things which I recall did happen there were:

My sister Phyllis was not happy in London and returned to live with us, for the first time I could remember, and she got a job in a shop in Shaftesbury to which she cycled to work. The roof of my maternal grandmother's cottage at Cheselbourne finally succumbing to the ravages of age and the turkeys, fell in, and Gran came to live with us. She was then 81, had only one eye and also suffered from leg ulcers. My mother had to bathe these daily and I remember how dreadful they looked and smelt. Jack, father's faithful old sheep dog died at the age of 17, he was much mourned by us all.

I cannot yet determine whether we left Charlton in the autumn of 1938 or the spring of 1939, but our next move was to a cottage at Field Barn about a mile outside the village of Tarrant Monkton where my father had been promised the job of managing this mixed dairy and arable farm for an old farmer friend of his, a Mr John Bugg. Living in the cottage at Field Barn was to be a temporary arrangement until we could move into the Manor Farm house down in the village and near to the farm buildings.

As a nine year old, my memories from now on are much clearer and more detailed. Our house was less than a mile from the perimeter of what had been an army and Prisoner of War camp during the first World War and was then downland and covered in gorse. We acquired at this time a black puppy which we named Grip and he was my only companion. We used to wander over the downland chasing, and often catching rabbits which we took home for Mum to cook. Rabbit was the mainstay meat for us and many other poor families as they were plentiful and easy to come by. Something I always found puzzling was that chicken was then and right up to recent years, considered to be a luxury food, even in the country. Perhaps it was because the battery production processes, now so common, had not then started.

At this time, the spring/summer of 1939, the war was pending and I well remember the 'Caterpillar' tractors moving on to the old army camp and making tracks and clearing the gorse. They set fire to the gorse and I was on hand to chase the rabbits, some of them on fire, as they ran for cover. There were some old concrete bunkers there which I used to play in, I believe they were used to hold German Prisoners of War during the First World War. In a very short space of time the whole area was covered in tents, and then as the numbers of soldiers grew, some Nissen huts with concrete bases were erected.

I recall that the road between the Manor Farm and the cottages at Field Barn was a dirt track road and there was a 5 bar gate at one point to keep the cattle from straying. We children used to wait by or play near the gate in order to open it if a car went through in the hope of getting a couple of pennies. Unfortunately the amount of traffic probably averaged less than two cars per day so we did not make much out of this practice.

My sister Doris had to go to school by bus at Spetisbury which was about five miles away. I attended the village school, the Head Mistress and, indeed, the only teacher was a Miss Rawlings and she managed the little school of about twenty-five pupils ranging from the ages of 5 to 11. I had great respect for Miss Rawlings, she lived in a small cottage about 100 yards from the school and she was very kind and understanding. She took particular interest in me and three or four other children of the 9/10 year old age group and groomed us well for our Eleven Plus examinations, I think they were called Grammar School Scholarship examinations in those days.

During the summer and autumn of 1939, all talk was of war and when war was eventually declared on 3rd September 1939, I recall vividly that we had not been issued with respirators or gas masks as they were then called. This was probably because we had moved house recently and our records were not with the local authority. The lack of gas masks was a very serious calamity to me. Mother kept some old blankets in water to hang up round the doors in the case of gas as this was advice given to us. Another piece of advice I remember was to lie down and breath as near to the ground as possible. I recall lying in the field practising to breath with my face buried in the grass and being very frightened.

A German bomber came over us in late September or October and dropped a few bombs on the Army Camp, then to be called Blandford Camp. Blandford Camp is now a very large establishment and the Headquarters of the Royal Corps of Signals. In later years, as a Royal Navy Signals Officer, I had many occasions to visit this now very modern establishment and it always brought back the memories of the burning gorse and the rabbits with their fur alight during the summer of 1939. The bombs frightened me even more and I spent much time worrying about gas attacks. My mother was also concerned but was too busy and too worried about how to look after the family (we still had Gran with us), to waste time on it.

My father didn't worry about such trivial matters, he worked long hours on the farm, fell out with his boss on many occasions, I suspect over matters of policy, principle and the quality of his work. For the first time ever, my father was given a tractor to drive. It was a big International and very difficult to start. My father, with his poor eyesight and not being mechanically minded had a lot of trouble and I recall the farmer, John Bugg, accused him of putting water in the fuel tank, whether this was so I do not know. I only knew my father started to worry about his job and detested the tractor and longed for his beloved horses again. He was quite happy to continue to use a two horse plough and plod up and down the field all day, stopping only to rest and feed and water the horses. His furrows would never have been straight enough to win a ploughing contest, but the horses knew what to do!

It was at Field Barn where I first developed my love of wild birds and I began to learn their names and habits.

We had no radio and relied only on the Daily Mail for news. The lack of radio meant that we never knew the time. My father always liked to keep all clocks and watches about thirty minutes fast, and as none of them was reliable, we were often up to an hour early when we needed to keep a timed appointment, such as catching a bus and me going to school. I used to go to school, which was about a mile and a half away over the fields, and often arrived before eight o'clock instead of by nine o'clock. This meant I had to embarrassingly wait about in the play ground until the others arrived about quarter to nine. My mother went to great lengths to ensure I was clean and tidy but I began to be aware that we did not have the money or security that many of the others had.

One incident I recall from Field Barn days was watching the farmer, my father and another farm worker trying to get a cart horse which was hitched to a wagon to move. The horse was a *"Jibber"* as they called such horses, it suddenly decided to stop and not go on. No amount of beating would budge it, even lighted paper under its tail failed to work. In the end the farmer hitched the horses halter to his car and pulled. The horse held out until it suddenly dropped down dead, I suppose of a broken neck. I expect there was a good reason why the horse would not go, perhaps it was sick and knew it couldn't get the wagon up the hill, we shall never know.

We remained at Field Barn for about six months and then moved, as was promised, into the Manor Farm house which was sited in the village of Tarrant Monkton. We did not have the house wholly to ourselves as the front (the best) portion was partitioned off and let to an army officer from Blandford camp. We had plenty of room however, and it was needed as shortly after we moved in, sometime during 1940, my Aunt Annie's employers from Tolpuddle, could no longer put up with her and without warning she arrived by car with all her possessions. Our family then comprised of Mum, Dad, Gran, Aunt Annie, sister Doris and me. All to be looked after by my mother.

My mother remained cheerful and hardworking, maintaining her lively interest in all events and even when an army sergeant and his wife were billeted on us, she managed to cope with the restrictions caused by food rationing without complaint. She used to go without to ensure that father and we children were properly nourished. My father continued to work hard and to have frequent rows with his employer. He had ceased drinking to excess after the loss of his farm and he only went to the pub on Saturday nights. He loved us all dearly but did not, or could not, communicate well. He seldom had a conversation even with my mother, let alone we children. The fact that mother was wearing herself out looking after Gran and Aunt Annie used to make him angry and was often the cause of angry words.

The stability of living in one place and with father keeping one job was to continue for three whole years, during which time I gained confidence at school, made friends with other boys of my own age and retain many happy memories or my boyhood in the Dorset countryside, the Tarrant valley being particularly pleasant. An incident which stands out in my memory was a day in May 1940 when Miss Rawlings came into the classroom one morning and burst into tears as she us told us of the fall of France and that the Germans would be swarming over us within days. As an already frightened little rabbit, this did not help me one bit.

I will recall memories of play. My chums were boys called Michael Gale and Norman Smyth. Together we roamed the hills and fields and river. The River Tarrant was a particular delight as it contained many trout, both brown and rainbow and although we had no fishing lines, our method of catching them was by "tickling" them and at which we were most successful. The aim was to stand in the river up to our knees and look for the trout in the clear water. They usually lurked under the weed, much of which was watercress, and if one ran one's fingers along the body very gently until reaching the gills, then squeezing hard into the gills and throwing the trout onto the bank. Another method was to wrap the weed around the trout and swiftly throw the whole bundle onto the bank. I took home many fine trout of between one and two pounds for mother to cook.

Reasons which helped us to be successful as fishermen were: as the war was in progress, there was no one to manage the water way or supervise the trout. I suspect there will be a gamekeeper or river warden to prevent young lads from doing such things today. Secondly, the summer of 1940 (or 1941 ?) was very dry and the river level fell dramatically. This allowed us to scavenge the river more easily. We also caught many eels, but mother didn't like them and they were usually cooked for the dog, Grip. We spent many hours leaning over the road bridge to the south of the village with bottles on strings. The bottles contained carbide and water and the object was for the bottle to explode under the water and kill the trout. The bottles often exploded, sometimes dangerously when we were not expecting it, but I do not think we ever did more than frighten the fish and leave broken bottles in the stream.

Grip accompanied me on all my expeditions. He was particularly helpful when we were searching for duck's eggs, moorhen's eggs and lapwing's eggs. The adult lapwings, or green plovers or peewits as we called them used to get very angry and dive bomb both me and Grip when we searched for their nests. I have on many occasions taken home up to two dozen plovers' eggs for mum to fry up. The same fate awaited the eggs of the duck, moorhen, pheasant and the occasional partridge. Once again, the game was not supervised due to lack of gamekeepers and we had free range of whatever came into our hands.

It was in 1940 that I started my birds egg collection and I roamed far and wide in search of eggs during the spring/summer of 1940 and 1941. I amassed a superb collection of eggs ranging from crows and rooks to tree creepers, cuckoo, nightjar and even goldfinches. I expect I had nearly every wild countryside bird egg possible to get, in all I believe I had over ninety eggs and was keen to make the number up to a hundred. There were of course no seabirds' eggs and to this day, even after 49 years in the navy, I find that I have little interest in seabirds but can recognise nearly all countryside birds by their flight patterns and their behavioural characteristics. Unfortunately I had kept the eggs on cotton wool in a large cardboard box with a glass lid and when I was 14 and shortly after we had moved once again, my mother accidentally knocked them from the top of a tall cabinet and they were all broken. That ended my egg collecting hobby.

We boys spent much time foraging in the woods, fields and hedgerows, hunting for rabbits, foxes, badgers and anything else of interest. I recall on one occasion we chased a family of red squirrels and cornered them in a small sapling. The poor squirrels must have been frightened out of their skins by us boys shouting and waving sticks to get them down. They eventually jumped down and we chased them away. Fortunately we never caught one. Red squirrels have long since disappeared from the Dorset countryside although there are still some on Brownsea Island in Poole Bay and also on the Isle of Wight.

Another hobby of mine was collecting butterflies. There were many more about then than there are today and butterflies such as Purple Emperor, Painted Ladies, Swallowtail, Red Admiral, White Admiral, Chalkhill Blues, Peacock, Tortoiseshell and Yellow Brimstone were common. As with the birds eggs, we had no idea of conservation and killed many hundreds for no good reason other than to take them home and keep them in our collections. I kept mine in cardboard shoe boxes and killed them by pinning them to a cardboard sheet with a pin through the head.

Whilst at Tarrant Monkton we all attended church regularly, (except father who went regularly once a year at Harvest Festival). I became a choir boy and spent my time eating sweets and giggling in the pews with my friends and being grumbled at by the lady organist. My sister Doris became 14 in 1940, left her school at Spetisbury and she came to work at the village school looking after the five and six year olds as an assistant to Miss Rawlings. She was very good at this and Miss Rawlings tried to encourage her to study and take the exams to become a properly qualified infant teacher but for whatever reason this did not happen.

I recall Miss Rawlings going to the toilet and coming back into the classroom with her dress tucked into her knickers. The poor lady could not understand the sniggering which went on from the class of 8, 9 and 10 year olds. I cannot recall how she found out the reason for our mirth, maybe one of the girls told her.

My eldest sister Phyllis obtained a post as a children's nurse to a family in London but was unhappy there as they expected her to be a 7 day a week domestic servant in addition to looking after the children. She came home to stay with us for a while and then got a job as a shop assistant and live-in help in at a small General Stores in the village of Cattistock about ten miles north of Dorchester and owned by a Mr and Mrs Shergold. She was most happy there and remained for many years, until she married and remained a very close friend of the Shergold family until their deaths. Indeed she and her husband still have many friends in Cattistock and visit the village regularly.

My school career was given a good grounding at Tarrant Monkton. Miss Rawlings spent much time on me and the other Scholarship potentials and as a result I passed my Scholarship to go to Blandford Grammar School at the age of 11. My other three friends did not pass. One other pupil also passed, her name was Christine. She passed a year ahead of me and had already spent a year at the grammar school when I started. However she was company for me to cycle the five miles to school. A bonus for passing my scholarship was that I was given a £5 grant to buy a bicycle. This bicycle gave me a freedom which I had never had and I was able to tour the countryside and devastate the birds nests even further afield. My dog Grip came with me either running alongside, or if he tired he loved sitting on my lap with his paws on the handlebars.

Blandford Grammar school took me into a new world inasmuch that I was now mixing with children of a higher social class than the farm workers' children with whom I had mixed at my primary schools. I quickly became aware that my family did not have as much money or as nice a house as most of the others. This made me very self conscious and I tried to hide my family background. The only thing I remember about the academic side of Blandford Grammar School was that we spent much time being taught how to write properly using big rounded letters. Whether this was a good thing or not I do not know. I think it may have destroyed the individuality and even flow of the writing style of many pupils.

There were three ways of getting to Blandford from Tarrant Monkton. To cycle to Tarrant Hinton on the main Salisbury to Blandford road, leave the cycle in the hedge and catch the bus. It was common practice to leave our cycles by the side of the road near the bus stops. I do not ever remember anyone having their cycle stolen or vandalised. Another route was to cycle via Tarrant Rushton and approach Blandford from the south east. The other and shortest route was to cycle through the Blandford army camp. We were given special passes to do this, I am not sure why. It may have been because we had army personnel staying with us.

A treat which I well remember was that the Army captain who lived in the other half of our house sometimes took us to the Garrison cinema to see a film. This was the first time I saw a film and it was a most exciting highlight. There was one other occasion when I was 10, which sticks in my memory. We, that is Father, Mother, Doris and I were going to the cinema in Blandford on a Saturday afternoon. This was to be my first trip to the cinema and the only time I ever remember that my father planned to attend with us. I was very excited and couldn't wait to go and as my mother and father were not ready at the time of the first intended bus, I was allowed to go on the bus to Blandford without them. They should never have let me do this. I got to the cinema and waited about outside for them for what seemed like hours. I had no watch. Becoming worried, I then caught a bus home. This bus crossed with the bus taking my family going into Blandford. They couldn't find me so went to the police. Lots of worry and confusion when they all came home and found me. None of us made the cinema and I know my father never ever saw a film again. I recall that both Mum and Dad were very understanding but Doris was most angry with me.

CHAPTER EIGHT

MY CHILDHOOD YEARS

(AGE 12 TO 16)

"Keep true the dreams of thy youth"

Fredrich von Schiller (1759 - 1805).

In the late summer of 1942, the brief stability of our family living in Tarrant Monkton for three whole years came to an end. My father had exasperated his employer on too many occasions and was asked to leave. This caused much upset and worry. His next job was again as a farm labourer at a farm at Long Crichel. I remember our cottage was up a long dirt track in the woods, at least a mile from any other habitation and the village. The only other thing which sticks in my memory was that the toilet was in a brick shed sited down the garden and it had a three seat bench. One large hole, one medium and one small aperture for a child. This may seem most incongruous in these days but if one remembers that to go to the toilet in the dark entailed taking a candle or a torch and walking down a long a garden path, it was nice to have company.

There was a pub in the village called the 'Drum and Monkey' which was owned by an erstwhile friend of my father. The name of the owner was Maidment and the family also ran a cattle haulage business, this being how my father knew him as he used to transport my own father's cattle when he had his own farm. Father visited the pub on Saturday nights as was his wont. It was his only relaxation as he continued to work six and sometimes seven days a week, virtually from dawn to dusk. Both mother and father were most concerned about my education. Having had one year at grammar school they wanted it to continue. It was too far for me to go to Blandford and the nearest Grammar School was at Wimborne which was 7 miles away.

I therefore started at Queen Elizabeth's Grammar School, at Wimborne in September 1942 at the age of 12. It was a good school but I was not happy there, I did not know anyone and somehow felt even more self conscious that my family did not have the money, nice house or stability of the others. It was shortly after I started at this school when I learned a salutary lesson which was to last me throughout my life. Talking to some other boys one day, I was asked where I lived and what my father did. I told them that my father was a farmer and when questioned further, I told them we had twenty cows, many pigs, chickens etc. My lie was soon found out as also attending the school were the two sons of the Maidment family, also from Crichel. I was derided by the other boys and this naturally made me most unhappy, but it taught me a lesson. I have never since deliberately told a lie to anyone on any subject and have tried to instil into my own children the importance of the truth in all their dealings.

I did not have a particularly strong constitution and the long cycle ride in all weathers took its toll. I became ill with flu' and was generally 'run down'. I think I was away from school for most of the Spring Term of 1943.

During this period my mother continued to look after Gran, Aunt Annie and of course, my father and me. My eldest sister Phyllis was happily working at the shop in Cattistock and living with the Shergolds and my sister Doris took a job as a children's nurse in Salisbury and only came home once every two or three weeks. I used to cycle up to the main Salisbury to Blandford road to meet her. This was about two miles and we used to take it in turns to ride the bike. One cycling ahead for about 400 yards, leaving the bike and walking ahead, and the other walking to the bike and riding past the other for 400 yards and then repeating the process. She later took a job at the American Red Cross in Salisbury and shared a flat with some other girls. She enjoyed this work and the company and remained there until the end of the war when the establishment closed. She has recently regained contact with one of her girl friends from those days who now lives at Witchampton and as both of them are now widowed, they meet quite frequently.

By the autumn of 1943 the inevitable happened. My father lost his job and we were again in danger of becoming homeless. All farm workers cottages were 'tied cottages' which went with the job , thus we could only get a home if father got a job. He was fortunate in a way that so many younger men were away in the services and that jobs were available, although he went for many interviews which were unsuccessful after the prospective employer noted his poor eyesight, hearing and unsteady walk. My father always walked as if he was crossing a ploughed field, even on the most even of surfaces. I am sure that had he seen a doctor and been properly diagnosed as a diabetic, his condition could have been stabilised. My father and mother were now most concerned about my education and the accessibility of a good school was a factor in my father's decision of where to apply for work, but unfortunately he was not really in a position to pick and choose.

In September 1943 we moved to Morgan's Vale in the county of Wiltshire, a then small village near to Redlynch and about a mile from Downton. My father's job was to run a small farm of about forty acres for two brothers who were successful businessmen (Coal Merchants) and kept the farm as a hobby. It was really an ideal situation for father as he was left to his own devices to look after a few cows, I think about six, a cart horse, two or three pigs and some chickens. A sad incident which I recall was that one day my father was backing the cart horse with a cart into the barn or machinery shed when the floor gave way beneath the horse and it fell down into a pit. The shed had previously had a car inspection pit about six foot deep which had been boarded over. The horse broke its back and died very quickly and I shall always remember the sight of the dead horse sitting up with its head above floor level and its feet resting on the ground as if begging. My father who loved horses so much was very upset.

Our bungalow was very small and we were very cramped as we still had Gran living with us. We could no longer have Aunt Annie and she went to Barnet to live with Uncle George (her brother), and Aunt Dora.

Once again I had to change school and this time I was sent to Bishop Wordsworth's School in Salisbury. This was an excellent school with a good reputation, it was in fact a Public School and listed in the Public School Year Book. The headmaster was a Dr F C Happold, who I remember as a very remote figure (to a 13 year old). Many of the teachers were away to war, most of those I remember were old (probably in their 50s or 60s), and had been at the school for many years.

Indeed I often felt out of place when the teachers spoke to other boys in the class and recalled teaching their own fathers. It was an all boys school. This, as well as my now increasing inferiority complex was heightened by the fact that most boys were from settled and 'well off' families and there were very few country yokels like myself. One teacher in particular stands out in my memory, the French master, Mr Hellman, a Frenchman who had already taught at the school for 40 years and knew and had taught, nearly every boy's father. He kept an old plimsoll in his desk with which he frequently used on our bottoms should we misbehave or fail to do our work properly.

Another disadvantage was that as this was my third grammar school in as many years, the continuity of subject teaching was lost. Somewhere along the line I missed the term or terms at school when certain parts of English History was taught, this proved to be my weak subject for many years - and probably still is. I also missed out on a thorough grounding in mathematics although I think I regained this omission just in time.

During this period I was on my own a lot, particularly during the long winter days and evenings and I became an avid reader and read any book I could lay my hands on, often in bed and with candlelight. As there was no television and we had no radio of any use, (the batteries were usually run out), I would read the very few books we had over and over again. There were two books in particular which I reckon I must have read each a hundred times. One was called 'The Scalp Hunters', a tale of the Wild West and Apache Indians. The other was called

'Chums at Last' a story about two very different boys at a boarding school. Neither were 'classics' but they were all I had and I nearly knew them by heart. One great source of knowledge was a set of Children's Encyclopaedias (ten volumes) by Arthur Mee, printed in 1933, these, similarly, I read and reread so many times that I can recall many of the tales and items of interest to this day.

Although I felt disadvantaged and was a nervous and often frightened pupil, I enjoyed the majority of my time at Bishops Wordsworth's School and made some good friends. I was once given six strokes of the cane by the headmaster for allegedly misbehaving in Art classes, I was supposed to have knocked over a desk but the 'crime' was actually done by two other boys This upset me very much as I was 'not guilty' and felt I had been picked on. Many of the 'sons of the fathers etc.' committed much worse crimes and got away with them.

I did well academically and although my family moved several more times over the next three years I remained at Bishop Wordsworth's School until I had taken my Oxford School Certificate and gained a matriculation. A 'Matric' was achieved by getting five Credits in the final exams, a credit was a mark of over 60%, a Pass was over 45%, and a Distinction over 75%. Those pupils who gained a 'Matric' were strongly recommended to stay on at school for a further two or three years to take their Higher School Certificate. This was slightly higher than the present 'A' Levels. Staying on at school was, however, out of the question as my family circumstances were such that we were unlikely to be living near enough to Salisbury for me to continue, and in any case, although Mum and Dad were prepared to sacrifice much for my sake, they just couldn't afford to keep me. There were no grants in those days, or at least none that we knew of.

Other memories of Bishop Wordsworth School days. I remember at the end of the war time when a young Royal Navy Lieutenant in his very smart uniform came to Assembly and he was introduced to us by the Headmaster as a teacher who had been at the school before the war and had been called up and was now about to be demobbed and would start back at school shortly. His name was William Goldsmith who later won the Nobel prize for Literature for his book *'The Lord of the Flies'*. Another boy with whom I became friendly became an RAF fighter pilot and test pilot and was killed when his plane crashed on Salisbury Plain in the mid 1950s.

An usual circumstance associated with Bishop Wordsworth's School was that, because of the German bombing of Portsmouth, the pupils and teachers of Portsmouth Grammar School were evacuated to Salisbury and they attended the school during the afternoons. We only had lessons in the mornings, which also included Saturday mornings. There were some sports on Wednesday afternoons, Rugby in the winter and Cricket in the summer, but I did not excel at either of these and only attended when forced. This meant that we had the afternoons off and so the boys often went to the cinema in Salisbury before going home. I could only go occasionally as my mother and father did not have the money to give me as did many other parents. Bless them though, they always gave me what they could afford.

As Bishop Wordsworth's School was sited virtually in the grounds of Salisbury Cathedral we often attended services there and on one occasion I was a member of the choir which made a recording, later to be broadcast by the BBC and to America. I left school in July 1946, before I had received the results of my School Certificate examinations and applied to join the Royal Navy as a Boy Seaman.

During my time at Morgan's Vale, besides school, I led a busy life. I joined the Downton Boy Scouts, did well and became a Patrol Leader. We were due to spend a week camping with another troop of scouts at West Bridgeford near Nottingham in August 1945 and all was arranged and I had paid my money when we realised the date clashed with my sister Phyllis's wedding to Robert Giblett. This was on 15th August 1945, VJ Day. I had to make a decision and decided to go camping and miss the wedding. I have since been reminded many times since of this error of judgement. I believe that whilst courting, Phyl and Bob had a tiff and were only brought back together by my mother putting pressure on Phyllis to make it up.

I also recall our own scout troop spent a week camping in the water meadows at Bemerton, a village just outside Salisbury on the banks of the River Avon during which time we were inspected several times a day and took part in many competitions. The result was that we won and the prize was a two week trip to Paris or St Germain-en-Leys which was on the outskirts of Paris, one week to be spent camping and one week living with a French family. This was to take place in the late August/early September of 1946.

This caused me much panic at the time as having applied to join the Royal Navy in July 1946, I received my joining papers to report to HMS ST. VINCENT at Gosport on 3rd September, two days before I was due to return from Paris. What should I do? Cancel the Paris trip which I had been eagerly anticipating for nearly a year or tell the Navy I couldn't join. I was most worried that he RN would turn me down for ever if I didn't obey my joining orders.

My mother, always the reliable and supportive stanchion of my childhood days, wrote to the navy and they very kindly agreed that I could join on 10th September 1946 and must report to Temple Meads station in Bristol.

Also whilst at Morgan's Vale, I joined the local youth club which was run by a Methodist minister and for a whole year I attended the Methodist Church so regularly that I eventually got to read the lessons on Sundays. Another reason why I was keen on the Youth Club and the Methodist Church was that at the age of 14/15, I was in love with a girl called Doreen who also attended both church and the Youth Club.

Another hobby of mine at that time was model aeroplane making using balsa wood frames. My chums and I spend much time making, flying and breaking these delicate models.

During the year we lived at Morgan's Vale, I recall spending much time cycling through the New Forest area, visiting Rufus's Stone with my cousin Joan, who came to stay with us when on leave from the WRNS, and generally enjoying the lovely countryside. My pals and I found the wreckage of a crashed 'Lightning' fighter aircraft and there were hundreds of packets of radar jamming tin foil, or 'chaff' as it is now known, which we took and scattered about the New Forest countryside as we rode home on our cycles. Litter louts we were indeed. I broke my left arm whilst swinging from a beam in a barn with other boys at the age of 14 and had the arm in an 'aeroplane' splint for six weeks. It was most awkward boarding and taking the bus journey to school every day and I was much teased.

The 1ˢᵗ Downton Scout Troop. 1944

Another hobby of mine was fishing in the River Avon, we spent many happy hours along the river banks, particularly to the north of Downton, where trout, dace, roach and carp abounded. Again, due to the war there were no river wardens to stop us fishing where we pleased.

A good friend of mine at that time was a school chum and also a Scouting companion, his name was David and he lived at Downton. When I left school I lost touch with him but met up with him in the Royal Navy many years later, he had remained at school till he was 19, taken and passed his Higher School Certificate, then studied to be a dentist. He rose to the highest rank for a Dental Officer in the Royal Navy, to Dental Surgeon Rear Admiral. I remember that his School Certificate results were not as high as mine and often muse as to whether, had I had home stability and my family had the money for me to stay on at school, I could have risen to such great heights. As it was, I started in the RN as a Boy and after working my up through the ranks I did gain a commission and eventual promotion to Lieutenant Commander. Very few achieve this as every step on the way was by merit, tough examination and character assessment. This is unlike those who join the Royal Navy from University or High school as a direct entry officer. They gain promotion to Lieutenant Commander automatically without any special examination test of merit, other than a few months 'accelerated promotion' to those of greater ability. This fact I used to make very pointedly to tease my General List colleagues in the navy in later years. That is another part of my life which will be recorded in later chapters.

An incident I recall vividly was D-Day, 6th June 1944. I counted over 1400 American Dakota planes each towing a glider, I think they were mainly Horsa gliders, made entirely of wood, as they passed overhead on route from their bases on Salisbury Plain to Normandy. I was very interested in all aspects of the war which I followed closely in the Daily Mail. Marking and cutting out the maps as the allies closed in on the Germans from both the Eastern and Western fronts. We had by this time obtained a battery radio, but it was very temperamental, required expensive HT and LT batteries plus a lead-acid accumulator which had to be recharged at the local garage every week. The result was that it was only ever put on by my father for the evening news and, very exceptionally, we were allowed to listen to Tommy Handley and Workers' Playtime. Therefore we never listened to music on the radio and although we had an old wind up gramophone with a few very scratched HMV records, it was seldom played. Perhaps that is why even now I have no musical appreciation of either good classical or modern music. We do not have a 'Hi-Fi' in the house.

By the summer of 1944, the inevitable happened, my father was sacked from his job and we had to move on again. A top priority for mum and dad was for him to get another job in an area near enough to Salisbury for me to continue my schooling. We moved to Landford, a village on the very edge of the New Forest, we had a nice house and garden sited just opposite the village pub, which was and still is, called 'The Cuckoo'.

To get to school in Salisbury I used to cycle, or sometimes walk, the mile down the road to the A36 road and catch the Southampton to Salisbury bus to and from school. Again I used to leave my bicycle at the side of the road and there was never any thought of it being stolen. My dear mother continued to look after us all; Grandma, Aunt Annie, father and I, and welcome all visitors and friends. She worked very hard as housework was hard in those days without the advantages of modern appliances.

Whenever she could she also took cleaning jobs to supplement my father's meagre farm labourer's wages.

A thing which always upset my mother was that, as she loved nice things, the frequent moves from house to house had resulted in nearly all of her nice furniture and things being damaged by rough handling or discarded due to lack of room and by then we only had basic furniture and very few remains of the nice things Mum had when she was first married and lived in the farm houses at Cheselbourne, Chapel Farm and East Luccombe. When we moved we never had a proper furniture removers, it was always a cattle truck, and that not always properly cleaned out, there were no proper packing cases and the 'helpers' only had experience of moving cattle, thus our furniture and few possessions were never well handled or cared for.

Despite the upsets when father lost his jobs and the trauma of moving, having to make new friends and organise the new house, ensure that the electricity supplies were connected and the bills were paid etc., my mother, on to whom all this work fell, because by this time father could not see to read or write very well, remained cheerful, kept our spirits up and remained the strength of the family.

In 1945, my father again lost his job and we were forced to move from the nice cottage at Landford. My schooling remained important to my father and mother and thus the Salisbury area was the area for a job search. We moved to Swallowcliffe, a village on the A30 Salisbury to Shaftesbury road and about 14 miles from Salisbury. I liked Swallowcliffe, although our farm labourer's cottage was not very nice. I made some good friends in the village and as a 15/16 year old we played hard and toured the area on our cycles. I took the bus to school at Salisbury every day and completed my education whilst living at Swallowcliffe.

During this period I was aged 15 to 16 and was really into getting interested in girls and I spent much time wooing various lasses, both from the village and from the girls' grammar school in Salisbury. I remember that they wore green blazers but I cannot remember the name of the school. I attended my first proper dance at the village hall at Swallowcliffe and was most embarrassed as the, to me rather mature, lady singer in the band took a fancy to me and kept taking me on to the floor to 'teach me to dance'.

Although I did relatively well academically, I was never really at ease at Bishop Wordsworth's School. I had, not unnaturally, an inferiority complex with respect to my own and my parent's status in life and this led me to be very shy and reserved. In spite of their problems, both Mum and Dad did their very utmost to support me and I have much to be grateful to them for in standing by me during the crucial years of my schooling.

My decision to join the Royal Navy was taken with mixed feelings. I was 16 years old, I knew that my parents could not continue to support me at school and that I must find a job. There were only farm labourers' jobs in the Swallowcliffe area, my parents were in any case about to move again as by August 1946 my father was again about to be out of work and house. My father had always wanted me to join the navy - *'like Uncle George'* - ever since I could remember. I loved my parents and did not really want to leave home. Neither I, nor my parents, really knew anything about the Royal Navy. The decision was made and I signed on for 12 years from the age of 18, which meant I was committed from the age of 16 until I was 30 years old. The story of my career in the Royal Navy will be recounted in later Chapters.

CHAPTER NINE

THE CLOSING YEARS OF MY PARENTS LIVES

(1946 to 1989)

"Forever honour'd, forever mourned"

Homer (Eighth century BC) Greek epic poet. Iliad

To recapitulate. In 1946, I left home to join the Royal Navy, my father was then 59 years old. His undiagnosed diabetes had by then caused him to be very poor sighted, he would not go to an optician or a doctor as I have previously stated and the few teeth he had left he cleaned once a month with soot from the chimney and pulled out bad ones himself. He never showed pain and always made light of the many cuts, scratches and bruises he got working on the farms. His unsteady gait was often the cause of him falling over and into ditches. He continued to ignore pain or any other form of discomfort, including weather. His short temper and stubbornness' was also partially caused, in my view, by his diabetes. To make matters worse, he loved fat from the meat and always had a large helping of it and also he liked strong mature cheddar cheese and puddings such as apple pie with lots of sugar and custard. All these foods, we know today, being the worse things a diabetic can eat.

My mother was 54 years old, thin and worn and still working hard to keep the house and her last few nice things together. She took house cleaning work when she could but was not a well person, probably because she had denied herself so much to ensure that we were all fed properly, particularly during the war years of rationing and shortages. Although I had left, she still had grandmother Emily Thorne (her mother) and Aunt Annie (her sister), to look after.

As I had left home to join the Royal Navy in September 1946, my knowledge of day to day events in my family from then on are less detailed. However, I believe it important to record what I can remember and also information gathered from my sisters to complete the life story of my mother and father. My mother wrote to me at least once and often twice a week until her death in 1979. She wrote well and descriptively and so I heard all family news. I responded by writing to her equally frequently in return. Additionally I always visited home whenever I had leave when I was in the UK. This was every 4 months and I also visited more regularly in later years, my own family circumstances permitting.

Within weeks of me leaving home in September 1946, my father lost his job and their next move was to Lyndhurst in Hampshire. I only visited home a couple of times as I was then at HMS GANGES, the RN Boys training establishment in Suffolk. My sister Doris was by then living at home as her job at the American Red Cross centre in Salisbury had finished as the war had ended. Lyndhurst was a nice place, I know my mother was happy there and went shopping with friends she had made. During my Seasonal Leave from the Training Establishment, HMS GANGES, as a 17 year old, I was bored and remember cycling in to Totton to a fun fair for a bit of excitement, other than that I went for walks in the New Forest with our dog, Grip, who was always pleased to see me. I know nothing of father's work, only to know he only lasted a year at it and when I went home on Christmas Leave for 1947, it was not to Lyndhurst but to Fonthill Bishop in Wiltshire.

Whilst at Lyndhurst, my sister Doris had met the man who was to be her future husband, Frederick John Wearn. When father and mother moved to Fonthill Bishop, Doris and Fred married at the church in Fonthill Bishop and father and Fred worked together on the same farm. This was not a satisfactory arrangement as not only did my father not get on with his employer, for reasons by now so well understood, but he did not get on with Fred, and vice versa!

I came home on leave from the navy twice whilst they were living at Fonthill Bishop. Once on the occasion of Doris and Fred's wedding and the second time was during April 1948 when I recall my father taking me down to the pub, The Kings Head, and buying me a half pint of beer, it being my 18th Birthday. Mother continued be cheerful and to do her best to keep things together and used to cycle in to Hindon twice a week to do her shopping.

The next time I went home on leave was in the summer of 1948 and by then mother and father had moved to Tisbury. I remember very little of the house and did not even know which farm my father worked on as I was only home for two weeks. Once again I do not know the reasons for my father losing this job but when I went home for 1948 Christmas leave it was to Wincanton in Somerset. Again they were in tied house and when, in the autumn of

1949, my father lost his job, my family were again potentially homeless.

It was whilst I was on leave in Wincanton that I met my future wife, Gladys Audrey Oaten. She never liked the name Gladys and has always preferred to be called Audrey to which name I will refer from now on. It is of interest to note that my mother, a born matchmaker, organised my introduction and first date with Audrey, she arranged it all before I came home on leave. Similarly, it was mother who arranged my sister Doris's introduction and first meeting with her future husband Fred. This was while they lived at Lyndhurst and as mentioned previously she also helped to ensure that my sister Phyllis did not part from her future husband when they had a 'tiff'. So my mother had a significant influence on the future partners and marriages of all three of her children, all of which were successful and, I am sure, in no way regretted by any of us.

Losing yet another job and with it the family home was by 1949 a more serious problem as the men had come home from war and there was now no shortage of able bodied men to take on farm work, additionally, modern machinery and farm practices meant than less men were required. My father could not therefore get another job. As they therefore had no home to go to they had a problem. The employer and house owner therefore obtained an eviction order to get them out. This was a blessing in disguise as this caused the Wincanton Council to have need to re-house them. They were re-housed in a council house at Yarlington, a small hamlet about four miles from Wincanton.

I was away at sea in the Mediterranean at the time and was unaware of the problems at home or the worries of my parents. My father obtained a job as a council labourer looking after the roadside verges. He would go off in the mornings with his reap hook and work the hedgerows on the country lanes around Yarlington and Galhampton. He was working on his own, had no one to nag him or tell him how to do it, other than a Council foreman who visited him once or twice a week to see how he was getting on, bring his wage packet and perhaps to instruct him which roadside verges to do next. He liked his foreman and I suspect that not too much was expected of him and he was content. In fact, my father told me that the period between 1950 and 1953 when he was 65 and had to retire, was the happiest time of his life. Poor father, he had spent his life slaving away, albeit rather inadequately, to ensure that his family were housed and fed and only in the evening of his life did he have the chance of contentment inasmuch that he was not in a tied house and was happy at his work.

After he retired at the age of 65, he did odd jobs for his neighbour and farmer with whom he got on well, he had to work and was willing to work all day for nothing such was his work ethic and his good nature. During this period his old sense of fun came back and for the first time for 40 years he was able to enjoy himself insofar as his meagre pension would allow. He went to the local pub, The Stag, once or twice a week and enjoyed the company of the farming community folk who frequented it. He became a 'character' and was well known for sitting in his favourite seat in the corner by the bar, and buying drinks for his friends whenever he could afford it. He was well known for poking people with his stick when he wanted to talk to them, or even trying to trip up some of his old mates. He was content and happy. Similarly, my mother no longer had the worry of moving house every year and as my maternal grandmother died in 1950 shortly after they had moved to Yarlington, mother no longer had any family living at home to look after. She made many friends, did house cleaning work for several, looked after the cleaning in the local church and helped with the flowers. She was content. The one thing my parents then lacked was money, they only had their state pensions, but they managed.

During the 1950s and 1960s my two sisters probably visited mother and father more than I as I was often away for long periods on naval business. I do however, have many good memories of Yarlington, not only because it was such a nice little village and the folk were all so friendly but because when, during the years of 1949/50/51, I came on seasonal leave or on weekend leave I brought my future wife out with me from Wincanton and we used to walk the country lanes during our courting period. I well remember the period in 1950/51 when myxymatosis was raging and the rabbits were dying by the tens of thousands. I recall killing dozens to put them out of their agony as we walked around the lanes where they fell from the banks in our path.

In the early 1950s, my parents actually took a holiday and went to London for a week to stay with Uncle George and Aunt Dora. They had a lovely time and it was the only time either had been to London or indeed taken a holiday. We all visited home as much as possible and they were naturally very proud of their grandchildren, Phyllis and Bob had three daughters and we had one daughter and one son between the years of 1948 and 1965.

By the early 1960s I had bought a house in Fareham, Hampshire to be near my base in the Portsmouth area and I also got my first car, (that is to say, my first car in England, as I had run a 1938 Standard 10 whilst in Ceylon as will be recounted in later chapters). I was thus able to

My mother, Alice Foot, Aunt Dora (Thorne) and my father George Arthur Foot in Trafalgar Square (Mother and father's first and only visit to London in 1953)

My mother, Alice Foot, daughter, Linda , wife, Audrey and my father, George Arthur Foot - 1964

visit Yarlington more easily and even to bring my mother and father down to us for a holiday. By the middle 1960s my father was in his late 70s and his hearing and eyesight even worse. He had still not been medically examined and we still did not know that he was a diabetic.

I remember them coming down to Fareham in early December 1965 and whilst they were with us I had an accident with my car on the way to work which wrote the car off. I quickly hired another one and did not tell them about it at first in case they worried. The problem was the old car was maroon and my new one was white. Father looked out of the kitchen door on to the drive the next morning and observed that it had either been a very hard frost or it had been snowing. I had to tell him then! Whilst we were staying with them at Yarlington in about 1964, I took father for a car ride and took him round many of the places he used to live, including Pallington farm house at Tincleton where he was born. He got me to stop at a butchers in Sixpenny Handley and in he went and asked for an old butcher friend of his,('Nobby' Clarke). On being told his old pal was down the garden in the slaughterhouse he plodded down the path with me in tow and burst in on his friend who was butchering a lamb, poked him with his stick and they had a very jolly chat about old times. They had not met for thirty-five years. It was during this period and that leading up to his death that my father and I really conversed for the first time, although even then it was difficult as his hearing was very very poor. As I have previously noted, when I was a child he seldom spoke more than a few words to any of us.

In about 1966, my father, who still continued to try to look after the very large garden at Yarlington, knocked his toe with the garden spade. This resulted in it turning sceptic and swelling up. He didn't go to the Doctor at first as this was not his way. The foot got worse, (a common problem with diabetics), and by the time he eventually allowed my mother to call a doctor the foot was very much worse and he had to go into Yeovil hospital and his whole leg was amputated. Then and only then was he diagnosed as a diabetic. Too late to save his eyesight or hearing. He still had a strong constitution and recovered from the operation, became very popular with the staff in the hospital such was his character and personality and made strenuous efforts to use his false leg for the next two years, but without much success as he did not have much sense of balance. He even came with mother down to Fareham to stay with us for a few days and I had the privilege of pushing him around the town and in and out of the shops in a wheelchair. I say privilege as I loved my father for all his faults and know that he always did everything for others without thought to his own welfare.

Father became bed bound by the autumn of 1968 and died in January 1969 at the age of 81. He is buried at Yarlington Churchyard in a double grave in which we put my mother to rest ten years later. Within days of my father's funeral I sailed in a ship to the Far East so was unable to do much for mother who was left alone in the cottage. My sisters however, gave her as much support as possible and she was shortly to be re-housed by the council to a very cosy old persons bungalow in Wincanton. She was happy there, but lonely. Once again she made several friends and we all tried to visit her as often as possible, myself after I had returned from the Far East. I also brought her down to stay with us a couple of times a year. She also went to visit Phyllis and Doris for a few days when they could have her.

My mother, Alice Foot, with her grandson David in 1966

My father, George Arthur Foot, after having his leg amputated in 1967

Audrey, mother, David and Linda - 1966

This kept her active and she would plan and look forward to visiting her family and also to our visiting her. She was very brave and never complained but, in retrospect I wish I could have done more for her in her later years. But I was busy at work and we had two children at school which precluded us doing much more. Similarly my sister's husbands were busy with their occupations, but we all did our best.

Mother complained of chest pains during her latter years and the doctor gave her pills but we never really knew that her heart was in such a weak state. I brought her down to Fareham for Christmas 1978 and due to snow she stayed with us for nearly three weeks before I could take her back to Wincanton. We all had a lovely Christmas and she really enjoyed the company, especially of her two grandchildren. She enjoyed walking slowly with me or Audrey down to the Fareham shopping precinct and sitting on the seats and watching all the people doing their Christmas shopping.

I took her back to Wincanton in early January 1979 and did manage to call in to see her once more in mid January whilst on my way back to Fareham from Bath on business. She was with a friend who had come to call and although she looked frail, was cheerful and alert as always. A few days later she was poorly and the warden of the old peoples homes called my sister Phyllis who went with her husband Bob to fetch her and they took her back to Dorchester to stay with them. After a few days she appeared to be better but one evening on going to bed she suffered a heart attack and died at the age of 84. We were all naturally upset but I feel grateful that she had such an enjoyable Christmas and New Year with us and that she died with one of her family whom she loved so much and for whom she had made so many sacrifices throughout her life.

I often conjecture how my mother with her sharp brain and endless energy would have got on had she been able to free herself from the ties of her family and the restrictions imposed by the of lack of money and opportunity. One of her dearest wishes was to own and run a small Tea Shop or Cafe. It would have had to be in the country and with a nice garden in which she would grow and fill with flowers. I can just imagine her serving tea and home made cakes, which I know she would want to make herself, and chatting to her customers. If only.

Mother left a hand-written 'Will' which I shall always treasure. I loved her greatly and these simple words always bring tears to my eyes:

"For my three dear children.
To be read after my death.
The money I have in Lloyds Bank and what Fred has got in his Bank of mine which was £230 and of course there is interest in the few years.
   I wish it to be divided amongst my three dear children. And the Prudential Insurance will cover expenses, I hope.
   And God Bless you all,

   Love Mum"

Poor Mum, her total assets amounted to less than £1,200 after a life of hard work and deprivation whilst trying to keep her family fed and clothed during many trying years. The greatest asset she left us was of course her love, which is worth more than any material thing.

*David, mother, son-in-law Martyn and daughter,
Linda and my wife, Audrey - 1978*

I still visit my mother and father's grave at least once a year, they are buried together in a double grave at Yarlington. Indeed I visited it on Mothering Sunday of this year, 1997, together with my wife, daughter, son and granddaughter. We put a small vase of flowers on the grave and remembered them with fondness. They are not forgotten.

THE END OF PART ONE

PART TWO

CHAPTER TEN

AN ACCOUNT OF

MY LIFE IN THE ROYAL NAVY

THE EARLY YEARS

(1946 to 1947)

"Things at the worse will cease or at least climb upwards to what they were before"

William Shakespeare (1564 - 1616)

I left home on September 10th 1946. My mother packed a small case for me and came up to the bus stop at Swallowcliffe to see me off. I had been sent a rail warrant from Salisbury to Bristol Temple Meads station where I was to report to Rail Transport Officer (RTO). Mother tried to be brave but both she and I cried when I got on the bus as I had never been away from home before, except on two scouting trips, and I really knew nothing about the Royal Navy or of the place I was to go.

Arriving at Bristol Temple Meads, I soon met up with several other young lads, who were just as lost and bewildered as myself. We were shepherded into another train by the RTO who I believe was a Leading Patrolman and after a long tiring journey and changing trains in London we eventually arrived at Ipswich station, were bundled into a lorry and eventually arrived at HMS GANGES in Suffolk in the very late evening.

We were taken to what was referred to as The Annexe, which in fact was a separate part of the establishment where new recruits were isolated and processed. We were to stay in this Annex for 6 weeks and the nickname given to all New Entries was "Nozzers". We Nozzers had to wear white Duck Suits, a coarse linen trouser and tunic outfit which needed scrubbing every day. During this time we were under constant and strict supervision, we rose at 6 a.m. and lights out was at 9 p.m.

We were each given a sheet of brown paper to bundle up all the clothes and possessions which we had brought or worn when we arrived and these were parcelled up and sent home. The only personal possessions we were permitted was pen, pencil and writing paper. We were issued with every piece of clothing, shaving gear, soap etc. We were all given close shaven haircuts. Many a big lad was in tears after leaving his golden locks at the barbers. Another task was to sew our names into every item of kit we had, even socks, this took many days, especially as few of us had ever held or threaded a needle before. This was particularly difficult for those with long surnames.

We were taught the basics of parade ground drill and spent much time marching up and down to orders with a rifle, a Lee Enfield ·303in., on our shoulders. They were quite heavy, especially after twenty minutes or so marching and doubling about. Discipline was strict and we were wholly at the mercy of our Class Instructor who was a Petty Officer. To us he was God and fortunately for us this particular one was a nice person.

Here is a copy of a document I found among my old papers which reflects the official view of the Royal Navy with respect to Boys at HMS GANGES, and was given to parents to reassure them of their son's welfare.

CONDITIONS OF SERVICE IN THE ROYAL NAVY

These notes are intended to act an explanation of the Official Regulations.

PAY

At first 9d. a day; after about 9 months 1/3d a day, provided that the Boy has worked hard enough to have obtained the qualifications necessary for Boy 1st Class. Board and lodging are free. A complete outfit of uniform is provided free on entry and Boys are afterwards credited with an allowance which should be sufficient for replacements and repairs.

Boys are issued with 1/- to 1/6d a week from their pay as pocket money; the remainder is placed to their credit.

The cost of football boots, railway tickets when proceeding on leave, washing of clothes that the Boys do not wash themselves, and repairs of boots and clothes over the allowance mentioned above, are charged against this credit. From this credit a Boy may allot Home 2/6d a week as soon as the credit will permit, that is about 6 weeks, and 5/- when rated Boy 1st Class.

LEAVE

While in the Training Service leave is given 3 times a year. Easter and Christmas 2 weeks and 3 weeks in August. A boy need not take his leave unless he wants to.

During the time he is on leave a sum varying with the cost of living (at present 2/5d a day) is credited to him; this represents the Board and Lodging. This allowance is paid, should the Boy desire it, to those with whom the Boy has been given permission to spend his leave. The Boy is also given pocket money, 10/- to £1. should his credit permit, to see him through his leave.

It will be seen from this that a Boy is self-supporting from the day he enters the Navy, and that after about 6 weeks he is in a position to send money Home. If he does not send money Home, the money he is earning mounts up to his credit, but he may allot part of it to the Dockyard Bank if he desires. In any case he cannot have his money to waste, and is not allowed to have more than 2/6 in his possession.

There was no date on the above document but it generally applied to the time I was at HMS GANGES.

Boy 1st Class L G Foot - HMS GANGES - 1946

During the initial six week period we were given various intelligence tests in order that we could be graded and our abilities assessed. The broad assessment being that the top group would become Communications ratings and the remainder Ordinary Seamen who would later be specialised into Radar, Gunnery, Torpedo and other Seamen sub branches

I was selected for the Communications group. This group was further sub divided into Wireless Telegraphy (W/T) and Visual Signalling (V/S) specialisations. Again the rule of thumb procedure was that the top two thirds would be W/T and the lower one third V/S. In all these selections there was some scope for personal preference but not much. I did not know enough about what was going on to have any preference.

Something which became evident when I joined was that my Grammar/Public School education was to stand me in good stead, my educational standard was considerably above many of the other boys. But not all. There were a few like myself who had a good education and we stood out quite markedly. Another shock to my system was that as a country lad and coming from a hard working and honest family without much knowledge of the world, I was suddenly to be thrown in with some very different kinds of person, many of whom had very poor moral and personal standards. I did not smoke or swear, many of the boys did just that all the time. If I was told to do something I did it not only because I feared the consequences but because I knew it was the right thing to do. Many boys spent much energy and useless effort in avoiding doing their work properly and of skiving off work when opportunity allowed.

We had Scots, Irish, Geordies, Scousers and Brummies in our class, I could not understand what they said at first and I and several other innocent and naive boys were the butt of their bullying and suffered their coarse behaviour.

After six weeks at the Annexe, we were moved to the main part of HMS GANGES and commenced our proper training.

I am sure that many before me have graphically described life as a boy at HMS GANGES and I will not attempt to describe it in detail, but just to record my own memories. I was in a class of about thirty boys which was part of a Division called Drake Division. Drake 219 Class was our title. Our class had two Class Instructors permanently allocated to us, they took it in turns to be with us from 0600 till lights out at 2100. Their word was law. There was an officer who was called our Divisional Officer but we seldom saw him, I believe he was a navy tennis player, and in fact the only boys who came into contact with him were those who had committed heinous crimes and required to be punished even more severely than was permitted by the Class Instructors.

There were several Divisions as in all there were nearly two thousand boys at HMS GANGES in 1946/7. We lived in large Nissen type huts heated by one coke burning stove. The floors were of wooden block bricks which we had to scrub till they were nearly white about once a month and then polish them with a wax floor polish every day until they shone. Each metal bed frame had a set of four wooden bed chocks, wooden blocks which also had to be scrubbed daily. Woe betide the boy who made marks on the polished floor. Inspections of our personal selves and our beds and kit and of our accommodation were carried out at least twice daily. We rose daily at 6 a.m., or at 5.30 a.m. twice a week, when we were marched to the laundry where we had to scrub all our clothes and bedding with hard yellow soap and scrubbing brush, then show it to the class instructor before it went into the dryer. We also had to shower and wash ourselves and be inspected naked by the instructor before we were allowed to dry and dress ourselves. We had to shower daily in cold water, there was seldom any hot.

Another memory was of the meals. We had to collect the meals in large trays from the galley, which was about 150 yards from our accommodation hut. The food was then dished out under the supervision of the Instructor and when all was done, we were allowed to eat. I do not recall having a hot meal in the 15 months I spent at HMS GANGES. The food was awful and never enough and I need not describe the cold grease which we all ate up so ravenously. A typical 'punishment' by our Class Instructor was to fall us in outside the hut, often in our pyjamas, and leave us to attention for 10 or 15 minutes. This often happened just before or even during a meal with the consequence that the meal was truly uneatable by the time we were allowed to finish it. By then we were often too cold to want it any anyway.

I was very homesick, I did not like many of the boys I was forced to mix with and I was always cold and hungry. The winter of 1946/7 was very severe in East Anglia and snow drifts of 10 to 12 feet deep lay around for many weeks or to me it seemed like months. We spent much time clearing snow from the paths.

Another iniquitous punishment doled out by the Class Instructor was to double us as a class up and down a series of steps called Faith, Hope and Charity, to fit young men this was OK for the first five or ten minutes but after thirty or more minutes it was exhausting and painful. Both of our instructors were, I suppose in retrospect, sadists, one in particular, as he often punished individual boys or sometimes whole groups by striking our bare bottoms with a doubled up piece of electric flex. It drew blood after the first strike and six strokes were often doled out by him for the most trivial offence, such as talking, being just a few seconds late in falling in, or not having clean boots. There was no recourse to justice, the Instructor's word and actions were law.

Official punishments doled out by the superior officers were just as severe, six strokes of the cane (No. 6's) was often given, also 'Jankers' (No. 8s), which was doubling round the parade ground for an hour between six and seven in the morning and between five and six in the evening for periods of up to fourteen days. Detention or Cell punishment was also common for periods of up to twenty eight days.

Meek, frightened boys like myself accepted all this with fear and dread and we all regretted ever joining the navy but we were committed for the next fourteen or so years, twelve years from the age of eighteen, and although I was sixteen when I joined many boys were only fifteen. A few boys however rebelled, some ran away, they were always caught and punished with detention, strokes of the cane and Jankers. One boy in our class would not be quelled, he ran away many times and spent many months on punishment and was caned many times. In the end he won and was discharged from the navy. He did it the hard way but there were very few who could have withstood the punishment and pressures to which he was subjected.

On the plus side, I made several good friends with like minded and educated boys and we commiserated together and kept together. We were send to the classroom from 8.30 a.m. until 4 p.m. where we were taught general education subjects, especially mathematics, plus some basic radio theory. In addition to the subjects to train us for life at sea, the most important subject we were to learn as communications ratings was the Morse code, we were trained to transmit and receive up to twenty two words per minute and our handwriting had to be good and legible.

We were also taught to type on old Imperial Typewriters with all the keys blanked out. Woe betide the boy who even looked down at the keyboard. We had to look up on the wall at a big keyboard layout and touch type without looking down. The instructor's ruler came down across our knuckles if we dared to look at the blanked keyboard. I did well at the school work and at Morse and typing and the other miscellaneous communications subjects.

On some afternoons, at weekends and also on summer evenings we had sport. I did not excel at any of the ball game sports but played as directed, I was a reasonably good hockey player as I had played at school. The one activity which I did fairly well at was cross country running and I usually came in within the first twenty, sometimes in the first ten, out of the many hundreds of runners during the cross country races. My lungs were good and I had the stamina and determination to keep going on those gruelling runs.

The famous mast at HMS GANGES was another activity which I enjoyed, I had no fear of heights and even climbed to the button on several occasions. Perhaps my tree climbing days when looking for birds' eggs stood me in good stead. The achievement of climbing the last ten feet up the vertical pole and standing on the button, holding on only to the lightning conductor and looking down was most uplifting.

The only shore leave we were allowed was, after putting on our best uniform suits, on a Sunday afternoon. After being inspected, we were allowed to walk out of the gates at 2 p.m. and stroll up the road. There were a few houses, but it was mainly country road. We had to return by 4 p.m. and again be inspected. I tried this once for the sake of getting out but it was all too much trouble and very few of us did it twice.

The instructional terms were planned so that there were 105 days of instruction followed by two weeks seasonal leave at Christmas and Easter and three weeks leave in the summer (in August). As we were wakened by the Reveille every morning at 6 am, and as the reveille was commonly called 'Charley', the term '105 Charleys to leave' was on our lips on the day we returned from seasonal leave and we all kept a tick off chart of the number of 'Charleys to Leave'.

I cannot remember my full pay, it was about £2.10s.0d per week, but we were only allowed 2/3d for ourselves. The remainder was remitted to our parents or to a savings account. After a year we were promoted to Boy 1st Class and then we were paid 3/- per week. I spent my pay on writing paper, envelopes and stamps in order to write home and the remainder went on sticky buns at the canteen to assuage my constant hunger.

As I did not smoke I managed reasonably well, but the smokers were always short of money. Another disadvantage of being a smoker was that the rules of where and when one could smoke were very strict and it was inevitable that they were often broken. This resulted in the smokers being punished far more than the non smokers. The lack of money in a few cases resulted in a boy stealing from another. This was treated most severely and anyone caught thieving invariably suffered a caning and was sent to detention. In addition, because thieving was considered to be such an heinous crime, the boys themselves usually doled out their own punishment in addition.

I remember one boy caught thieving to be so battered that his face was unrecognisable for several weeks. This was the only departure from discipline to which the instructors turned a blind eye as they knew from experience that thieves had no place in the close proximity in which we lived and in which we were to live when sent to our ships.

My overall memories of HMS GANGES are not good. I spent 15 months being very frightened and always hungry and often cold. Perhaps it did me good. It certainly hardened me up and made me self sufficient in my personal affairs. It made me fit and it broadened my horizon by contact with other boys from all over the British Isles. Perhaps the most important lesson for most of us was that HMS GANGES taught us to obey orders and to be properly dressed at the right place and at the right time.

I passed out of HMS GANGES in November 1947 and was sent with about ten other boys to join HMS DUKE OF YORK at Portsmouth. One of the boys was one of my close friends so I had companionship in the great adventure of going to a seagoing ship at last.

CHAPTER ELEVEN

MY FIRST SHIPS (1947 to 1952)

"Those that go down to the sea in ships"

I was $17^1/_2$ when I joined HMS Duke of York as a Boy 1st Class in November 1947. As boys, we were accommodated in hammocks in the school room and it was there that we began to feel that we had some freedom at last. As we were permitted to buy duty free cigarettes I started smoking, as did nearly all the others who had resisted the habit during their GANGES days. Our accommodation and our mess was deep down in the ship below the waterline and the Communications offices in which I worked were also mostly down below.

The ship had a 14 inch thick steel armour plated waistcoat all around as an anti-torpedo measure so we were well and truly secured from the outside world. I found therefore that I went for days and I suspect sometimes a week or more without going up on deck or seeing daylight. I was really afraid to go up on the upper deck outside of my environment as there were so many things going of which I did not understand and I would invariably be shouted at for being in the wrong place and/or wearing the wrong rig.

HMS DUKE OF YORK 1947

The Quarter-deck was huge and a hallowed place. The wooden deck was scrubbed so often it was nearly white. It was always staffed by many officers and very fierce Royal Marine sentries. I once caught a glimpse of the Commander-in Chief Fleet himself, Admiral McGrigor, he was a very short man and known as *'wee Mac'* or *'Titch McGrigor'* - but not by me, to me he was a remote figure akin to God. I stayed away from all that. I enjoyed my work as a communication rating and the senior staff of Petty Officers were reasonably kind and easy to get along with. In practice, other than some communications training, particularly at Morse, I did very little else but scrub out the many Communications Offices and Transmitter Rooms. As boys, we were not allowed to man 'live' radio circuits on our own and were supervised continuously. The only moments of peace and quiet and freedom from worrying about whether I was doing anything wrong for me was in the evening, after supper, when I could retire to the school room where we boys had to sleep, (separately from those rough sailors!), get into my hammock and read. It was there that I started smoking, this was probably from boredom and wish to imitate my companions and also the ready availability of 'duty free' cigarettes.

In April 1948, I became 18 and was advanced to the rate of Ordinary Telegraphist, with six months backdated seniority for my good work and good examination marks. This meant a bonus of about £15 additional in my pay packet. This lifted me a lot and when in early May 1948 I was drafted from HMS DUKE OF YORK to HMS CADIZ, a Battle class destroyer, I really felt that life was improving.

Joining a Home Fleet destroyer, not as a trainee but as a fully qualified Ordinary Telegraphist, passed for Telegraphist, as part of the ship's complement, was a big boost. I had freedom, I was trusted to keep watches on my own and do the job I was trained for, albeit that there was much more training to come and much more to learn.

A lasting memory of HMS CADIZ was the food system. It was a system called Canteen Messing. This system allocated each mess a sum of money to feed itself. We bought our food from the on board victualling stores (or ashore if we could find something cheaper), and prepared it ourselves. It was then taken to the galley where it was cooked for us. There were two serious drawbacks to this system. Firstly, if we did not spend all the money on food each month we could divide the 'mess savings' up between us. As we were only paid about £3 per week, of which a sum also had to be remitted home, the aim was to spend as little as possible. We therefore lived on cheap beans, potatoes and meat. There was little variety and seldom a pudding.

The reason for this was that we had to prepare the food ourselves. As we were all busy watch keeping, there was little time for this, neither did we know how, furthermore I suppose we were too lazy. The result was that often there were no potatoes peeled and sent to the galley and the same applied to vegetables. The favourite meal and the easiest to prepare was 'pot mess'. This comprised of chopped up meat, potatoes (provided someone had peeled them), many tins of vegetables, beans and tomatoes thrown into a big pot and sent to the galley. To have enough money to go ashore for two or three beers, go to the çinema and then have steak, eggs and chips was the whole aim of life. Breakfast seldom consisted of anything more than toast with beans or jam.

During my time in HMS CADIZ we visited the Port of London and moored at Woolwich to act as Guard ship for the Royal Navy Field Gun team at Earls Court.

HMS CADIZ - 1948

The author as a "Jolly Jack" in 1947.

Whilst there I visited my Uncle George and his family at Barnet, to travel in London and on the Underground for the first time was an adventure. My chum and I met a couple of ATS girls at a dance and took them out whenever we had shore leave. The problem was that the girls had to be back in Woolwich Barracks by 11.30 p.m. and after we had said goodnight to them we had to walk back to the dockyard. By this time the gates of the dockyard were usually closed and the last boat back to the ship had gone. This meant we had to walk about all night until the first boat at 0630 in the morning. Although it was June and the weather was good, it got very cold at night. We spent a couple of nights in the Woolwich tunnel, one in a lorry parked near the dockyard and one night at the police station where the police kindly put us up in a cell but told us not to make a habit of it. I did not keep in touch with my girl but my pal eventually married his and I next met them in Ceylon in 1953. She was most attractive, indeed beautiful, but had a roving eye and played a bit loose with some of the unmarried lads. When they returned from Ceylon they split up and I last heard of her in the later 1950s when she was working as a prostitute at Southsea. I had fancied her much more than mine too! But my chum got to her first!

We also spent time at Invergordon, once the home of the mighty Home Fleet, and various ports in Scotland but the best run ashore of all was Londonderry, in Northern Ireland. The girls outnumbered the men in Londonderry by about 10 to 1 as there was little employment for men but the shirt making factories employed nearly all women. This meant we had lots of lovely girls fighting over us and we all looked forward to returning to harbour each evening and rushing off to the nearest pub for a drink and then going on to a local dance hall.

In the autumn of 1948 we sailed with the whole of the Home Fleet for the West Indies. This was for me, and indeed many others, my first trip abroad and was most exciting. These visits were to be the first courtesy visits, as opposed to operational visits, by Royal Navy warships since before the war and we were given a tumultuous welcome everywhere we went.

Our first port of call was San Fernando in Trinidad, this was followed by a few days in Port of Spain, the capital of Trinidad. Visits to Barbuda, Barbados, Antigua, St Lucia St. Kitts and other islands followed. The islands were at that time completely unspoilt by modern buildings or tourism and very much the paradise islands of which one had read so many times.

Memories of this trip are of the hundreds of sharks which were everywhere, we caught many using butchers meat hooks. I recall one shark falling off the hook with its mouth gashed open by the hook and all the other sharks smelling the blood tearing it to pieces as it tried to get away.

Rum was about 4d. for a large measure, probably about 4 ordinary tots. This of course led to many young sailors over indulging and I must confess that there were times that I saw much abuse of the hospitality offered to us. Sex with the local girls was anything between 2d. and 2/-. I abstained as I was afraid of catching V.D. which was rife in all the city and port areas. (He would say that wouldn't he!).

One incident in Trinidad which I recall was that I had been ashore in the afternoon with a chum and had enough to drink and wanted to return on board. We were at a club about a mile from the ship and my chum, not wanting to return yet asked the Military Police patrol if they would be kind enough to drop me off at the ship. They agreed and I got in the Patrol Jeep with the Patrol Team which comprised a Royal Naval Patrolman, a US Naval Patrolman and a Local Trinidadian policeman. All would have been well had they gone straight back to the jetty. But they went to a part of the town which was out of bounds to us servicemen. They stopped the Jeep outside of this club, told me to stay where I was and then went inside. After a few minutes, or maybe only moments, I decided that I was lonely and went to follow them. I went through an open door and was starting to go up some stairs when a crowd of both American and British sailors came rushing down the stairs, having been turned out by the Military Police. I was knocked over, not being too steady on my feet in any event. I was not hurt but my white suit was totally messed up. The Patrol coming down the stairs picked me up, somehow forgot that I was the chap they had brought to the place, and I was taken back on board and charged with being in an 'out of bounds' area. Who ever said life was fair !

  Whilst passing off the coast of Antigua we lost a young sailor overboard and although we turned and searched for several hours next morning he could not be found and the appropriate telegrams were sent to his next of kin. A great surprise about 3 days later when he was found ashore in Antigua. He had jumped on purpose and swam ashore. The miracle was that the Navigation Officer told us that the closest we had steamed to the shore was 3 miles and he had somehow survived the sharks - maybe they did not see him the dark !

  Having left the West Indies we called at Bermuda for a brief visit. I only went ashore for a few hours and other than recalling the main street in Hamilton with the policeman directing traffic from his pedestal under a canopy, and that egg and chips cost me 7/6d. which was a fortune to a young sailor in those days, I have little other memory. Little was I to know that I would be returning there to live with my family 26 years later!

In the summer of 1949 we were seconded to the Mediterranean Fleet and sailed for the Mediterranean, we visited Gibraltar, Malta, Cyprus (Limassol, Kyrenia and Famagusta) and Lebanon (Beirut). Then to Port Said and the Suez Canal, Port Suez (Port Tewfik) and then to the top of the Red Sea to Aqaba where we spent six weeks as the guard ship. It should be remembered that at that time Israel was our enemy and we were on guard against air, and special boat squadron attacks by Jewish saboteurs. Aqaba is in Jordan and sited at the top of the Red Sea with the borders of Israel, Egypt and Saudi Arabia all within a few miles. At that time we had 600 troops in tents in Jordan. I recall no sign of life in the Saudi Arabian or Egyptian sectors. But in the Israeli sector, there was a tented encampment of Jewish soldiers, no buildings of any kind. This spot is now the very popular and modern Israeli holiday resort of Eilat and I would like to visit it one day.

Whilst we were in the Red Sea area, and indeed throughout my time in HMS CADIZ, I was watch keeping in the W/T Office. Long periods of watch keeping are most debilitating and the Captain noticed that I and two other Telegraphists in particular were looking pale and less healthy than the rest of the ship's company and he ordered us to be issued with camp beds and to sleep on the upper deck to get more fresh air. It was very kind of him but one could not get proper rest on deck, and even out there it was sometimes cold at night and it sometimes rained on us. I used to creep down below and in to my hammock at every opportunity!

An incident at Aqaba which I will always remember was that one night whilst I was on watch in the Wireless Telegraphy (W/T) office, the Signalman called down the voice pipe to tell me we were being fired on. I, like a foolish young 18 year old, left the office and went down the passage and on to the iron deck to 'see what was happening'. I crouched under the Captain's motor boat just as some machine gun fire hit the boat and a splinter flicked on to my forehead and caused it to bleed. I rushed back to the office and told no one as I knew I had no business to leave the office. The cut on my forehead was of no consequence and was gone in a couple of days. The reason for the firing was that the Signalman who had been told to illuminate any vessel which came near, had, in illuminating an Arab fishing boat, shone the searchlight on the Jewish encampment. The Jews responded in a manner which we now know as being most characteristic, by immediately firing at us in retaliation. I kept quiet about my injury and it turned out that it was the only time I was ever fired upon or injured in my 49 years of naval service.

At about this time I had my first connection with Spiritualism. My best friend from HMS GANGES and who also served in HMS DUKE OF YORK with me, had been sent to another destroyer, HMS SCORPION at the time I went to HMS CADIZ. i.e. May 1948. Just before we sailed to the Mediterranean, I met my friend for a drink one evening in the Portsmouth Dockyard canteen and he told me that he was involved in Spiritualist meetings and that a certain Petty Officer, Torpedo (TAS) specialist, who had been in HMS SCORPION and who was now in HMS SAINTES had been instrumental in his interest. My friend was an extremely clever man. He was one of the few who on joining the navy at the age of 16 like myself, already spoke French and Spanish and had gained 8 or 9 Credits in his School Certificate examinations. He told me that the

Petty Officer in question was in the destroyer HMS SAINTES which was berthed alongside my own ship and that it was sailing the next day at noon. My friend, (I will not name names of those who are still alive of who I give account of their actions during my Naval service), told me that I should make contact with this Petty Officer who could do me a lot of good. As he persisted, I half promised that I would go and see him in the morning. But I did not go, as like all young sailors I was nervous of senior ratings and particularly wary of homosexuals. We sailed for the Mediterranean a few weeks later and when in Malta, I was waiting for some friends outside a pub (Tony's Bar) at Sliema Creek, when a Chief Petty Officer approached me and said that he sensed that we had a mutual friend in common and that it was a close friend of mine who was at that time serving in Scottish waters. I was slightly alarmed, but putting two and two together, seeing HMS SAINTES moored in the harbour and the Torpedo badge on his lapels, and knowing that my pal was in HMS SCORPION in the Invergordon area, I guessed who he was. I said my pal's name and he concurred. I was not happy and wanted to get away as my pals were arriving at any minute. He asked me to meet him later at the VERNON Club. I said no I am sorry but that we were off somewhere else. Anywhere else would have been OK by me! My friends arrived and off we went and I naturally told them of my meeting with this 'funny' chap. They were all amused, especially as my friend from HMS GANGES was also known to them. As chance would have it later that evening we were near the VERNON Club and my friends persuaded me to go in.

The chief in question was at the bar drinking orange juice, (this made him suspect to us hardened 18 year old beer drinkers), and my pals pushed me up near to him and then drew back giggling. The Chief looked at me and said "*I knew you would come*". I felt a fool. For conversation I asked him if he corresponded with my pal. He said no but that they 'tune in' sometimes. He told me that Spiritualism would be a great help to my friend and that he was sure that he would become an officer one day. I remarked that as my pal was particularly clever I would not be surprised . He told me that I could do well also and he would like to have a longer chat with me sometime. I had enough by then and I made my excuses, joined my friends and we left. I met him once more by accident on a bus in Valetta, Malta. He sat next to me and our conversation was general but he said that my pal had told him about me and that he was sure that Spiritualism could help me. I got away as quickly as I could.

The aftermath of this story was that much later, in 1957, when I was a Petty Officer instructor at HMS MERCURY, I was telling the above story to my colleagues in the instructor's room at a coffee break and I finished the story with the words *"--- and I do not bloody well believe in Spiritualism"*. As I said the words a wooden rack with cases and Anti Gas Respirators above our heads collapsed and fell on top of us. This put us all into spasms of laughter and I was teased for weeks and dared to say it again. My friend did indeed become an officer and in fact was the only one of my original class to do better than I as he ended his career as a Commander in the Royal Navy. I still meet him every year at the Signal Officers' Reunions and he is still a spiritualist. He doesn't broadcast the fact, neither does he hide it although few of his colleagues know of his convictions. He was kind enough last year to promise to pray for my daughter who has Rheumatoid Arthritis. Although I scoffed at spiritualism as a young man. I would not scoff at it now and I retain an open mind.

Other memories of HMS CADIZ. In order to destroy confidential waste paper it was necessary to take the paper in hessian sacks down to the ship's boiler room. To get to these one had to go through the double doors which kept the boiler room pressure high, this was an adventure in itself to me. The boiler rooms were very hot (naturally!), and the stoker would open the furnace doors for me to empty the sack. It was only necessary to hold it open in front of the furnace and the in-draft would do the rest. This sounded simple in theory but I seldom managed to retain the sack as it either got sucked out of my hands or the end caught fire and I had to let it go. The Petty Officer Telegraphist in charge of us used to blow his top every time I came back from the boiler room without his sack. These were in short supply as were many things just after the war.

Another time I got into trouble was at Aqaba where the mackerel used to teem round the gangway lights in their millions. It was easy to catch them with an unbaited hook or even just scoop them out of the water. I had a brain wave. I took the basket work waste paper basket from the W/T Office, tied a piece of rope to it and lowered it over the side. Of course the weight of fish and water in the basket caused the rope to break or come undone, I cannot remember which now. I lost the waste paper basket. I was in trouble again. Nevertheless the Petty Officer Telegraphist was a good man with a sense of humour.

Whilst at Cyprus, I recall that someone in my mess caught 'crabs', from sleeping with a lady ashore I suppose. The 'doctor's' remedy was for all of us to shave all the hair from our private parts. Just imagine a dozen young sailors, all naked, sitting on sheets of newspaper on the floor, all with razors, trying to shave themselves. It was hilarious. When the hair started to grow again in a few days/weeks it was most uncomfortable and itchy.

In January 1950, I left HMS CADIZ and went to HMS MERCURY, the Signal Communications Training School for a 3 month course to qualify to be a Leading Telegraphist. I passed the course in early April and on the 23rd of April, I was rating up to Leading Telegraphist. This being the earliest possible date any one could be advanced as 20 years old was the minimum age of advancement to this rate.

In May 1950, I was sent back to sea to another Home Fleet ship. This time to HMS SCORPION, a Weapon Class Destroyer. I was to spend one year in HMS SCORPION, during which time we spent most of our time trialling a new Anti submarine mortar then code named 'Limbo'. It was later to enter service as the very successful Mortar Mark 10. My lasting memory of this ship was that it was overcrowded. For the whole year I did not have my own hammock billet. I had to wait until all the others in the mess had slung their hammocks and then sling mine crossways over the mess table. This meant I had to go to bed last and get up first to keep out of the way of the others getting up. As I was also constantly watch keeping this was quite a strain.

We had a very pleasant man as the Chief Telegraphist, he nicknamed me 'Hoof', instead of Foot, but I had much respect for him. I recall that we had a young Lieutenant as our Divisional Officer. (He had been in HMS AMETHYST during the Chinese communist rebellion in 1949 when the ship was shelled and severely damaged and had therefore seen much recent action). He was however, an inexperienced man with regard to looking after men and I remember that one day he was talking to me in the corner of the W/T Office with regard to my career, and in his nervousness he was twiddling the knobs on a nearby Radio Transceiver. The Chief seeing him shouted to me *"Smack his hands Hoof! Smack his hands"!* I was much embarrassed and the Lieutenant blushed and left the office. Thereafter whenever I was seen near my Divisional Officer, one of my chums would call out *"Smack his hand Hoof"*!

I must have done well in HMS SCORPION as in May 1951 I was drafted to HMS MERCURY to await a Petty Officers Qualifying course. Bearing in mind that I was only just 21 and still too young to have a Good Conduct badge which was awarded for four years good service from the age of 18, I was doing very well. Whilst waiting for my course, I was drafted temporarily to HMS ZEPHYR or HMS ZEST, (I cannot for the life of me now remember which!), a destroyer on exercises in the North West Approaches. Whilst there I had the chance to visit Londonderry again and renew some old acquaintances from the shirt factories.

When I left HMS ZEPHYR/ZEST I was dropped by boat at the end of Blackpool Pier and had to carry my kit bag and hammock down the pier to a naval transport waiting at the end to take me to the railway station. I found out how long that pier was the hard way! I arrived back at HMS MERCURY about midnight and the next morning was despatched on another temporary draft to Fort Southwick at Portsdown where I spent two weeks watch keeping in the underground bunker which had been used by Generals Eisenhower and Montgomery and their Staffs when controlling the D-Day landings. I recall that there were three hundred and sixty six steps to climb when coming off watch, and at 2 a.m. or 8 a.m. after a busy six hour watch they seemed more like a thousand.

The author with his then fiancee Audrey Oaten in 1950

Whilst this turbulence was happening I was at the same time trying to plan my own wedding. I had met Gladys Audrey Oaten, from hereon referred to as Audrey, at Wincanton in 1949. She lived a few doors away from my parents and our meeting was contrived by my mother when I went home on leave. Our courting consisted of occasional weekend meetings, lots and lots of letters and, later, when my parents had moved to Yarlington, of us sharing our time between our respective parents when I went home on weekend leave.

Getting to Wincanton from Portsmouth for a short weekend was always a problem, the best train left Portsmouth at 1215, this got me to Templecombe in time to change to get a train to Wincanton by about 4 p.m. This was super, but the problem was to catch the train, as Weekend Leave did not start till 1200 and it was a long way from the dockyard to Portsmouth Rail Station. If I missed this train I did not get to Wincanton till about 6.30 p.m. The same problem occurred on Sunday nights, to get the last train from Templecombe meant that I had to leave by 5 p.m. My weekends were therefore very short and sweet. Whilst I was at HMS MERCURY I generally got a lift by a pal of mine who lived at Chard and came via Wincanton to pick me up on Sunday evenings. These trips were memorable as my pal had a little red 3 wheel Morgan with an air cooled engine. He drove fast but it seemed even faster as one was seated only a few inches from the ground. I recall one of his habits was that on coming up to a crossroads at night where we did not have the right of way, instead of stopping he would switch off his headlights and if it all looked dark he would continue across the crossing without even slowing down. It was not an uncommon practice in those days on country roads where traffic was light.

Our Wedding 2nd August 1951.

(From left to right) My father, mother, best man Frederick Wearn (Bro. in law), bridesmaid Gillian Giblett (niece), myself, Audrey, Lily Howell (Matron of honour), bridesmaid Valerie Thorne (niece), Albert & Jane Oaten (bride's parents).

I proposed to Audrey in the summer of 1950 and I had to hope that I would get leave in the August of 1951 to get married. By chance it all worked out OK, but all the arrangements had to be made by her and our parents as I was away and out of touch. Of course neither of our parents had a telephone. I booked our honeymoon at a Guest House at Burnham-on-Sea. I cannot remember why or how I did this. Perhaps it was because Wincanton was on the railway line which ran from Bournemouth to Bath and it was possible to change at Bath and go direct to Burnham. Alas all these local rail services are long since closed. Our honeymoon could only be for 6 days as I only had 14 days leave. I recall we paid 15/6d per night for the room. This included breakfast and evening meal.

I returned to HMS MERCURY at the end of August 1951 and was placed on an advancement course for Petty Officer Telegraphist. There were 16 in the class and I was the youngest, still being only 21, whilst several of the others were well over 30. I did well on course but here came up against the first hurdle to prevent my rapid advancement. At that time the navy was divided into three Port Divisions, Portsmouth, Chatham and Plymouth. Each division had its own ships and establishments to fill and ran its own advancement rosters. As it happened that both Chatham and Plymouth were short of Petty Officer Telegraphists but Portsmouth had too many, the ratings on my course from Chatham and Plymouth therefore had only to wait a few weeks before being promoted to Petty Officer. As I belonged to the Portsmouth division I had to wait for a vacancy. This took four and a half years and I was eventually advanced in 1955. In retrospect this did not matter too much as during this period I gained very valuable experience and, in short, matured into an experienced person.

CHAPTER TWELVE

CEYLON WEST WIRELESS STATION (CWRS)

(1952 TO 1954)

"A good place to visit but a poor place to stay"

Anon

Having completed and passed the qualifying course for Petty Officer Telegraphist, I was then given a draft to Ceylon West Wireless Station (CWRS or HMS HIGHFLYER). This was considered a plum job and it was to be 'married accompanied' so I could take my wife with me, or rather, the complex rules of the navy were that I had to go out first and find accommodation and then send for her. I sailed in the troopship HMT DILWARA on 6th February 1952. There was great excitement that morning as I, together with others who were going to various places ranging from Gibraltar to Korea, boarded the ship at about 9 am, (We had been accommodated in the Royal Naval Barracks at Portsmouth the night before), and we were due to sail at noon. At about 11 am it was announced that the King (King George VI) had died. We all speculated that our sailing would be postponed. It wasn't, we sailed at noon.

Life on a troopship was very austere, but less so than on a warship. We were ruled by a Regimental Sergeant Major as the majority of the 'passengers' were soldiers going to Korea. The one privilege we ten sailors had was that we had to muster at the Purser's office at 11 a.m. every day and receive our tot of rum, this made us feel most important and superior to the soldiers.

The troopship, as were most of the other troopships, was old and could only proceed at about 12 knots. The journey therefore took slightly over four weeks, the latter two weeks being through the Red Sea and Indian Ocean during which time living conditions were most trying as there was no air conditioning and the sticky heat and cramped conditions made us all most uncomfortable.

I, together with three others disembarked at Colombo and was taken to CWRS where we were accommodated in Bhandas, which were large thatched barn like sheds with partly open sides, no glass windows. There were about 30 of us to each Bhanda. We slept under mosquito nets as the mosquitoes were most persistent. I was immediately put into a watch where I remained for two whole years.

This meant working 24 hours about from Monday to Thursday and then 48 hours about for the period from noon Thursday to noon Saturday, then from noon Saturday to noon Monday. There were advantages to this type of watch keeping for short periods as it gave one a nice break during the 48 hours off, but to do this continually for two years was a very heavy drain on one's constitution and this combined with the damp tropical heat had a debilitating effect on one's health. Many lads were poorly, I remained fit but lost weight and when I left Ceylon I weighed only 8 stones 12 pounds.

HMT EMPIRE WINDRUSH (1952)

Having settled in as a single man, I then had to find accommodation which had to be approved by the Officer in Charge as there were no married quarters in those days, and I was then entitled to apply for my wife to join me. This I did and after much red tape, my dear young wife left home for the first time, boarded the troopship HMT EMPIRE WINDRUSH at Southampton and sailed to join me. She was nearly five weeks at sea in yet another slow non air conditioned ship which also broke down twice on the way, she was alone and I know worried to death. She arrived safely, but her baggage was broken into whilst waiting collection from Colombo docks and she lost several items of value.

We had very little money, indeed I had none and had even got Audrey to send me her only savings of about £100 to enable me to buy an old car so that we had transport when she arrived. It was a 1938 Standard 10 car. I knew nothing about cars, it was always going wrong and I am sure the local Ceylonese garage mechanic saw me off regularly when I took it for repair. I recall the windscreen wipers were operated by air suction from the engine. When going uphill they slowed down and when the engine stopped they stopped. This was most inconvenient during a monsoon storm and I had on many occasions to pull into the side to wait for the rain to stop or abate.

Dear Audrey, I put her in a bungalow with a Ceylonese cook who spoke only a little English and a Tamil houseboy who spoke almost no English at all. These two servants did not like each other and were forever telling tales about each other. The Tamils are still fighting the Singhalese to this day! Our nearest white neighbours were nearly a mile away and as I was away watch keeping and virtually working a 94 hour week, my wife was on her own for very long periods. She was very brave, put up with the mosquitoes and other insects and the snakes, there were vipers and cobras by the dozen in our own garden or to be more accurate our own bit of jungle, which adjoined a paddy field.

From there we sometimes saw a cobragoya, (or some such spelling!) a large lizard like creature about 4 feet long, they looked most fearsome but I do not think they ever hurt anyone. The snakes did. A young electrical rating from the camp was bitten by a viper and died within a couple of days. There were also scorpions. We were all advised to carry a razor blade and a piece of rubber in order to cut across a snake bite and then suck out the venom. I recall a pal of mine, when we were getting up at 0130 one morning to go on watch at 0200, he put his bare foot into his sandal in which was a scorpion which bit him on the toe. He very quickly attempted to cut out the sting with his razor blade. He did not suffer from the scorpion's bite but managed to cut off half his big toe!

We had a big pig at the camp which roamed freely in the jungle, ate scraps from the galley and was always poking around us wanting it's back rubbed. As there were no doors or windows on our Bhandas, or in the shower rooms, the pig always waited for someone to go into the shower and then went in with them to share relief from the heat. It died of a cobra bite as did so many pets. Also in our garden were many coconut palm trees with chipmunks running up and down them and chattering all the time. The main predators of the chipmunks were the rat snakes. These were not poisonous but grew up to six feet long and were forever seen slithering round our veranda and even up on the roof. Huge water buffaloes with large horns came from the jungle which adjoined our house and often frightened us at night by scraping their horns on the window bars.

All our windows were barred as thieves abounded. We lost the sheets from the bed one night. Audrey had turned down the bed shortly before we were to go in and when we went to bed the sheets were gone. A thief had pushed a forked stick though the window bars, twisted it on the sheets and pulled them out. A friend of mine awoke one night to see his alarm clock going out the window in a similar manner.

As Audrey was on her own so much I got her an Alsatian puppy which she adored. It was a constant companion and kept away the continuous stream of beggars who were always at the gate, as well as intruders as burglary and theft was a way of life to the locals. Because we were white we were considered to be very rich.

Other memories of Ceylon. The country had only just achieved independence from colonial status and was feeling its way. There was poverty, but not I believe as much as now, fifty odd years later !

The climate was tropical monsoon, when it rained it rained and rained and rained for what seemed months on end. It was warm rain however and we made the most of the beautiful beaches with the huge Indian Ocean rollers being broken up by reefs which formed lagoons which made it safe for swimming.

I recall taking my driving test. Every few minutes and especially when I made a slight error, the examiner sitting beside me saying over and over again, "*I am a very poor man sir*". He wanted me to know that to pass I had to tip him. I knew some who just gave the examiner 50 rupees and passed without the test but I was determined to pass the test in order to give myself the confidence I needed. I continued to the end and then he consulted his colleague who had been following on a motor scooter and then came back to me saying that I had passed and that he was a very poor man. I gave him 20 rupees and we were all happy. (A rupee was worth about 1/6d.).

Our Alsatian dog, Rajah, contracted distemper and in spite of paying out a large sum in vets fees it died. We then got a small mongrel, terrier type puppy which was a bundle of mischief and a super house dog. It detested all coloured Ceylonese people, probably because our houseboy Martin used to tease him with his broom or polishing cloth. Martin was always coming to Audrey saying "*Lady the dog has bitten me*" and Audrey had to put dettol and plaster on his hands or ankles. Audrey told me that one night whilst I was away, an old beggar came to the door and before Audrey could restrain the dog it had pulled off his sari and the poor man dropped his torch (a burning brand) and hared off down the road very partially clothed. Another incident with the dog was when it went for the Pekinese belonging to our neighbour, a Ceylonese lawyer, it pulled the skin off the back of the poor peke. Suffice to say we were then no longer on speaking terms with our neighbours.

When we left Ceylon we had the dog put down as we loved it and did not want it to fall into the hands of the locals who were often very cruel to animals. There were many feral dogs, that is, domestic dogs which had been left unattended and had become wild. These roamed about in packs and rabies was rife. Everyone was therefore afraid of all dogs. I recall one incident when Audrey and I were having a drink on the veranda at a neighbour's house, he was a Frenchman, an engineer working on a Bridge building project. He had been showing me his rifle which he used for shooting bears up in the mountains and his two young sons were playing in the garden. We heard a commotion in the road and about a dozen Singhalese people were running down the road being chased by a rabid dog. The dog turned into my neighbour's garden, his sons ran up towards us and my neighbour picked up his rifle and shot the rabid dog only 10 yards from his son. A very near thing and a frightening experience for us all.

Another incident with dogs was when the Station Administrative Chief, who had a shotgun and had orders to shoot all dogs which came within the perimeter of this very large Wireless Station on sight, accidentally shot the dog, a spaniel, belonging to the wife of the Officer-in Charge. To make matters worse the poor little critter took three days to die. We teased this poor Chief, who was a very nice man, and a good Chief, for many weeks.

After two years I had a break from watch keeping and we went on two weeks holiday to Diyatalawa, a Services Rest Camp, it was in the mountains about 6,000 feet up and the climate was beautiful and gave us much needed respite from the damp heat of the coastal region.

Of my work, I spent most of my time running the Merchant Shipping desk during my watch and operated the ship to shore and shore to ship broadcasts to all the P & O and other passenger, cargo and tanker vessels which operated in or passed through the Indian Ocean. We took thousands of telegrams from the ships every day, all sent and received by Morse. The strange thing is that I can remember to this day the W/T callsigns of many of these ships but I cannot recall the callsign of even one of the many warships I have served in or operated with over the past 50 years.

The ships I recall are those with famous old names such as:

SS ORCADES/GCNB, SS ORONSAY/GMCD,
SS HIMALAYA/MCDY, SS CHUSAN/GGZY,
BRITISH SKILL/MCMD, STRATHEDEN/GCGD
SS ORION/GKYD

(Perhaps I have a couple of the above callsigns wrong, memory plays tricks sometimes).

and so many others. I even used to work the QUEEN MARY/GBTT whilst it was crossing the Atlantic Ocean. The big liners were busy transporting emigrants from Europe to Australia, particularly from the UK, Italy and Greece. Many others, including the troopships were busy transporting troops to and from Korea, Malaysia and Hong Kong.

Another source of huge batches of telegrams was from the Pilgrim ships going from Malaysia and Indonesia to Mecca. Everyone on board seemed to want to sent a telegram and it was not unusual to receive 80 telegrams in Malay from one of these ships. As it was my job to check the number of words in each telegram in order to ensure that the charge was right, the languages often gave real problems. This, however, made the work more interesting and I thoroughly enjoyed my work at CWRS but the debilitating climate, the insects and the less than satisfactory working and living conditions gave us no regrets when the time came to return home. We were allowed to travel home together and left Colombo in HMT EMPIRE HALLADALE in early June 1954, arriving mid July.

As it was another troopship, we were not allowed to stay together, Audrey was accommodated with the other women and I was accommodated down on the troop deck. We were allowed to meet between 11 a.m. and 12 noon, and again from 2 p.m. to 5 p.m. and from 7 p.m. to 9 p.m. But under strict supervision. The Regimental Sergeant Major in charge ensured that no hanky panky was allowed, whether married or not!

CHAPTER THIRTEEN

BACK TO SEA

HMS BOXER AND HMS GLASGOW (1954 TO 1956)

"Travel and change of place impart new vigour to the mind"

Seneca (c. 59 BC - c. AD 40) Roman rhetorician.

Arriving in UK, I had about seven weeks leave to come. We had no home and so Audrey and I went to Wincanton where we shared the leave period between staying with her parents and with mine at Yarlington. My mother and father were pleased to see us and it was the longest period I had been at home since joining the navy eight years before. Mother was involved in helping with cleaning the church, looking after the flowers and making friends with everyone as always. She was happy, but they lived four miles from the nearest shops either at Wincanton or at Castle Cary, there were no buses and had to wholly rely on the groceries and meat delivered by the local rounds men. Alas these rounds men do not exist any more. As she had made many friends, some of them had cars and she had the occasional trip to town with them. Father was still working for the council and was also happy. He and I used

223

to go down to the local pub, *'The Stag'*, every Saturday night and he enjoyed having me with him and also the company of his cronies. I did not have a car and so Audrey and I cycled or sometimes walked, the four miles to and from Wincanton as we had done in the past. During this period Audrey became pregnant.

I had to report to my next ship in early September 1954. It was to be HMS BOXER, based at Portsmouth. HMS BOXER was an old Landing Ship Tank (LST) which had been converted into a radar training ship. She had been given four masts and was a most distinctive vessel going in and out of Portsmouth harbour.

I was, by this time a very experienced Leading Telegraphist and very ready to be advanced to Petty Officer Telegraphist. The work in HMS BOXER was reasonably demanding but I was not over stretched and thoroughly enjoyed this period as we went to sea most days of the week and I therefore managed to get home to Wincanton most weekends. Audrey lived with her parents in Wincanton and we generally went out to Yarlington to see mother and father when I came home.

Our daughter, Linda Jean was born on 3rd May 1955, she weighed eight pounds and was three weeks late in arriving as Audrey had a difficult pregnancy and had been sent to bed with pleurisy by her doctor in early April and I believe he forgot about her and the baby grew too big and the delivery was by caesarean section at the maternity hospital at Templecombe. Audrey then suffered from swollen legs (White leg) for several weeks and was unable to get about very much. She had much help from her mother and was greatly proud of her baby as we both were and the little money we did have went on ensuring that our daughter had the best we could afford.

Our concern was where were we going to live, as Audrey's parents did not really have room for us. Fortunately, my sister Doris who was married to Frederick Wearn, had a roomy house with a half an acre of land at Verwood in Dorset where they kept goats and rabbits as a hobby. Fred worked at the local nurseries and Doris had her work cut out looking after the goats and rabbits. They offered us a bedroom, living room and kitchen at their house. We were delighted, moved down to Verwood in the summer, August, of 1955. Doris and Fred gave or lent us many basic items and we went to Ringwood to buy our first pieces of furniture.

The Chief Telegraphist in HMS BOXER was a pleasant man, nearing pensionable age but he totally lacked interest in his job. He had served through the war, but appeared to have totally lost interest and was not up to date with procedures or the latest technical equipment. This did not matter too much as I was very much up to date and keen and the communications tasks were not too demanding as we usually sailed at 0830 and returned to harbour about 1700. We thus got into a routine which entailed me supervising the cleaning of my mess deck every morning until about 0815, then going to the office, stirring up the Chief who would be looking at magazines with the young operators, with no work being done, making them scrub out the office and set watch on the appropriate circuits. The Chief who had come from his home in Portsmouth at about 0750 would then gather up his magazines and papers and retire tc his mess and we often did not see him again that day. This led to an amusing situation when we were, for a change, going to spend a few days at sea. On the third day at sea the Squadron Communications Officer (SCO), called down the voice pipe from the Bridge and asked for the Chief. I replied that he was not in the office at that moment but I would let the Chief know he wanted him when he came in. (Intending to ring the Chief's Mess and tell his that he was wanted). A few minutes later the SCO came into the office, pulled me aside and told me that the Chief was not on board. I, and all the rest of the staff had not realised he was not with us. Although I suspect the SCO thought I was trying to cover up for him - which I would have done - as despite his inadequacies the Chief was a nice man and I would not have knowingly got him into trouble.

In September 1955 I was promoted, at last, to Petty Officer Telegraphist and was drafted from HMS BOXER to HMS GLASGOW which was the Flagship of Flag Officer Flotillas (Home Fleet). This was very hard work, I was away at sea most of the time, carrying out exercises with the Fleet. During this period I visited Gibraltar, Tangier, Hamburg, Kiel and several other UK and European ports. I had the consolation of knowing that Audrey was not alone and had the support of my sister and her husband.

I stayed in HMS GLASGOW for just over a year, I had worked hard and was highly recommended for my work. In the autumn of 1956 the Suez crisis occurred. We in HMS GLASGOW were armed, stored, took on dozens of additional crew to put us on a war complement and got ready to sail for Suez as part of the large fleet being deployed by the Government, then led by Sir Anthony Eden. Unfortunately, or fortunately for me, HMS GLASGOW, an already old ship, developed serious engine problems. Therefore when we sailed from Rosyth, instead of heading directly for Suez as planned, we headed for Portsmouth where the ship decommissioned for scrap.

HMS GLASGOW leaving Portsmouth 1955

The Communications staff on the Fo'c'sle of HMS GLASGOW 1956

HMS GLASGOW's sister ship, HMS BELFAST, is now moored on the Thames and open to visitors daily. I will pay a nostalgic visit one day!

CHAPTER FOURTEEN

NEW ENTRY INSTRUCTING

HMS MERCURY

(1956 TO 1957)

A little learning is a dangerous thing, but ignorance is just as bad.

Alexander Pope

I was sent to HMS MERCURY, the Signal School, which by then was half empty and very short of Instructors as every available man had been sent to the Suez war. I was given the job of instructing new recruits into communications. This was a pleasant job, I could get home on weekend leave most weekends, but this was not enough for me. I applied for and got a married quarter at Lovedean which was a few miles from HMS MERCURY. We moved in January 1957 and had the first home of our own at last. I got home every night, except when duty which was about once every ten days, and enjoyed married life with my wife and daughter, Linda, who was by then about 18 months old.

The married quarter was fully furnished and very comfortable, our own furniture and few belongings at Verwood we left in situ, paying Doris and Fred a nominal rent until we knew where we were to go next. During our time at Lovedean, Audrey's father died and she and Linda went home to Wincanton for the funeral. I was too involved with my work to be able to get away, in those days the navy was far less liberal when it came to giving one time off for 'compassionate' reasons than it is today.

One harrowing incident occurred when we were in married quarters. I had just arrived home from work and Audrey was preparing the tea when Linda who was then $2^{1}/_{2}$ toddled to the edge of the table and pulled the teapot full of freshly made tea over her. She was very badly scalded and we had to rush her to Queen Alexandra Hospital at Cosham. They treated her as best they could but she was in much pain for some time. Poor Linda she still has the scars of that accident to this day.

I did well as an Instructor, I was by now an experienced Petty Officer Telegraphist and had gained the confidence which enables one to do one's job well and enjoy it. My first class were National Servicemen who were all Royal Naval Reservists in civilian life. They were therefore all most interested and keen and it was a joy to teach them, indeed one of them still comes to the Signal Officer's reunions every year. After he had completed his two years National Service he continued in the RNR and his promotion through the ranks to Lieutenant Commander almost exactly mirrored my own promotions. The second class I took through were normal newly entered ratings and were of a mixed bag, some were keen but several did not seem to try or care. At this time I believe I developed a hardness which I did not have before and I found I had little time for those who did not try. I soon had them back classed or taken off course altogether. Indeed there were some who I recommended as 'unfit for further training' and they were sent home without more ado. This came as quite a shock to them and to their parents who then wanted to know why 'little Johnny' was sent home without notice. Another example of my new found 'hardness' was when duty, it was the job of the Duty Petty Officer to ensure that everyone got out of bed at 0630, went to breakfast in the right rig, changed into the correct uniform before supper and went to bed with lights out by 2200 etc. There was much scope here for catching lads getting it wrong and I, together with a couple of colleagues sometimes vied with each other to see who could get the most 'defaulters' during one days duty. I led for some time with thirty nine defaulters in one days duty. The disadvantage of doing this was that one had to spend the first hour or more next morning at the defaulters table giving evidence, this meant that my class was then without an instructor if I could not get someone to look out for me. After a time I found that my reputation went ahead of me and my duties were most peaceful! I had learnt that to enforce discipline and to ensure proper punishment in minor matters led to a significant reduction in more serious offences. I think there is a moral here for our present justice system!

In November 1957 I was pleasantly surprised by being given a draft to Slangkop Radio Station which was situated about 25 miles from Capetown in South Africa. This was to be another *'married accompanied'* draft and for another period of $2^1/_2$ years, but with the important difference that we could sail together by the Union Castle Line and not suffer the indignities of the troopship life. We gave up our married quarter and Audrey and Linda went back to Verwood for a few weeks whilst we were preparing for the journey. We put our furniture in storage in Ringwood until our return. We had a last minute panic as Linda developed bronchitis and was very poorly and we had quite a battle to persuade the doctor how essential it was for us to sail.

The author as a Petty Officer Telegraphist in 1957

CHAPTER FIFTEEN

SOUTH AFRICA

SLANGKOP W/T
OR
HMS AFRIKANDER

(1957 TO 1960)

The proper means of increasing the love we bear to our native country is to reside some time in a foreign one.

William Shenstone (1714 - 1763)
English Poet

We sailed on a Thursday in mid November 1957, as did every Union Castle line ship going to South Africa, in the Arundel Castle, circa 20,000 tons. We had a lovely trip on this very fine old liner and arrived refreshed and eager. Linda recovered in the sunshine during the trip. We stayed with naval friends for a few weeks when we arrived until we could find a place of our own. This was quite an adventure as we went to estate agents and were taken round many fine old houses, and flats. One incident which stands out in my mind was when we were looking at one old house which had been empty for many months we looked down at Linda's legs, she was wearing long white stockings, and they were completely black, also our trouser legs. Audrey screamed and the estate agent calmly brushed off the thousands of fleas from his trousers and said, *"That's nothing to worry about, it always happens when houses have been empty for a while, flea powder will soon get rid of them"*. This in fact was a perfectly true statement as fleas lay their eggs and die if they have no one or no animal to feed on and the eggs lie around in houses or in the jungle or wherever for years until disturbed by a passing animal or person when they all hatch at once and leap on the their food source. Although we liked the house there was no way Audrey was going to live there.

We eventually decided on a modern ground floor flat in the small town of Fishoek (VishHoek). This was sited about 200 yards from one of the most beautiful beaches one could imagine. We loved it there. The South African people in the area were mostly ex British and all very friendly and we soon settled in. An additional advantage was that Fishoek was a whites only area and no colours or blacks were allowed to live in the town. They were allowed of course to come in to work. This meant we did not have fears of being burgled, robbed or assaulted as we did in Ceylon, the police being particularly efficient. We had no car, but this did not pose a problem as there was naval transport from Fishoek to Slangkop which was about five miles distant, at regular intervals to fit in with the watch keeping pattern. Also there was a very efficient electric train service to Capetown, which was then and I am sure still is a very beautiful city. We had all we wanted, our lovely daughter was $2^1/_2$ when we arrived and 5 when we left so she did not have to go to school. Audrey could take her to the beach every day and I also went with them every other day when I was home from work. We made some nice friends, some of whom we are in touch with even to this day.

U.C.M.S. ARUNDEL CASTLE - 1957

I was watch keeping again at Slangkop Radio Station doing a job very similar to that at Ceylon West Wireless Station in the early 1950s. The merchant shipping traffic was heavy as by this time the Suez Canal was in the hands of the Egyptians who were not yet ready to take the volume of traffic of previous years and, in addition, the big oil companies were then bringing in very large tankers of 100,000 tons and over which could not at that time transit the canal.

Another major source of merchant shipping telegrams was from the Whaling Fleets. There were many large factory ships, the majority belonging to the British and the Norwegians. These spent the summer (our winter), in the Antarctic and they were always very careful not to disclose their whereabouts in order that competitors did not know where the best whaling grounds were. They even encrypted their weather reports, which of course contained a position. All whaling has now of course been banned from Antarctic waters, except I believe the Japanese continue for what they call 'scientific purposes'.

A peculiarity of Slangkop Radio Station was that it was situated 5 miles from the nearest large village or town and 10 miles from its parent naval base which was called HMS AFRIKANDER and where the Admiral, the Commander-in Chief South Atlantic, and his staff plus the administration services were situated. The Officer-in-Charge of the radio station therefore lived and worked in HMS AFRIKANDER and only visited us about three or four times a month and then generally only to bring our pay and to see to requestmen and defaulters. This situation should have been ideal, i.e. we were left alone to get on with our work, which, being a radio station we were working directly into and largely controlled by Whitehall Wireless Station back in the UK.

Unfortunately the day to day administration and running of the station was actually in the hands of a Chief Petty Officer Telegraphist who was, in my view then, and it still is my view, an out and out crook. He lived only a few hundred yards from the station in the only married quarter. He paid little attention to the details of the radio circuits we operated as he did not understand much of it. He did however rule with a rod of iron the administrative side of life such as the discipline and cleanliness of the area. He was not a very clever man, crafty rather than clever, and invariably resorted to shouting and bullying when he wanted his way. The young unmarried lads who lived in the accommodation huts were particularly liable to his bad temper. One of the things he did was to take down the netting around the tennis courts and use it as a pen for his chickens. This upset the younger lads, among whom I must admit there were a few hard cases and they resolved to get their own back for this and many other unnecessary restrictions placed on them.

One morning the Chief arrived to find that someone had shot several of his chickens with arrows and left them hanging up on the wire. He immediately called the police and blamed all and sundry, even I, who had been on watch in the radio station all night, was accused of having a hand in it. This incident together with many others, particularly to do with transport which the Chief seemed to regard as for his own and his family's private use caused much unhappiness among the young lads. At one time a battery for the bus went missing, it was reported by one of the South African civilian drivers and the Chief immediately called the police and there was yet another investigation. Chief again implied that I and several others had something to do with it - and I did not even have a car! We were later to be informed, long after this Chief had gone, from one of the other South African drivers, that the Chief himself had taken this battery, and had called the police when the driver had reported it missing. We could not of course verify this story but it was most probably true and typical of this man.

Another source of discontent was the food and the price of items at the small Canteen which were controlled by the Chief and who the lads suspected of being up to dirty business with the Caterers. One night they wired up the gate to his house and smeared grease on it, the consequence was that when he came out in the morning he got grease on his white uniform, I believe his daughters were also caught when going off to school. Whilst not actively concerned so much with the goings on of the young lads living on the camp, I was concerned for their welfare inasmuch as that some of them were in my watch and I remonstrated with the Chief several times with respect to certain of his actions. His reaction each time was to blow his top and tell me to mind my own business. He then found fault with minor items which occurred during my watch and told the Officer-in Charge that he was not happy with some aspects. I also attempted to tell the Officer in Charge on one of his rare visits but he would not listen to me, or indeed to the other Petty Officers who ran the other three watches and who were also similarly concerned. Looking back, I now find it incredible that this very nasty situation could have been allowed to occur and carry on for so long with no senior officer being the slightest bit interested in the welfare of the 50 or 60 ratings at this isolated wireless station.

As with all radio stations, although we only had about 12 men in each watch and the total complement was about 60 persons, the area of the station was large because of the many receiving aerials. There was therefore about 60 acres of bush which was fenced to keep out intruders. A constant danger was bush fires, when a bush fire broke out it could travel for many miles at a tremendous pace, faster than one could walk in many cases and the 'standby watch ' was always to be ready to fight these fires within the camp perimeter. We had many fires and many scares but with the aid of a very efficient local police and Fire Service we managed to save our accommodation although we lost an aerial or two on occasion.

The 'Standby Watch' was the second watch on duty but not actually on watch in the radio station, we had to be there on camp all the time and thus we were all effectively required to do a 94 hour week. A habit of the Chief which also upset those who were married and wanted to get home to sleep after a 24 or 48 hour stint, was that if there was anything wrong the Chief would keep us back for an investigation and he often told us that the Officer-in-Charge was coming out. On many occasions I came off the night watch at 0800 and instead of being able to go home to my family I had to wait for the Officer-in-Charge. On many occasions, I and others waited all day and were then told he couldn't come as he was too busy. I then was able to go home just in time to have supper and go to bed and get up next morning to go away for another 24 or 48 hour stint.

This uncaring attitude made this Chief the most detested man I have ever met in my life. I have met some, but not really very many, people during my life whom I did not like but never anyone so detestable as this man. The uncaring attitude of the Officer in Charge, who I cannot believe did not know what was going on was also a factor.

We all knew the Chief lied to the Officer-in-charge about us, particularly the young lads when they were at defaulters charged with minor offences. A very good chum of mine, a Petty Officer, when on 'Standby Watch' one night received a phone call from his wife to say the their youngest son was having a screaming fit. As he had his own car he informed his 'second in command' and went home for about an hour between 3 a.m. and 4 a.m.. In the morning he told the Chief, who, instead of being understanding, charged him with being absent from place of duty and he was sent to the Administrative headquarters at HMS AFRIKANDER for trial and he received a severe reprimand. This reprimand was enough to ruin my friend's career in the navy and he never recovered. The irony of it all was that no one would have known that he had gone home if he had not innocently told the Chief of what he had done and the reason for it. The Officer-in-Charge was again, in my view, weak, and did not stand up to this Chief with such a powerful personality.

The antics of this Chief spoilt, together with many others, my first year in South Africa to some extent. But a new Officer-in-Charge arrived after I had been there about 15 months and he actually took an interest in our isolated Radio Station, he even arrived at 0700 on some mornings to see how we were getting on. He even talked to us! He took only a few weeks to size up this problem Chief. He relieved him from any involvement with the actual running of the Radio Station, and ensured he only looked after the most basic of administrative affairs, and these he double checked. He charged him with misuse of Naval transport and had a full audit of the catering accounts. I did not find out the outcome but the catering management was changed and food was much improved.

The person who came as Officer-in-Charge and put everything to right, is now (in 1997), 80 years old and I occasionally see him in a pub in Fareham, I always buy him a drink and remind him of the good he did so many years ago. The obnoxious Chief left the navy, stayed in South

Africa and got a job selling vacuum cleaners. I heard later that he knocked on the door of one of the young naval wives whose husband he had formerly persecuted so unfairly. She had much pleasure in telling him where to put his vacuum cleaners!

During our time in South Africa my '*12 years service from the age of 18*' expired and I therefore had the option of leaving the Royal Navy. I was sorely tempted to do so as I saw no prospect other than becoming a Chief eventually and soldiering on until I was 40 and then would have to leave on completion of pensionable service. I also realised that it would be much easier to get a job in civilian life at the age of 30 than at the age of 40. Additionally, I had the opportunity to leave the navy in South Africa and take a job there. This was very tempting as the climate was perfect, the people were pleasant and of my kind of thinking and the job opportunities were most attractive. All these things made me think hard but I believe there were two factors which decided me against.

Firstly, the Sharpeville riots of 1960 took place whilst we were there and it was plain that, whilst I believed that the white supremacy would be able to last for at least another 30 years, it was evident that after that the blacks would take charge and the country would inevitably slip into anarchy. I did not want my children to inherit this future. This belief has proved itself to be largely true as the white government did last for 30 years and there is now every sign of all the wealth which has been built up in that beautiful country over the past 300 years being destroyed as indeed has happened in most other African states.

Secondly, my parents were, by then, both in their seventies and I did not like the thought of not going home to see them. Had I stayed I may not have been able to afford to go home for many years. Audrey's mother died in 1959 and she therefore did not have parents to go home to so she was prepared to stay if I wished to do so.

I therefore decided to re-engage for a further 10 years to complete time for my pension at the age of 40.

We left Capetown in the Union Castle liner SS WINCHESTER CASTLE in early June 1960 and arrived in UK in mid June. It was another perfect cruise home in a lovely old ship. Linda was by then 5 years old and able to enjoy the fun and experience.

CHAPTER SIXTEEN

FINDING A HOME, BACK TO SEA, HMS WAKEFUL

INSTRUCTORS COURSE AND PROMOTION COURSES (1960 TO 1962)

*Seek home for rest,
For home is best.*

Thomas Tusser (1524 - 1580)
Writer

On arrival in UK we had to decide where we were to go. We could not go to Verwood to my sister's house as they had by then re-let the rooms which we had lived in. Audrey's mum and dad were dead and their house no more (it had been demolished). We went to my mother and father at Yarlington. They had room and were naturally pleased to see us but we knew we could not live with them for long as I would have to go off to sea again and Audrey, with a 5 year old daughter and without transport, could not live in this isolated hamlet for long. Neither would it have been fair on my parents.

We stayed at Yarlington for about 6 weeks. During this time I wrote to an estate agent in Fareham for brochures on affordable houses, these we perused and then went to Fareham to view them. We stayed in a boarding house for a couple of nights and trudged around Fareham looking at likely places. I remember it was a very wet two days and we both wished we were back in Capetown. We eventually settled for a 3 bed semi-detached house right in the town. The house had been built in about 1928, using not the best looking of bricks but it was solidly built and had a reasonably large garden for a town house and it was in a secluded street. The house cost £2,450, a lot of money for us. We had saved about £1000 since we married, most whilst we were in Ceylon, and so we took out a mortgage for £1500 which was as much as I could afford on my Petty Officer's pay at that time.

Why did we choose Fareham? Basically because I had no car, it was on the main railway line to the west country where our relations lived, it was convenient for me to get to the Royal Naval Dockyard at Portsmouth by either the Gosport/Ferry route or directly to Portsmouth via Portchester and Cosham.

In those days the A27 road was so congested that it was much quicker and easier to go by bus to Gosport, take the ferry across to Portsmouth Hard and then walk to the Dockyard. Also I could get to HMS MERCURY at Leydene easily as a special naval bus ran from Gosport via Fareham to Leydene daily.

Whilst I was on leave and making all these arrangements I received notification of my next ship. It was to be HMS WAKEFUL, a frigate which was based at Portsmouth and would generally be operating in and out of Portsmouth on a daily basis, carrying navigation training classes. This suited me fine. I joined in August 1960 as the Radio Supervisor in charge of the communications department. It was a lovely job, I was my own boss and slept, not in a hammock but on a camp bed in the transmitter room. This I kept as my own office and only reluctantly let the radio engineers in for essential maintenance, most work I did myself and I also kept it clean and used a lavender wax polish on the floor. The Captain always made a nice remark when he inspected this office during his weekly rounds. It was the cleanest office in the ship.

As we were carrying out navigation training, of which I knew nothing, the Captain suggested to me on several occasions that I should get out of the Wireless Office and go on the Bridge for Bridge Watch keeping and ship navigational experience. This was because I had been recommended for several years, ever since HMS GLASGOW, as a possible candidate to be given a Special Duties Officer commission. However, I was not really interested in this at that time. I saw my future as eventually taking the Radio Communications Instructor's (RCI) course at HMS MERCURY and becoming a top grade instructor as a Petty Officer and then as a Chief Radio Supervisor until I was 40 and had completed time for pension. My other main aim in life was to get home to my wife and lovely daughter as often as I could. I therefore always found an excuse of being 'too busy' when the Captain tried to get me on to the Bridge. How I was to regret this later !

I was highly recommended for my work in HMS WAKEFUL, it must have been the lavender floor polish!, and I got my wish. In August 1961 I was drafted to HMS

MERCURY for the Radio Communications Instructor's (RCI's) course. I was delighted, I was placed on course with 12 other experienced Petty Officers and Chiefs. The course was to last about 9 months and was intended to bring us all to the peak of our professional training. We were all very competitive and worked hard to get top marks. There were to be 14 final examinations in various communications subjects and it was necessary to pass all of them. The pass mark in most subjects was 80%, with the exceptions of Radio Theory where the pass mark was to be 60 % and certain practical subjects such as Morse and typing where the pass mark was to be 96 %. I vied for top place, as the top of the course student had his name put up in gold letters on an honours board in the Senior Ratings' mess.

At the end of the course we were all anxious to hear our results for various subjects. The course officer gave out the various marks and then announced that I was top. This was great, although there was not much in it. However, the following week, my best chum, who had got a copy of the printed marks added them up for himself and found that he had beaten me by four marks out of the total of 1400 possible marks. Being a nice chap, and indeed a good friend to this day, he said, *"Never mind Len, leave it like it is."* I said *"No way"* and we went to the Course Officer, pointed out his mistake in the additions and my chum was then pronounced *'Top of the Course'* and his name is on the honours board to this day. Looking back I wonder why we made such play of how many marks we got, it was sufficient just to pass, but it was the competitive spirit in all of us which drove us to pursue perfection.

Having completed the course, I was to be drafted to the Royal Naval College at Dartmouth as a Communications Instructor to the Officer Cadets with the rank of Acting Chief Radio Supervisor. This was fine. I wasn't sure whether Audrey and Linda would come with me or not at the time as Linda had by now started infant school and we did not want to move her unnecessarily. We decided to wait till I got down to Dartmouth and I had found out the pros and cons of getting a married quarter before deciding. Meanwhile I went home on summer leave.

On the very evening of the day I was to start my leave I got a message that I was to report to the Training Commander at HMS MERCURY the next morning (Saturday). I reported accordingly and was told that I had been selected for the next Special Duties Officers Course which was to start in 3 weeks time, early September. Did I want it ? He noted that I had not had gained my Bridge Experience Certificate which was essential before being placed on this course. How I wished I had made the effort when my Captain in HMS WAKEFUL had urged me!

I was given until the following Monday to make up my mind and told that if I wanted the course I would have to go to a ship right away for a crash Bridge Experience Course. I went home in a daze, talked it over with Audrey, pointing out the hard work involved and the chances of my being away from home for long periods. She did not stand in my way, nor has she ever stood in the way of me advancing my career, in spite of the difficulties which she may have been put in to. I decided to go for it. Gone was my planned easy life instructing at the top of my profession as a Chief Radio Supervisor and Radio Communications Instructor for the remaining eight years of my naval service.

I reported to the Training Commander on the Monday and accepted the offer. I was told to report to HMS MALCOLM at Portland that very day for two weeks 'Bridge Experience' training.

I was given the job as Assistant Officer of the Watch on the Bridge. I did not have a clue, although I had several years before, whilst in HMS GLASGOW, passed the requisite Navigation Theory exams. We went to sea every day and I slowly got used to learning how to keep the Log, take fixes and generally learn about what was going on the Bridge and how to run the ship. How I wished yet again that I had paid attention whilst in HMS WAKEFUL. At the end of two weeks I left HMS MALCOM with my Bridge Experience Certificate signed by the Captain. I felt a fraud as I still did not really know what was going on. I had spent all my life at sea in the Communications offices of ships and had never really put myself out to broaden my horizons by finding out about ship navigation, and ship handling generally. This was to change.

I enjoyed the (SD)(C) Course and had no trouble with the professional side with regard to communications. I worked hard and also did well at the General Service subjects and did extremely well at Navigation, Gunnery, Anti-Submarine Warfare, Radar and Action Information Organisation subjects.

Navigation training was carried out in HMS WAKEFUL, my old ship. I recall working very late one night to prepare a passage plan and anchorage in the Solent for the next day. This was to be my final examination in Navigation. The passage plan went OK, but as I was running in to my anchorage position I had to change course to avoid the RMS QUEEN ELIZABETH. This threw my careful calculations right out and I had to continue to the anchorage with a quickly revised plan, most of it in my head. It worked. I anchored exactly where I had been told to. More by luck than skill perhaps, but I passed my Navigation Examination with high marks and came 4th overall out of 16 in all the examinations throughout the course so I was well content.

On the 18th June 1962, we reported to the Royal Naval College at GREENWICH wearing the uniform of Sub Lieutenants for the final part of our course. This was to be in various subjects including Naval History and Staff Paper writing and as a general broadening of our education and outlook. We all worked hard and enjoyed this lovely college. I invited Audrey up for the Summer Ball which was in the Painted Hall and a particularly grand occasion.

Whilst there, I recall Admiral of the Fleet Lord Louis Mountbatten, who was then Chief of the Defence Staff, coming to a mess dinner and he brought along Douglas Fairbanks Junior as his private guest. Apparently Lord Louis had invited himself and his guest to the mess dinner and the Admiral President of the College was not over amused at this pushiness. He showed his displeasure when Lord Louis and guest rose to leave the table, we all stood up in deference to the great man. The Admiral President, red in the face, gesticulated violently for us to sit down. Politics!

CHAPTER SEVENTEEN

MY FIRST SHIP AS AN OFFICER

(1962 TO 1964)

The secret of success is constancy of purpose.

Benjamin Disraeli (1804-1881)

My first ship as a Sub Lieutenant was HMS NUBIAN. She was brand new and I joined her at Portsmouth on a Sunday evening prior to sailing to Portland for what was then called the Flag Officer Sea Training Work Up . This was a very intensive six week period during which time every aspect of the ship's machinery and weapons and every officer and man was placed under maximum stress. I was Communications Officer, Assistant Fo'c'sle Officer and Assistant Officer of the Watch. The Officer of the Watch task was my main occupation as I needed the experience and the training to enable me to pass my Bridge Watch keeping certificate. I learned much in a very short time and gained confidence in my abilities. I was and am still most grateful to the Captain of HMS NUBIAN, Captain Ian Jamieson, he was a super man. He was an Anti-Submarine Warfare expert, a senior Captain and one of the kindest and understanding persons I have ever met. His guidance helped me to become proficient as an Officer and in particular to achieve my goal of being granted a Bridge Watch keeping Certificate within one year of joining the ship. This certificate entitled me to take charge of any warship as the Officer of the Watch on my own by day or by night. I also learned much with respect to Anti-Submarine warfare and management of the Operations Room organisation.

The winter of 1962/3 was a particularly severe one, there was much snow and Portland and Weymouth were cut off from the rest of Dorset for several days. The cold weather lasted right through January and February. As Fo'c'sle officer I was required to be on the Fo'c'sle to take charge of berthing when entering and leaving harbour and also of anchoring and mooring the ship. I froze up there every day and I recall we had to chip the ice off the guard rails and iron deck before we could work. What had I let myself in for ?

In HMS NUBIAN, we worked hard and sailed for the Persian Gulf in April 1963. The Gulf, as we were encouraged to call it so as not to upset the Iraqis or Saudis who did not like it being called the Persian Gulf, was very different in those days to what it is today. The only really oil rich state was Kuwait which I remember we visited and was most impressed with the brand new Italian architect designed houses, the new hospital fitted out with the most up to date, (mainly German), equipment, the wide roads and street lights and the Ruler's new palace which he was building especially for his guests was nearing completion. We were shown round it, it had sound proof bedrooms, gold fittings on all doors, windows and in the bathrooms. There was an enormous chandelier in the main entrance which I recall was made of German crystal and had cost a million pounds. That was a lot of money in those days.

The rest of the Gulf was relatively poor and undeveloped, especially the Trucial States. These were small Sheikhdoms which were supported and semi protected by Britain and a major reason for us being there. There was a small force of Trucial Scouts, led by British Army officers who kept the peace between the often warring Sheikhdoms. We had to be most careful that we accorded the various Sheikhs their due ceremonial as to accord one greater or lesser respects than his due could easily provoke a diplomatic incident or even a war.

I recall attending a banquet given by a minor Sheikh. It was a lunch time affair, it was very hot, the humidity was over 95% and we were wearing white dress uniforms with swords. The Sheikh's body guards were armed with several pistols, rifles and knives each and they watched us all the time. We had to take off our swords when we sat down to eat. The meal was the traditional Sheep or Goat stew flavoured with a very hot and red sauce. It was the custom for the host who may have taken a tasty piece of mutton from the big central pot to hand it to his guest. We ate with our fingers and I recall that my white suit was not only soaking wet with the sweat and humidity but my sleeves and the front of my tunic were covered in this red sauce. We all felt a mess, but did our duty as diplomats in this politically highly charged region.

Another of our duties was to patrol and try to prevent arms and illegal immigrant smuggling. Unfortunately we were built as an Anti-submarine patrol frigate and our top speed was about 24 knots. Indeed the top speed which we could sustain for any lengthy period without using up too much fuel was about 19 knots. There were two problems, firstly, the Arab Dhows which were used for smuggling usually had large Lister, or such make, diesel engines which could move at up to 18 knots and secondly, the waters in the Gulf are very shallow and there were many areas close to shore where we could not go, but the Dhows could and so we were not at all successful in this task. Indeed, the only Dhows which we ever stopped and searched were those which wanted us to stop them so that they could get some free fresh water from us. I never discovered whether the Foreign Office officials and the Admiralty Board had ever thought through the policy of sending such frigates to this area.

Another first. HMS NUBIAN as a Tribal class frigate, was one of the first frigates to be built with a built in air conditioning system, consequently we had no scuttles. To say the least the system had its teething troubles. It frequently broke down and we had some most uncomfortable periods. At one stage we had to go into Bahrain, tie up alongside and we all had to live ashore for several days, leaving only a minimal duty watch on board, until the system was repaired.

Whilst practising mooring ship, I recall that as Fo'c'sle officer, I had trouble raising the anchor, it was lodged on some rocks on the bottom. After much trouble and getting the Captain to go slow ahead and really wrench it free, we got it up. It was horribly bent and I was teased for what I was alleged to have done. I was most surprised to find that this anchor, designed to hold a 2,500 ton frigate was hollow and not made of the strength of material I would have expected. However I must assume that the Naval Architects who designed it knew their business. We had to get another anchor flown out from the UK. As it weighed a lot, I believe about thirty hundredweight, this cost a lot in civil air freight charges.

We were then friends and allies of the Persians (the Iranians), and visited their ports and ships and also carried out sea exercises with them. The Shah was at that time modernising his armed forces with considerable help from

Britain and we were keen to show his navy what we had to offer.

A port visit I particularly recall was the visit to Muscat. Muscat was then ruled by a despotic ruler and was kept firmly in the 19th century. He would have none of the modern world. There were no cars in the streets, all women were in purdah, there was a curfew at night except for those who had proper business and carried an oil lantern. All his political opponents were locked up in a huge castle dungeon, many of them not for long as the death penalty was freely used. We held a 'Sea Day' for some relatives of the Ruler and took them to sea to show off our new ship and modern weapons. I was tasked to look after a fierce looking individual who I believe was the Ruler's uncle. He spoke little or no English and I did my best to guide him round.

He had a very expensive looking camera and took many photographs. The amusing thing was that some months later we returned to Muscat and this man came aboard again, again with his camera and this time he kept shielding the lens with his hand from the several radar aerials which we had operating. I managed to get from him, through an interpreter, that none of the last lot of photographs he took had come out and that he thought that I had allowed him to take photographs only to secretly wipe them out with the radar. I did my best to explain that we didn't mind what photos he took, but he didn't believe me and kept hiding his camera from the radars. I never found out if the second lot came out. I suspect the camera was too complicated for him.

Sub Lieutenant L G Foot - HMS NUBIAN 1963

One port which we visited which has now changed so notably was Dubai. Then it was a busy commercial trading port from which the Dhows operated throughout the Gulf and to India and Pakistan. Gold smuggling was among the business transacted. In discussions with the manager of a local British bank I was told that it was legal to put gold into a Dhow and sent it to India and the only illegal act was the actual landing it as contraband in India. Much money was being made and this particular Bank employee actually had a part share in a Dhow which was operating this trade, which was quite legal in Dubai. Dubai is now a very wealthy and modern city and I am sure I would not now recognise the changes which have now occurred to the dusty streets and Arab market stalls of 1963.

To give us a break from the heat and long periods of boredom whilst patrolling in the Gulf, we visited the Seychelles and Mombasa. I particularly recall arriving at Victoria on Mahe, then the only town in the Seychelles and seeing green vegetation for the first time for many months. The Seychelles were a marvellous visit for all of us. At that time there was no airport and apart from a seaplane which came out from Mombasa once a week with the odd official passenger and mail, the only way to get there was by a ten day sea voyage from Mombasa. There was thus no tourist industry and the Islands were largely unspoilt. It is very different today as the reader will be well aware.

We really visited Mombasa for what was called an Assisted Maintenance Period. Routine maintenance was to be completed by ship's staff engineers assisted by a small team specially flown out from the UK. Kenya had, at that time, in 1963, only recently achieved independence and Mombasa was a lovely port and it was quite safe to walk the streets and beaches and there was no malaria consequent to the British colonial policy of continual spraying of mosquito larvae. During this period I went on safari to the Tsavo national park and recall that with my recently purchased camera, bought in Aden, I took hundreds of slides of animals. These slides are in the cupboard now and I never show them, as, without a telephoto lens, one has to explain to the viewer that; *"There is a giraffe behind that tree if you look hard enough"*. or *"Can you see the ears of that rhino"?* *"What rhino?"* The Tsavo National Park was then and I am sure still is, a fantastic place to visit and an unforgettable experience.

I also had my first experience of deep sea fishing from Mombasa. The Engineer Officer, Supply Officer, Electrical Officer and myself set off in a hired boat at 0800 one morning and we were taken about 20 miles out into the Indian ocean. At half past nine we started fishing. There were 3 harnessed seats for us. All was quiet for about a half an hour and then suddenly we all had strikes of yellow fin tunny. I managed to get mine aboard, so did the Electrical Officer, (sadly now dead). But the Supply Officer, a delightful man (also sadly now dead), suddenly had a very considerable additional weight on his line. His fish had been taken by a very large shark. We played this shark for 4 hours. Every time we got it near to the boat and could see what appeared to be its vast size, and I suppose, it saw us. It just swished its tail and took the line away. We all took it in turns to play it but it was of no use. It must have tired of the game as at about 1300 it just rushed off so hard that it took the line with it. That was the end of our days fishing as by then it was time to go back to harbour.

Another series of visits which we made to give us a break from the Gulf was to Karachi, Bombay and Cochin. My lasting memory of the Indian sub continent was 'people', particularly in Bombay where the streets were thronged with people day and night, some prosperous and many very poor. It brought home to us the size and huge population of India and the immense problems they have and will continue to have, in the population explosion which they are unable to control.

On our return to patrol in the Gulf we continued to visit the various Sheikhdoms, I recall one old stone built 'palace' which we visited had no sanitation and there were ordinary gutter pipes protruding from the walls at various levels from which the effluent fell straight down to the ground. This attracted flies and the flies carried a particular disease which affected the eyes and most Arabs seemed to have some sort of eye infection. I am sure this has all changed now.

Whilst visiting Bahrain we played hockey, I believe against a Royal Air Force team from the RAF base, we played at 0700 in the morning to avoid the heat. I got a knock on the leg and thought nothing of it but it developed into what I think is called 'white leg'. The leg swelled up and became very painful. I was confined to bed for several days and this was during a period when the ship's air conditioning was again broken down. The temperature in my cabin was unbearable and the Captain insisted that I used his day cabin for a while. He was busy in the operations room and not likely to need the bed anyway. I didn't want to do this but he insisted. The reader can imagine the ribbing I got from my fellow officers for being permitted to use the Captain's bed. I pleaded that I was better as soon as I could and got back to my own cabin. This was an example of the kindness of this man.

HMS NUBIAN at Cochin - 1963

HMS ARK ROYAL at 2 cables from HMS NUBIAN - Indian Ocean - 1963

We were in Bahrain again in early January 1964 and I went swimming in the pool at HMS JUFAIR, the shore base. This pool was actually cooled in the summer to prevent it being too hot for a comfortable swim, but in the winter it tended to get quite cool in Bahrain, I was told that once it actually snowed! I believe the pool had not been cleaned recently due to lack of use and I was taken ill a few days later whilst at sea. I remember the Gunner giving me a very large malt whisky and telling me to go to bed. This was the worse thing that he could have given me as I became so ill that I was taken by helicopter to the RAF Hospital in Bahrain and did not regain consciousness for nearly a week. I was diagnosed as having contracted hepatitis and was in hospital for a month.

In February, when the ship returned to Bahrain the Captain and some of my brother officers came to see me. The Captain told me that the RAF wanted to fly me home but he would like me to return to UK in the ship as a passenger to recuperate. I opted to return with the ship which was sailing for home in a few days. As the reader will be aware, recovery from hepatitis is a long slow business and one is not to drink alcohol for at least a year and for the first 6 weeks or so it is not possible to put one's mind to anything taxing without it causing a sort of relapse. I was therefore a complete passenger.

My chums had to do my work whilst I looked on, giving them of course the occasional word of encouragement! Another example of the Captain's kindness was that he lent me his sun lounger chair for me to lie on and sunbathe on the upper deck. I received many comments from the Officers of the Watch who could see me lying there whilst they did my watches. They used to amuse themselves by switching on the windscreen wipers and squirters at the front of the enclosed bridge, just to make sure I got wet now and then and didn't sleep too much!

We arrived in Portsmouth on 1st April 1964. I recall us entering harbour and seeing my dear wife Audrey and our daughter Linda, who was by then nearly 9 years old, waiting on the jetty and waving to me. Linda was wearing a new green overcoat and looked lovely.

One last remark about HMS NUBIAN and its Captain. The Captain was a lovely man as I have already stated and we all respected him very much. However, he was not a good ship handler and although it must be admitted that the Tribal class frigates were not easy to handle, having only one screw, he always had much trouble when berthing her. On our arrival in Portsmouth at the end of the commission we all felt particularly sorry for him as he damaged our own ship quite badly and also the guard rails and sea boat of another frigate at an adjoining berth which we were passing. For this to happen in front of Senior Officers from the Port Admiral's staff and all welcoming families was most embarrassing. This incident did not, however, appear to damage the career of the Captain as he went on to become Captain of Dartmouth College, a Rear Admiral, Flag Officer Gibraltar and later Chief of Staff to Commander-in Chief Fleet. Sadly he died whilst still in his fifties.

CHAPTER EIGHTEEN

ASHORE AND INSTRUCTING

HMS MERCURY

(1964 TO 1967)

Do not on any account try to write on both sides of the paper at once

W C Sellar (1858-1951)

On leaving HMS NUBIAN, I had a month's convalescent leave and reported to HMS MERCURY in May 1964 to take up the post of Course Officer and Divisional Officer, instructing officers and ratings in Electronic Warfare. This was not a subject with which I had much previous experience so I had a lot to learn, and learn quickly I did as it was a very busy and demanding job. During this period I bought my first car in the UK, (I had run a car in Ceylon in 1952/4 as mentioned before), as I needed to commute from Fareham to HMS MERCURY every day, a distance of about 13 miles. It was a maroon coloured Ford Anglia and it served us well for about 3 years until I wrecked it going to work. That in itself is an interesting tale. I left home at about 8 a.m. and took the back lanes to go to HMS MERCURY, it was early December and it was a dull misty morning in Fareham. As I went over Portsdown Hill the weather changed as it often does, and it was cold and icy. There was ice across the road and I saw it too late, braked and spun round and was hit by a large construction company lorry coming the other way, or rather I hit it, as by the time of the impact I believe he had stopped. My boot cover went over the hedge, the rear of the car was wrecked and I hit my offside door with such force as to bend it at an acute angle. Luckily I was only bruised and after getting the lorry driver to assist me to push the wreck to the side of the road and exchanging vehicle details, a chum driving the same route picked me up and took me to work. I rang my local garage and asked them to pick the car up. I rang them again at about noon and was told they had the car and that it was a write off, and by the way, the lorry driver had given me an incorrect detail with respect to his insurance and the correct detail was... whatever. I thanked the garage owner and then asked how he had met the lorry driver. *"He is still there"* I was told. Apparently, unbeknown to us at the time, the impact had broken the lorry front spring or suspension and he could not move. I felt very guilty about leaving him on that lonely country road after an accident which was wholly my fault. My insurance paid anyway.

Our son David George was born on 4th October 1965. Audrey had another caesarean section, this time at St Mary's hospital in Portsmouth. We were and still are very proud of our children and we found that as Linda was 10 when David was born, she looked after him like a mother and they became, and still are very close to each other.

Life was good inasmuch that I was home most nights and weekends, there were of course the occasional naval duties. In retrospect, I believe I was overly put on during this period by my senior officers as I was teaching for 5 or 6 sessions every day. In addition I was responsible for producing course syllabi, examination papers and marking examination papers and being Divisional Officer for up to 120 senior and junior ratings. I found that I seldom left my office until 6 p.m. and then brought home piles of personal reports and examination papers to mark which often kept me busy until midnight. Perhaps because I had made myself 'indispensable' in this job, I was kept on for a period of nearly three and a half years, which was most unusual in those days. I did enjoy the work and made many friends among the officers and ratings courses I taught. I remain in touch with many of them even to this day.

Recollections of those days are: The Turkish naval commander on one of my courses had brought his wife with him and stayed at an hotel in the Petersfield area. He was a charming chap, spoke good English and gave me no trouble whilst he was here. The problem came after he had returned home. The local police and the Guildford police courts all started sending me summonses for the parking offences he had committed during his month's stay. Why they sent them to me and whether they expected me to pay them I don't know. I send them all off to the Ministry of Defence to give to the Turkish Embassy. I believe that as a NATO officer he considered he had diplomatic immunity. I doubt if they were ever paid.

Some of the young sailors in my division started drawing expedition gear such as tents and camping equipment from the store. I was very pleased to see them doing these activities, as opposed to sitting about drinking every weekend and gave them every encouragement. This was to be short lived however as one Monday morning the Master at Arms rang me to say that he had four of my lads up on a charge and would I go to the Commander's table to defend them. Yes, my good young lads had been camping at Soberton, in a field next to the WRNS quarters at Soberton Towers and had been apprehended at an illegal party in the WRNS quarters. Some even managed to get the WRNS to their tents. This sort of behaviour was totally illegal in those days and of course they were punished.

As I had a car, I was able to visit my mother and father at Yarlington fairly regularly. They were naturally very proud of their grandchildren. I also brought them down to stay with us at least once a year, although it was always difficult to get my father to leave home. As with all old people, especially those with sight and hearing problems, they feel insecure outside their home environment. The last time they visited us together was in 1967 shortly after father had his leg amputated and I pushed him around Fareham shops in a wheel chair. He was most impressed at this modern town and all the shops. I often wonder what he would say today if he could see the size of the huge buildings housing what we today call Hypermarkets. I expect he would envisage a large herds of milking cows, beef cattle or pigs all being well fed, watered and sheltered in the space occupied by foodstuffs.

CHAPTER NINETEEN

BACK TO SEA

HMS ARGONAUT

(1967 TO 1969)

The Argonauts sailed in the galley Argo in search of the Golden Fleece.

Homer's Odyssey (6th Century BC)

In June 1967 I was appointed to join HMS ARGONAUT, a brand new LEANDER class frigate which was just completing build at Hebburn on Tyne. This appointment was just what I wanted as I was aware that I was in the promotion zone for Lieutenant and that my promotion to Lieutenant would be greatly helped by good sea reports. I knew that I had very strong recommends from the Captain of HMS MERCURY, but recommends from sea counted far more in those days than they do today.

The Captain of my new ship was a Commander whom I had known and much admired when I was serving at the Greenwich Naval College in 1962 and the rest of the officers were all good guys and we all got on well. We had a good team and a happy team. The ship was only at Hebburn-on-Tyne for about six weeks after I joined and we then sailed for Portsmouth for weapon system trials and adjustments. I recall on one occasion four or five of us officers were week ending down to Portsmouth and we did the usual thing for long train journeys; 'commandeered' a compartment to ourselves and stocked up with some cans of beer to while away the long journey. The silly incident which always stands out in my mind was when one of us said; *"Look at those pigs on the hillside"*. Another replied: "They are not pigs they are sheep". An argument ensued and in the end we all agreed that they were *"woolly pigs"*. To this day, when driving in the country, I, and my wife and children, always refer to sheep as *'woolly pigs'*.

On the ship's arrival at Portsmouth we were all kept busy getting both the ship and the men ready for war. The weapon systems were set to work and I was involved in Command Team Training with the Captain and the Command or Operations Room team. It was all very exciting and very hard work but we enjoyed it.

We completed the weapon and ship system setting to work in about December, had our Christmas leave and sailed for our Flag Officer Sea Training (FOST), work up at Portland in early January 1968. The work-up was hard but we survived and in fact did very well. Our reward for completing the work-up was visits to Dartmouth, Plymouth and Londonderry. The Captain of the Royal Naval College at Dartmouth was my Captain from HMS NUBIAN in the 1962/4 period. He invited me to lunch and tea at the Captain's house and was his usual most kind self. He told me he had been promoted to Rear Admiral and was about to be re-appointed.

Londonderry brought back memories of my days as an 18 and 19 year old, chasing the girls at the local dance hall. I was not politically aware of the Northern Ireland problems at that time and I do not recall that we were warned to be careful. I went over the border to a hotel/pub with my friends one night and many of us used the streets at night as one would anywhere else in the UK. One incident stands out in my mind. One of the Chief Petty Officers was attacked by a crowd of women with umbrellas for no reason when he strayed into what must had been a Catholic area. Only then did we perceive the mounting tensions in that unhappy province.

After some operational work with submarines in the Clyde area, we returned to Portsmouth for Easter leave. In May, I believe, we joined up with a United States Navy destroyer, USS GLENNON, a Federal German Navy destroyer and a Royal Netherlands Navy frigate and formed what was to be the first operational Standing Naval Force Atlantic. We were to be completely NATO controlled and a Commodore was appointed with a Staff to manage us. The Commodore was British, the Staff Officer Operations was Canadian, the Communications Officer was American and the Torpedo and Anti-submarine Warfare officer was Norwegian. These officers were to be in HMS ARGONAUT so we had to make space for them. For the next six months we were worked very hard indeed, and joined at times by Belgian, Danish and Norwegian warships for exercises. On the plus side, because this concept was new, we also paid official visits to many major European ports including Oslo, Copenhagen, Amsterdam, Antwerp, Belfast, Lisbon and Southampton. These visits were interesting but also hard work as the were many cocktail parties and official functions for the officers to attend. There were some times when we were glad to get back to sea.

Lieutenant L G Foot - HMS ARGONAUT - 1968

It is not my intention to recount details of day to day happenings in the navy but here are a few memories of that time. The Norwegian Officer was a charming man and we introduced him to the game of Liar Dice. He loved it, got hooked and wanted to play all the time. Even after breakfast he would plead for *"A quick game of liars"*. We were all too busy to play at that time but every evening we played and all thoroughly enjoyed this relaxation. We played for drinks of course!

The American communications officer was a nice chap, but inexperienced and rather naive. He was called the Squadron Communications Officer, the SCO. I was called the Ship's Communications Officer, the SCO. Something had to change. I decided that I would be called the *'Professional Communications Officer'* and put a sign on the door of my cabin to make my expertise known to the world. The Captain saw this and was most amused and from then on I was officially known as the *'Professional Communications Officer'*. My American counterpart took this slight jibe at his inexperience quite happily and we worked well together - most of the time!

A point which became very evident as the 4 nations worked together was that the British, Dutch, German and Norwegians all had a similar sense of humour and also because these nations all trained their warships at Portland and frequently worked with Royal Navy warships, our operational procedures and way of doing things were very similar. The Americans and the Canadians, who joined us for a short while, did not operate in the same way as us and their sense of humour was markedly different. These differences ironed themselves out over the 6 months we were together. I felt sorry for the USS GLENNON as she was an old ex-World War 2 Destroyer which had been converted to take modern weapons whilst the RN, FGN and

RNLN WARSHIPS were new build and modern. USS GLENNON was always breaking down in some respect and had many malfunctions of her communications and weapons systems.

In the six months we were together I do not recall this ship managing to get her sea boat into the water without one end dropping in first and the crew falling in the water or having to hang on for their lives. She had a radio robot controlled helicopter for target spotting but this was seriously affected by radar and radio signals and it usually went out of control. It ended up crashing into her own mast and quite seriously damaging her own radar. These incidents embarrassed her crew very much and they were very conscious of their limitations.

Two events helped to bring us together. Firstly, all USN warships are 'dry' and as we and USS GLENNON were always tied up alongside each other in harbour, we gave the USN officers wardroom mess numbers so that they could use our bar when they liked. Some made use of the facility but others were too proud. In return they told us to use their wardroom mess for a meal if we wished. I recall that on returning from shore one evening at about midnight, our mess was full of USS GLENNON officers and I and my chums went to their mess and had a beautifully cooked steak which was prepared by their Filipino stewards. Secondly, the USN ratings were not permitted to go ashore or return in civilian clothes. All our ratings were permitted to do this. The solution; the USN ratings brought their civilian clothes down to our messdecks and changed with our lads. Many friendships were struck over this period and an example of the camaraderie which occurred was when we were in Lisbon, turning over to our Royal Navy frigate successor. When the lads went ashore and the ratings of our successor ship, after a few beers, started deriding the

Americans, our sailors joined in with their American buddies and supported and battled with the 'new boys'.

We left the NATO Squadron in December at Lisbon, returned to Portsmouth for maintenance and leave and set sail for a Far Eastern deployment in late January 1969. My dear old dad died on 12th January and was buried a week later, I was not able to comfort my dear mother for more than a few hours as I had to return to my ship and sail away. It was fortunate that my two sisters were able to provide the support she needed at this time.

The day before we sailed, my Appointing Officer rang me and asked me if I would like to take up the post of Signal Communications Officer to Captain SM7 in HMS FORTH in Singapore. It was to be a *'married accompanied'* appointment and that I would probably have to join in the summer. I would have preferred in many ways to have remained in HMS ARGONAUT and completed the commission by encircling the globe east to west as was planned but my time was up and so I accepted the new post.

One incident on the way south is worth recounting. We had a new Captain and we were somewhere off Freetown, Sierra Leone where we had a rendezvous with an RFA tanker to fuel and after fuelling the RFA stayed with us so that we could do some practice Replenishment at Sea (RAS) approaches. I was Officer of the Watch and the Captain asked me if I had ever done a RAS Approach. I replied *"Yes but not on my own"*. He then said I could do the next one. I was not unduly worried as I knew what to do and knew he would be there to make sure all was well. However after I had made a good approach and was on a good parallel course with about 90 feet between the two ships, I caught the attention of a figure waving to me from the fo'c'sle. It was the Captain who shouted *"Don't you bloody well hit her"*. Realising that he was no longer standing behind me to keep me out of trouble I quickly made the distance 120 feet and carried on with the manoeuvre. It was nice to know the Captain trusted me so well as to leave me on the Bridge on my own during this exacting manoeuvre.

I heard no more about my new appointment until we had been on Beira Patrol for a couple of weeks when the RAF Shackleton mail drop included instructions for me to get home as soon as possible, do a specialist submarine acquaintance course at HMS DOLPHIN and fly to Singapore to join HMS FORTH by 1st April. I discussed this with my Captain and it was decided that I should leave the following week (it was already early March) by getting a lift in HMS ZULU which was also on patrol but due to leave for Mombasa the next week.

I duly joined HMS ZULU for the three or four day passage to Mombasa. There, I was accommodated at the Silver Sands rest camp, a special rest camp for servicemen of all three services to give them a break from the onerous duties in the Gulf and Indian Ocean area. It was of course once much used by our troops in Kenya. There was no one else there! I lazed on a beautiful beach for 4 or 5 days and then my relief in HMS ARGONAUT arrived from UK to await the ship's arrival at Mombasa. I knew him well so we spent three days bathing, drinking and turning over my old duties to him. It was very pleasant but I was beginning to panic as I needed to get home as quickly as possibly. I eventually got a flight in a small plane which took me to Nairobi via Tanzania and over Mount Kenya and many hundreds of miles of jungle and bush.

One thing that I was sad to see about Kenya, or at least the Mombasa area: in 1963 on my last visit which was just before independence, there was little or no malaria as the British Colonial administration ensured that spraying was carried out on a large scale. Now malaria was endemic and indeed, several sailors from ships died from it over this period. Also, in 1963, it was safe to walk the streets and beaches without fear or indeed thought of being mugged. This was no longer so. I was therefore not sorry to leave Kenya. I nearly didn't get away then as when I passed through Nairobi airport to catch my British Airways plane to the UK, the immigration official discovered that there was no 'entry' stamp in my passport. This was because I had landed at Mombasa in a warship and had not passed through any immigration control post. This official, an Indian lady, was most insistent that as I had not officially entered Kenya I therefore could not leave the country. It took me some time to persuade her that if she did not stamp my passport as leaving, everything would be OK as I had never officially entered anyway. I won in the end but nearly missed my plane.

I eventually arrived in the UK on 20th March and had ten days in which to organise the letting of our house, packing up our belongings, getting the family vaccinated and inoculated, visiting and saying farewell to my mother and the rest of our family, selling the car and doing a five day course at HMS DOLPHIN, the submarine training school at Gosport. We made it and on 1st April we flew to Singapore.

CHAPTER TWENTY

SINGAPORE

HMS FORTH

(1969 TO 1971)

Ship me somewhere east of Suez, where the best is like the worst.

Mandalay (1892)

On arrival in Singapore, we were met and taken to a lovely 3 bedroom furnished bungalow which had been obtained for me by my predecessor. It was situated about 5 miles north of Singapore city and five miles south of the naval dockyard where my ship HMS FORTH was normally berthed. My predecessor had also left me his car which was a Triumph Herald and although old, it just about served me for the two years I was to use it. About a hundred yards from our home was a small Chinese shop which sold everything - and if Mr Chan didn't have it he would get it and deliver it. One only had to ring and ask for a pound of butter and it would be at the door within minutes. The Chinese were and still are unsurpassed in providing service.

We once had a similar service in our English country village stores but they are, alas, no more. My daughter was then just 14 and my son 3 and they thrived on the new experiences. They only had to enter the shop and Mr Chan would give them sweets or some sort of little present. The Chinese also have the habit of giving their customers presents at Christmas, not as at home when they expect you to give them a tip. I remember we received quite as nice crockery dinner set from our grocer one year.

My ship, HMS FORTH, was an operational vessel but based in Singapore to provide support to the submarines based on or passing through the Far East station. It was then an old ship and had been converted to also support nuclear submarines, consequently it had many highly technical engineering facilities, large workshops and plenty of accommodation. For the first and only time in my naval career I was in a ship where space was not at a premium. My job as the Signals Communications Officer (SCO) to the 7th Submarine Squadron was a busy one but not over demanding and I also assumed the duties of assistant to the Staff Operations Officer (SOO).

This gave me plenty to do and was most rewarding as it enabled me to acquire new skills such as organising the berthing of submarines, checking their operational passage plans and generally requiring me to be very aware of all safety aspects of submarine operations. Captain SM7 was a much decorated World War II submariner with a double DSO and double DSC. He was an extremely meticulous man whose attention to detail was greater than any I had ever met in any aspect of life. This made him hard to work for in the sense that one had to do one's homework with equal thoroughness to satisfy his high standards.

I recall that on one occasion, shortly after I joined HMS FORTH, I took him a letter for signature. It was about a highly classified and technical subject, but one which I considered that I was quite competent to handle. He looked at my letter and then looked at me and said, "*That is not the way which I told you to do this. If you cannot do as I ask I will get someone else*". I got the message and thereafter was most careful to follow his guidelines. We got on famously after that and I had very much respect for him.

Unfortunately, there were several submarine Commanding Officers and other officers who did not get the message as clearly. They were given short shrift and several found themselves on a flight home within hours of upsetting him. I recall one submarine Commanding Officer storming in to me after coming alongside after being at sea and asking why he had been berthed in that particular berth. He, knew that I was generally in charge of berthing. I pointed at the signal which I had made. It was "*From Captain SM7*". As is the normal custom I had acted on behalf of my captain, and invited him to take the matter up with the great man himself. He declined as he knew well that my captain would have supported me and he would have received a severe telling off. In any case there was a very good reason for this particular berthing plan of which he had not been aware.

One other incident which caused me many anxious moments was when we, that is the ship, had sailed to Fremantle (Perth) in Western Australia and we were controlling British and Australian submarines in a large exercise. For this operation the operational control of submarines was in the hands of the Australians, and a small team of Australian navy submarine officers came aboard to do this duty. As communications officer I naturally continued to provide their communications support and was therefore much involved in the exercise. The fleet were at sea, it was Saturday afternoon, nearly everyone was ashore enjoying the delights of Perth when the Australian submarine controller, a commander, came to me and asked me to look out for him whilst he went ashore. He gave me the keys to the staff office etc. and off he went. I was in my cabin writing a letter at about 4 p.m. when the Signalman came to me with a signal from one of the British submarines reporting that "..... *whilst dived at 400 feet a loud bang was heard"*. The submarine had surfaced, investigated for signs of damage, found none, and had then dived again to resume operations. I didn't like the sound of this and so I went to report this to a more senior and more qualified submarine officer than I. (I was not a trained submarine officer). There was not one on board. All the submarine experts had gone ashore! I found a shipwright who was also not a submariner and asked for his opinion. He, like me didn't really know but thought it sounded potentially worrying. I was on tenterhooks, what should I do? Officially the Commanding Officer of the submarine had ultimate responsibility for the safety of the submarine and the 70 or so men aboard but I was also acting for the Australian submarine staff who were absent ashore. By this time it was 5 p.m. and I knew that if I was to respond to the submarine I had to make a signal now in order to catch the next four hourly schedule. I wrote a signal ordering the submarine to "*.......Surface immediately and make a further inspection and report"*. I then instructed my communications staff to hold the schedule for as long as possible, just in case a submarine expert returned on board. None did. I sent the signal and surfaced the submarine, knowing that it would disrupt the exercise for many ships in the south eastern Indian Ocean. At about half past six the Australian staff officers returned on board. I cursed them for leaving me in such a nasty and deeply worrying situation, told them what I had done and also told them I had to report to the Captain.

The Captain heard my story, fully supported my actions and gave my Australian colleagues a very severe talking to ("*for leaving Len who was only a Lieutenant and not an experienced submariner, to carry the can..!*"). An hour later the submarine signalled that it had surfaced and carried out a further inspection and had found a blown valve in the snorkel system and was returning to harbour. I was right, it was very serious and I had done the right thing. The submarine Commanding Officer, no names, no pack drill, also got a few choice words from me when he returned and I drank beer on him for many months to come, indeed years, as we met again several times over the following years and he became a Captain, then Commodore and eventually a Rear Admiral.

That will suffice with respect to work, this story is about my experiences outside the technicalities of my day to day duties.

As my wife did not drive, we found our bungalow was situated a little too far from the Naval Base and after about six months we moved to another bungalow nearer my work and nearer to other naval families. We had a housemaid who we called "Chop". She came every morning and did the basic cleaning and washing. My wife continued to do the cooking. Chop was only about 16 years of age and spoke little English but she was a good worker and easy to get on with. I recall that our son, David who was only 3 years old would follow her about and on one occasion he hid her shoes in a drain culvert and poor Chop could not find them when the time came for her to leave.

HMS FORTH - Singapore 1970 showing Audrey, Linda and David on the walkway.

HMS FORTH - 'Mothering' her submarines - 1970

We searched everywhere and of course David had forgotten where he put them. On another occasion he locked her in the outhouse where she did the washing. Audrey thought she had gone home and it was some time before we found a very tearful girl in the washroom. Chop was for ever wary of him after that.

David went to nursery school and mixed well with the other children. He made many friends and was forever going to birthday parties. We held a party for his 3rd or 4th birthday and hired a 'Gully Gully' man to do tricks. He also brought a couple of snakes which kept the children excited and amused. One of the snakes 'escaped' inasmuch that it wriggled under the settee. The excitement and screams of the dozen or so children was most entertaining.

There was a very good swimming pool at HMS TERROR, the shore base, and we spent many, if not most, afternoons around the pool. The children loved it and it was a perfect meeting place for us all. Linda went to the military secondary school in Singapore. It was a good school, very strict on discipline and she did well there, although all the children had to work hard and she used to bring home lots of homework.

Socially, HMS FORTH was an ideal ship for parties, both formal and informal and we had many, I was assistant social secretary for some of the time and consequently helped organise and attended all occasions. Additionally we were honorary members of the wardroom mess in HMS TERROR and also attended many social events there.

A regular Sunday lunch outing was to the army Garrison Mess in Singapore where we sat in the sun had a few drinks and ate Rijstafel or curry for lunch. There was usually a 'gully gully' man there to entertain us and the children.

Singapore city was a bustling modern city with lovely shops as well as the old Chinese market areas where bargains galore could be obtained. It was fascinating and often upsetting to stroll through the Chinese food markets where every type of animal was for sale. Particularly upsetting was the cruel manner in which the animals were kept or tied up. There were mice, to be eaten alive to cure stomach ulcers, there were lizards, trussed very cruelly, ducks and chickens tied in bunches and hung by the legs and still alive. Baby chickens and ducks, to be thrown live into boiling fat and then pulled out and skinned to be eaten as a tasty snack. Snakes, piglets and other exotic and some rare animals were similarly treated.

My wife and family were always particularly upset by the way the Chinese treated their pets, particularly cats and dogs. These were often starved, beaten and mutilated and thrown into the monsoon ditches to die in agony. I mentioned our concern at the way animals were treated to a Chinese friend one day and he shrugged his shoulders and reminded me that one never saw or heard of baby battering or child cruelty in Singapore as one did in England. I believe this was a largely true statement but it did not alleviate our feelings of abhorrence at the animal cruelty. Having said this, we found the Chinese people to be clever, hard working and charming and I have very much respect for them as a race. They have many qualities which we do not have.

We frequently crossed the Causeway into Malaya, where the bustle of Singapore life faded away and one could drive for miles through rubber plantations and to some very beautiful and largely deserted beaches. There was one particular Malay village, Kirkup, which was built on stilts over the sea where one could go for a meal. Choosing one's fish or crab or lobster live from the tank. The Malays were friendly pleasant people, easy to get on with but perhaps lacking the drive and industry of the Chinese.

For our summer holiday we went to the mountains in central Malaya to a place called Frasers Hill where we shared a holiday bungalow with friends who had children near to the ages of our own. The mountains were about 6000 feet up and although still near to the equator, the air was clear and most invigorating. The greatest relief for us was the absence of the oppressive, tropical heat of Singapore and the opportunity to have cool evenings.

Whilst at Frasers Hill my chum and I played golf most mornings. The wives and children either went for walks or followed us around and Audrey used whichever club I did not happen to need at the time!

During my time in HMS FORTH, the ship visited Bangkok on two occasions and Hong Kong once, these were fascinating cities which at that time were not yet fully on the map as far as world tourism was concerned and were thus largely unspoilt. That is if one can ever envisage Hong Kong as anything other than an artificial city which purely exists for commerce. I would love to return to Singapore to see the great changes that have occurred in the past 25 or so years, also to Hong Kong, but I suspect I shall now never be able to afford these luxuries.

During our last 6 months in Singapore the run down of British Forces there started to speed up and we were to some extent being replaced by Australian Forces. I recall going to a party (we all went to lots of parties!) at the radio station at Kranji in March of 1971 and I found that my wife and myself plus the Officer in Charge of the station and his wife, who had asked us, were the only non Australians there.

The Chinese did not take to the Australians who tended to be rather brash and less polite to the workers than we generally were. The Chinese are a proud race and give and expect good manners. These they did not receive, certainly in the initial stages while I was still there and there was some friction building up at that time. For whatever reason the Australians did not stay long in Singapore, the Singaporeans being perfectly competent to manage their own affairs, including defence.

The time for HMS FORTH to leave was 1st April 1971. I was asked to remain on board and carry out the duties of Officer of the Watch to help sail the ship home but unfortunately I had another appointment to take up at HMS MERCURY in late May and had I stayed in the ship would not have been home in time as the big old ship could only make about 10 knots and was going to take over 2 months to get home. I therefore stood on the jetty with my family and waved the ship and my shipmates good-bye and then flew home a couple of days later. My two years in HMS FORTH and in Singapore with my family had been wonderful years which we will always remember fondly.

CHAPTER TWENTY ONE

MY INTRODUCTION TO ROYAL NAVAL RESEARCH AND DEVELOPMENT

THE USER REQUIREMENT AND TRIALS SECTION HMS MERCURY

1971 TO 1973

"Either I will find a way or I will make one"

Sir Philip Sidney (1554 - 1586)

My next posting was to HMS MERCURY. When we returned to England we were able to return to our home in Fareham. Whilst away in Singapore I had put the house in the hands of an Estate Agent to let as furnished accommodation. The first tenant had been a Royal Navy dentist who stayed about a year and, according to the Estate Agent's reports was a good tenant. The next one was an Iranian Chief Petty Officer who was in the UK for a year doing courses at HMS COLLINGWOOD. I never met him or his family, which I believe comprised of his wife and several young children, as they had left before we returned home. But we were appalled at the state of our home. Decoratively it was now in a very bad state, I suppose one must accept that if a home is left with no normal maintenance for two years it is bound to deteriorate but it seemed awful to us.

The most upsetting thing was that the carpet in the lounge was very worn, stained and stank of curry. The settee and the tables were marked and scored by rough usage and of course, no work had been done to keep the garden in shape. I complained to the Estate Agent and although it was admitted that the damage was much more than *'Fair Wear and Tear'*, I got no compensation as the tenant had returned to Iran. All in all, the Estate Agent was less than helpful or concerned. I resolved never to let my home again or to use that particular Estate Agent for any purpose.

During the next 2 years I was able to get my home sorted out and my children were settled at school. Linda went to a good girls' comprehensive and David attended the local primary school. We were all together and happy. Many, if not most, of my Royal Naval colleagues put their children into boarding schools. Some from the age of 8 and most of the others from the age of 11. Whilst appreciating the desirability of giving one's children a settled and better than the norm education, we could never envisage letting our children go in such a manner. We believe that the advantages of loving parents and a settled home life far outweigh the advantages of the 'posh' education.

My own view is that children who have been at boarding schools from the tender ages of 8 or 11 become hard and independent too early and do not have the deep affection for their parents, or the ability to communicate as part of a family, as those brought up at home. Additionally, many children are sent to boarding school for the convenience of the parents, particularly the mother who wants to work and travel without being encumbered by children. Furthermore it is my opinion, formed by the observation of others, that young boys in particular, who are taken from their parents at such early ages and sent away to boarding school, tend to turn to other boys for comfort and consolation, this in turn leading to homosexual tendencies coming to the fore. The prevalence of homosexuality among the Public School class to my mind confirms this opinion.

Our children were, and still are, our pride and joy and all our actions were and are devoted to them. This we can never regret as both have grown up to be upright citizens and loving children. We are proud of them.

We visited my mother who was then widowed and lived in a small bungalow in Wincanton, as often as we could. She loved to have us and as it was usually a Sunday when we went down, she always had a lovely roast lunch for us. We also brought her down to us at Fareham once or twice a year for a break. She loved all this and being near her grandchildren. Mother was always cheerful and I have memories of her telling us how when she visited the butcher and bought some sausages, he told her they were; *'The best in the West'*. This little phrase always brings back fond memories. We also found time to visit my sisters Phyllis and Doris more than formerly so we kept in touch with our immediate family; but never with our cousins of whom we knew little or nothing at that time.

The Officer in Charge of the User Requirements and Trials Section at that time was an experienced and very relaxed Commander who was very pleasant to work for, he never fussed when things went wrong and was always supportive of his staff. He lived about 4 miles from HMS MERCURY and owned a large farm house with stables and some land. He owned several horses for use by his wife and family and in order to exercise them he often rode his horse to work in the mornings. His wife would drive the car, leave the car and ride the horse home, then do the reverse in the late afternoon. A very civilised way of life.

My work comprised of conducting and carrying out trials of communications equipments and carrying out ship inspections of the communications compartments and the associated communications facilities, also making recommendations with respect to the requirement for additional items of equipment or changes to the layouts or procedures used. This was quite challenging work. I travelled a good deal, not only to ships in Devonport, Portsmouth and Rosyth, but to ships being built in various commercial yards such as Barrow-in Furness, Edinburgh, Lowestoft and even to Harland and Wolff at Belfast.

Additionally, I attended many planning meetings at Bath and at the Ministry of Defence in London. I thoroughly enjoyed the diversity of the work involved. Sometimes I had to do inspections or trials whilst the ship was at sea so I also had a day or so at sea now and then to keep me on my toes.

The other important aspect of my work was to draft Staff Papers and letters regarding present and future communications requirements. I learnt a lot and this consolidated my practical communications knowledge which I had gained at sea. I was now truly becoming an 'expert'. I also got to know and gain much respect for my colleagues in MoD Civil Service, the Scientific Officers, the Project Officers and the Engineering Draughtsmen. I made many friends and soon found that by putting the right word in the right ear at the right time I could achieve much, and influence my masters in the Ministry of Defence much more than they may have realised. This way of operating of mine was to stand me in good stead when I returned to the User Requirements and Trials Section a few years later.

An example of my dedication and determination to do my job correctly was when, shortly after I had taken the job, I had to travel to Plymouth to a ship inspection, I think it was the first one that I had to do on my own. I left home and drove westwards along the A31 till I got to Puddletown when I realised that I had left my briefcase containing the marked up ship compartment drawings at home. I turned round and drove back, collected them and then without stopping, started the journey again. This put another 140 miles on the journey of 180 miles so I ended up driving 320 miles just to get to Plymouth. At the end of the day it had not really been necessary as the shipbuilder's draughtsmen had all the up to date copies of the drawings.

On another occasion when returning from Plymouth, which I left at about 1.30 p.m., it had been raining hard for 48 hours and when I got to Charmouth the road was flooded, the traffic piled up and all were advised to find another route. The reader may remember that it was the day when the holiday caravans at Charmouth were swept into the sea and I believe some lives were lost. We were also advised that there was 5 feet of water on the road towards Bridport. I turned northwards through the lanes to Beaminster in an attempt to avoid the Bridport area but the floods were there too, so I was forced to go northwards to Chard. I then took the A30 to Yeovil, which was also flooded but I got through them and proceeded towards Sherborne on the A30. Just past Sherborne the roads were again flooded and I was again forced to turn northwards to Wincanton. I carried on along the A303 and decided not to risk turning south towards the low lying areas of the Avon valley and Salisbury so continued to Andover where I stopped at a Little Chef for a coffee. By then in was 11.30 p.m. Sitting at the next table was a chap I had spoken to at Charmouth at 3 p.m. that afternoon. He was going to

Brighton, we commiserated together. From then on all was well as I took the A34 to Winchester and then home to Fareham. My boss didn't blink an eye lid when I put in an expense claim for an additional 100 miles and for a journey 'over 10 hours'!

One incident which demonstrates the liaisons I had made with colleagues in the procurement world was when HMS ARK ROYAL, not the present HMS ARK ROYAL but the navy's last real aircraft carrier, the 45,000 ton one, was returning from an exercise, she went through a very severe storm with the consequence that quite a lot of damage was done, even to so large a ship. One item of damage was the two receiving whip aerials sited at the starboard forward part of the ship were lost. The FlyCo who operated the planes and helicopters found that without these aerials it was much easier to operate the helicopters and that they could bring them in to land using a different and better flying pattern.

The Air Staff therefore persuaded the Staff Communications Officer to recommend that these aerials be removed permanently and a signal was sent to the Ministry of Defence accordingly. I received a phone call from London telling me about this and asking if I was happy. I responded that I would check. I got out the ship drawings and studied the aerial layout and noticed that the lack of these aerials meant that the ship had only one receiving aerial left, and that being a wire aerial which was largely horizontally polarised. I was therefore not happy, but who was I to prevent something which the ship obviously found to be advantageous, particularly to helicopter flying operations.

The ship had just arrived at Plymouth and I rang the Assistant Signal Communications Officer and asked if I could go down to Plymouth to visit. He agreed and I drove down to Plymouth the next day. I discussed the problem with the ship's communications staff and found that they were most unhappy that the 'Air Boys' were going to make them lose their two best receiving whip aerials. But they had been overruled by the Staff Communications Officer. He had by this time left the ship and returned to his Headquarters.

I returned to HMS MERCURY and the next day rang my boss in London and told him I was not happy. He responded that the Admiral's staff officer had recommended it and that is how it would be and that the ship had managed during the time the aerials were missing. I pointed out that during this period the ship was relatively close to UK but it would be much different if the ship had to be deployed overseas. I expressed my great concern and explained why; inasmuch that this large flagship would be reliant on one wire aerial for all of the reception of its operational traffic. I was overruled, the air operational staff being more powerful than I.

I then rang my engineering draughtsmen friends in MoD Bath and told them that I could not support the proposal but that the MoD in London were going to force it through. I suggested they contact their Constructor and ensure that he was aware of the consequence of the proposal. This they did and the result was a signal from MoD Bath stating that the aerials would be re-instated. I was delighted, the ship's staff were delighted, but the Flag Officer's Air staff and Communications officer were not. I had won by having contacts in the right places even then when I was only a relatively junior lieutenant.

As I was anxious to take the optimum job to give me the best chance of promotion, I wanted to go to sea again as the communications officer of a DLG (Destroyer, Light, Guided Missile) and was pencilled in by my Appointing Officer to go to HMS HAMPSHIRE. This job had first been offered to and been turned down by a close colleague with whom I worked and when it was offered to me I accepted eagerly. However whilst I was on Easter leave in 1973, my colleague changed his mind and told the Appointing Officer that he then wanted it. When I returned from leave I was told that the job had gone and that another DLG would be found for me in due course. But for some reason this did not happen and a few months later I was asked to go to Northwood on the staff of the Commander in Chief Fleet.

CHAPTER TWENTY TWO

ON THE STAFF OF THE FLEET AND NATO HEADQUARTERS AT NORTHWOOD

HMS WARRIOR

1973 TO 1974

"Never turn down a job because it's too small, You don't know where it can lead"

Julia Morgan (1872 - 1957)

My next appointment came in the spring of 1973 when I was appointed to HMS WARRIOR at Northwood in north west London which was and still is the administrative establishment for the National and NATO Fleet Headquarters.

It was not feasible to move my family as my daughter was then 18 and completing her school examinations, my son was 8 and attending a very good local primary school. My own childhood experiences of changing schools every year, together with the more recent experience of suffering the result of letting one's house helped us to decide that I would go on my own and commute home at weekends only.

This worked well, I had a good car, a 1.8 litre Morris Marina, and although the M.25 motorway was not yet opened, I had little trouble getting to Northwood late on Sunday nights and coming home again on Friday afternoons. Except when I was required for weekend duty of course.

My job was as the Deputy Officer-in-Charge of the NATO Communications Centre which was situated below ground in a very large operational complex. The Headquarters housed the Commanders of the UK National Fleet and Maritime Air Command, plus the Commanders of the NATO Eastern Atlantic and Channel Fleet and Maritime Air Commands, also the UK National and Nato Submarine Commands. There were also several other minor command groups. This large grouping of UK and NATO commands meant that there were many Admirals and Air Marshals and Staff Officers from every NATO country, ranging from American to Greek and Turkish. All of these generated signals, and my job was to manage the communications which connected the NATO countries and the Commanders with their ships and units. It was and still is, I am sure, a very big communications centre and the very large amount of traffic generated kept us all on our toes. During my stay at Northwood, the Officer-in Charge and my immediate boss was an RAF Squadron Leader. He was a super chap but unfortunately he suffered ill health and was away sick for much of the time I was there, this meant that I had the total running of the Communications centre to myself. I enjoyed this and although I was only a Lieutenant at the time, I had no trouble in managing the work. Watchkeeping in the Communications centre at any one time were a total of 60 personnel, comprising RN communications ratings, WRNS communications ratings, RN engineering ratings, RAF personnel and civilians. As there were 4 watches plus a spare watch and day workers to take account of leave, sickness etc., the total manpower was approaching 300. The introduction of modern techniques and computer equipments have now reduced this number very considerably.

I will relate one incident of work which may be of interest to the reader and which probably reflects my stubborn character inherited from my forebears. A very senior Fleet staff officer sent a signal to a ship with regard to his intended visit in 2 days time. The officer who actually drafted the signal was probably his Secretary, a Lieutenant Commander and this officer made the mistake of writing on the signal "......*The Captain of the Fleet will join ship at 0700 on Thursday 7th. Please arrange for a boat to pick him up at ......*". The signal was duly sent and the ship noted that Thursday was the 8th not the 7th and therefore signalled back to verify that the visit was to take place on Thursday 8th. This verification signal arrived at the Communications centre late one evening and as it held a precedence of 'Immediate', the Petty Officer of the Watch, after allegedly consulting the Fleet Duty Staff Officer made a response confirming the visit as Thursday 8th. This was quite a normal procedure and I was wholly unaware of this exchange until a few days later when the Staff Officer in question returned to Northwood in a great anger and instructed his Secretary to find and punish the culprit who had messed up his joining arrangements.

He had actually meant the signal to state that he intended to join on Wednesday 7th! Therefore the boat was not there to meet him and his joining arrangements very much messed up. The Secretary rang me, told me what had occurred and asked me to investigate. This I agreed to do.

Unfortunately the Petty Officer who had been on watch on that evening was by then away on leave and not due back for a week so I could do little but instruct my Warrant Officer to sort it out when he came back. A couple of days later the Fleet Communications Officer came to see me and said the Captain of the Fleet was still highly incensed and why had I not sorted out and charged the culprit. I explained that I had not yet completed my investigation and that as far as I was concerned I did not yet accept that my Petty Officer was guilty of any wrong action. When the Petty Officer returned my Warrant Officer investigated the happenings and the Petty Officer, who was a good and very reliable man, maintained that he rang the Fleet Duty Staff Officer on that evening and that it was the Fleet Duty Staff Officer who authorised the confirmation of the date and time being Thursday 8th. It then took me a few days to find and talk to the Staff Officer who had been on duty that evening as he was away on a visit to Scotland. During this time the Secretary, who had made the original mistake of writing the wrong day and date, rang me and ordered me to place the offending Petty Officer in the 'Rattle' (or on Report). I refused, saying that I was still checking the facts. He then went to his Captain and told him I was not carrying out this action. The Captain then sent for the Fleet Communications Officer to order me once again to charge my Petty Officer. I repeated my refusal, and knowing that those up in the Headquarters building above ground were by then very angry with me, I wrote two formal letters. One asking to be sent to another post and one resigning from the Navy. These I put in my 'IN' tray and awaited developments. When the Duty Staff Officer returned from Scotland I went to see him, explained the situation and asked him if he had authorised the offending signal. By now at least two weeks had passed and he could not remember, or said he could not remember, although he did agree that the Duty Petty Officer had rang him on that particular evening. This was enough for me. I sent for my Petty Officer and told him that I accepted his explanation but reminded him that in future he was not to accept verbal signals from the Duty Staff Officer, no matter how immediate. I then wrote a minute to the Fleet Communications Officer and the Captain of the Fleet explaining that I did not consider my Petty Officer had done anything wrong other than trying to help out the Duty Staff Officer by accepting a signal over the phone instead of in writing. I stated that I had spoken to and admonished my Petty Officer and that I did not intend to formally charge him or take any further action. This did not satisfy those in authority and I was again told to charge my Petty Officer.

I then sent a memo to my NATO Admiral who was my top superior with respect to the running of this NATO communications centre detailing all the facts and stating that I would take no further action against my Petty Officer. He was a Royal Netherlands Navy Admiral, a very efficient and a very hard man, especially with his senior staff officers, but someone I greatly respected and liked. I also knew he liked and trusted me. I heard no more of the matter but I knew I had to watch my back from those on the Fleet staff from then onwards! I kept my 'resignation' letters in my 'IN' tray for a couple of months then ditched them. (Stubborn old Len Foot!)

The above episode did not mean I did not enjoy my time at Northwood, I did. It was a very responsible and challenging job and I was very much involved in everything. The Royal Netherlands Navy Admiral mentioned above was very supportive of the problems I had in running so large an organisation and used to ring me and ask me to go up to see him when he was dealing with certain communications matters. I used to go into his suite of offices by his private door and not via his main office which was guarded by his Secretary. This used to upset the Secretary (another Lieutenant Commander) who liked to know who was with his Admiral. I always left through the Secretary's office to make sure he knew I had been there. The reader may get the impression that I did not like Secretaries; perhaps they are right!

As my work took me down to the underground complex at eight o'clock every morning, I usually stayed down there all day and was normally too busy to stop for a lunch break. I therefore used to 'emerge' from the 'hole' about five thirty every evening, go to my room, rest and read for thirty minutes, then have a bath and shave and go to the officers' mess at about six thirty where I met up with my colleagues, both male and female and we all had a couple of drinks together, then went to supper at about seven thirty. After that we sometimes went out to a local pub, sometimes sat and chatted and sometimes I went to my room to relax, read and get an early night. I was quite happy except that I was not at home. I always looked forward to Fridays when I could get home to my wife and children.

One amusing incident of note was that a young (mid twenties) and very attractive WRNS Officer was lent to me for a couple of months to help me out and to give her additional training and experience. She was a super girl, very outgoing and full of life. My office was always full of laughter and fun when he was around and she was moderately good at her job. As long as I could keep her concentration off the young sailors working in the underground complex! One day she beckoned me and asked *"Who is that ? What is his name ?"*, pointing to a very handsome, fair haired, well built young sailor. I told her he was an Able Seaman lent to us for messenger duties.

I thought no more of it until a few nights later I was out to a local pub with a chum of mine, a Commander, who was in fact the Fleet Security Officer, when I saw in the corner of the bar this WRNS officer cuddling up to none other than this above mentioned Able Seaman. I gave her a brief nod without letting my chum see me as I knew as well as she should have done that it was not permitted for officers to mix socially with other ranks.

As we were leaving my chum saw them and when we were outside said he thought he recognised the girl in the corner with the chap. Did I know her? I said I hadn't noticed and let the subject drop. I had no wish to get her into trouble and as the Fleet Security Officer my chum would have been duty bound to report her activities. The next morning I gave her a good talking to and told her to be more careful with whom she mixed. She took my telling off with good grace, said sorry and that was the end of it. Within a few minutes her warm cheerfulness reasserted itself and the office was again buzzing with fun. I believe she still continued to meet this sailor for a while, but well out of my cognisance.

During my time at Northwood, because I was the employer of a large number of WRNS ratings, I was asked to sit on a committee which was then exploring the possibility of using more WRNS, both ashore and at sea. I had, and still have, a very high opinion of most WRNS ratings and have found them dedicated and most competent. I was therefore very much 'pro' having additional WRNS in my communications centre. One good reason was that when a WRNS rating came she usually stayed for 18 months or 2 years, during which time she became a most valuable operator.

When a male rating came he usually came in from sea, and even before he had joined me I had received a draft order for him to go back to sea within 4 to 6 months. Therefore by the time the rating had joined, had the leave owing to him, learned his job in the organisation and then had his next seasonal leave it was time for him to go and I got very little value from him. Neither was the poor lad very happy at being moved about so much.

My Royal Naval, as opposed to my NATO, boss at that time was the Fleet Communications Officer with whom I got on very well and respected very much, (in spite of the incident with respect to the signal mentioned above which was not of his making). He gave me very good recommends and was pushing me hard for promotion to Lieutenant Commander. This had being my aim in life for some years as I knew that I had gone through for promotion to officer too late ever to get the chance of promotion to full Commander.

The next incident of note was that late one Monday afternoon I received a phone call from my Appointing Officer in London to say that there was a problem in HMS MALABAR in Bermuda and he would like me to go there as First Lieutenant and Communications Officer as soon as possible. I was stunned as I had expected at least another year at Northwood and was much involved in various projects which I wanted to see through to completion. He asked me to think it over and let him know first thing the next morning. I rang Audrey and asked her opinion, she like me was stunned for a while and then said she would be happy if I wanted it and that we could resolve the children's schooling as Linda had by then completed College and David, being only eight years old would not be disadvantaged. I rang my Appointing Officer first thing the next morning and said yes I would accept the appointment.

He thanked me and told me he would be making it official and forwarding details as soon as he could. During the forenoon of the Tuesday I thought it all over more calmly, found out more about the job and also discussed it with my boss, the Fleet Communications Officer. We discussed my career and the interruption to his plans to get me promoted. By the end of the forenoon I had come to the conclusion that it was perhaps not a very good idea and that I would be better off staying where I was for another year. The Fleet Communications Officer wanted to keep me at Northwood.

I rang my Appointing Officer during the afternoon and said that, having thought it over I did not want to go. I said to him that there must be many other Communications Officers who would give their eye tooth for so plum a job and in any case I had already had three full foreign accompanied postings. This was three times more than most of my colleagues. The Appointing Officer said he was sympathetic, (they always are!), but I had to go and there were very good reasons why it should be me and no one else. I knew that this emergency posting was being managed by my very senior adversary in the Headquarters building, the Captain of the Fleet and wondered if this was his revenge for my stubbornness in the instance quoted above. I later found out that this was unlikely to be so as the reason for this emergency posting was the incumbent First Lieutenant had got into trouble, domestically and also with regard to his relationships with the ratings and families in the very small and tight community and that they wanted an officer with the personality (and stubbornness?) to take his place and calm the then potentially unhappy situation.

When my colleagues heard that I was going to Bermuda with my family they were all envious and none would believe that I had tried to refuse it! I told them I would grin and bear this onerous appointment!

Events then moved fast. The officer who had been sacked from the Bermuda job was flown home and came to relieve me. I had a few days to turn my job over to him and he told me of the situation out there, or at least his version of it. He was an old colleague of mine, a clever and able man for whom I was sorry it had all happened, but he had no one to blame but himself for getting into trouble.

CHAPTER TWENTY THREE

BERMUDA

HMS MALABAR

1974 TO 1976

"A journey of a thousand mile must begin with a single step"

Lao-tze (6th century BC)

I went home, took ten days leave, and in late November flew to Bermuda with Audrey, Linda and David. As previously stated I did not want to let my house again so I investigated the pros and cons of: leaving it empty as it was, leaving it empty without furniture in order not to have to pay rates, disconnecting the electricity, disconnecting the telephone, and every other option I could think of.

I decided to leave the house just as it was. Our neighbours and good friends who lived next door at No.17 agreed to take the house keys and turn the heating on now and again in the winter and open some windows now and again in the summer, also to send on any mail which looked important. The neighbour the other side at No. 13 agreed to cut the lawns and keep general eye on the garden so he had the shed key.

We just packed our cases, walked out of the door and were then on our way. The navy provided a mini bus to take us and our baggage to Heathrow and we caught the British Airways scheduled flight to Bermuda and in a few hours we were there. The children were naturally excited, just as Audrey and I were. David especially so as he could not remember much about our last tour abroad to Singapore.

We were met at the airport and made most welcome by a brother officer with a minibus and we were taken to our bungalow which had been the home of my predecessor whom I had left behind at Northwood. The bungalow was quite spacious, it had 3 bedrooms and was plainly furnished and was situated about 3 miles from the naval base where I was to work. A beauty of it was that it was situated on a small farm which grew potatoes and fruit. The fruit trees which surrounded our bungalow were oranges, limes, grapefruit, avocado and some bananas. The landlord was a very wealthy American who was married to a Bermudan lady. He had extensive interests in the United States, plantations in Jamaica and also owned newspaper and printing concerns in Jamaica and in Bermuda. In spite of his many interests, he was always doing odd jobs around the small farm. He cut the grass tidied the pathways, picked and looked after the fruit and was for ever pottering about.

As we were in fully furnished rented accommodation all items and kitchen gadgets belonged to him and should my lawn mower go wrong or the iron fail, we only had to tell him and he would get it fixed. The snag was it always took a long time for it to be done. I found out why one day when he admitted that he repaired such gadgets himself and the item in question was still in his workshop waiting for him to find time to fix it. I suppose that is why he was a multi-millionaire and I am not!

The landlord did not mind us having fruit from the trees in moderation and so it was always pleasant to be able to say to my son: "*Go and get me a lime to go in my drink please David*". The trees which were the most prolific were the grapefruit. There were several dozen of these and when they bore fruit it was the delicious pink grapefruit which many readers will know are much sweeter than the others. I recall that my son David went out one morning with the landlord's son and between them they picked and graded eighty dozen grapefruit between 0700 and about 1000, and then delivered them to a local hotel. That was from only a few trees and there were many thousands left.

Another delight of living in that spot was that the landlord had two geese which lived in a barn just near our garden and they met and hissed angrily at all intruders. They soon got to know us and gave us no trouble. He also had two Alsatian dogs which similarly kept intruders at bay. We grew to love them very much and they visited us several times a day for a pat and perhaps a biscuit or bone.

I will not attempt to describe Bermuda in travelogue terms, but mention those aspects which are pertinent to my story. Suffice to say that the island is 22 miles long and has an average width of less than a mile. One main road extends the length of the island with minor, single lane, roads servicing the houses, hotels and bays and inlets. Bermuda is not a sub tropical island as are the West Indies. This mistake was often made by visitors, especially the American tourists who expected hot sun and warm seas to swim in all the year round. They did not expect the wind, which blew often and suddenly, nor the rain. Bermuda's average rainfall is about forty inches which is similar to and perhaps a little more than we get in the south of England. The Bermudan people do not generally swim in the sea between November and May but we hardy 'Brits' often braved the water throughout the year.

As Bermuda is a volcanic island based on volcanic rock with only a light subsoil it had not been possible, certainly up to that time, to lay underground water pipes or sewage services to the houses on the island, except in the two major towns of Hamilton and St. George's. In consequence all houses were built with underground or sometimes above ground water storage tanks which caught the water from the roof. We had a storage tank under the veranda and also alongside the back bedroom. As previously mentioned, the rainfall in Bermuda is about to 40 inches per year, about the same as UK and slightly more than we get in the south of England. This we found sufficient to supply all our needs as long as we were moderately careful. We never bought water during our two year stay. Of course the hotels and larger institutions bought water which at that time cost about 15 dollars for a thousand gallons.

When one considers the rainfall in the British Isles and the frequent water shortages one wonders why more effort is not made to conserve water here. All new houses could easily have storage tanks for rainwater, this could be connected to non drinking utilities such as the baths washing machines and toilets. In Bermuda we drank the rainwater just as it came out of the tank, it did us no harm and we did not spend time wondering what the birds on the roof had dropped into it or, indeed about the very large toads which occasionally fell in the tank and drowned.

The above reminds me of an incident when the wire mesh over the underground tank overflow outlet was pushed aside by a toad and this led to many dozens of the toads getting into the tank. Fortunately I discovered them within a day or so and removed the inspection hatch and peered down. There were all these toads in the water with no place to land and they were obviously beginning to tire without rest from swimming to stay afloat and they were also without food. How could I get them out? I borrowed Audrey's chip strainer and tied it to a cord and lowered it in on a broom handle to try to scoop them up. I didn't have to try very hard. The poor toads swam to what they saw as a resting place and I think I pulled about over 40 within an hour and another 15 or so later on. Only 1 or 2 died and sank to the bottom. I don't recall the water tasting any different afterwards!

Whilst talking of the toads, they were very big and there were tens of thousands of them. The unfortunate thing was that they would sit in the road at night and although one tried to avoid them when driving, it was not possible to miss them all and one heard the crunch and squelch of toads being squashed as one drove along. This was particularly so along the 400 yard dirt track which led from the main road, through the farm to our bungalow.

At the other end of the scale were the tree frogs. These made a tremendous noise, so much so that they kept us awake at night when we first arrived. But after a while we got used to them. They were green and very small and hid on the backs of leaves. On many occasions we went out at night with a torch to look for a particularly noisy one outside the lounge or bedroom window but they were very difficult to find. I think I only actually sighted two or three in my whole time out there.

Other than some very beautiful birds, that was the total of the wildlife on the island. But the great sport which I enjoyed most was fishing. The waters around the reefs teemed with fish and as I had ready access to the several boats which we kept in the dockyard, it was easy to go fishing. We spent many happy hours fishing. It was not uncommon to trail a line with 2 or 3 hooks on, without bait and catch a Red Snapper on each hook within minutes. I went out to the deeper water on some occasions and fished for larger fish such as Tuna and Groupers. David started to keep a record of the fish we caught but did not keep it fully up to date.

Here are a few examples:

Caught By.	Type.	Length.	Weight.	Where.
Dad	Snapper	10"	1 lb	Rocks
David	Squirrel Fish	8"	6 oz	Dockyard
Dad	Red Snapper	12"	2 lb.	Rocks
Dad	Hind	16"	2 lbs	Rocks
Mum	Moray Eel	24"	2 lb.	Rocks
Dad	Chubb	20"	8 lbs	Reef
David	Barber	10"	1 lb	Reef
Dad	Moray Eel	18"	2 lb.	Rocks
David	5 Red Snappers	12"	2 lbs	N. Channel
Dad	Black Fin Tuna	19"	13 lb.	Argus Tower
David	Moray Eel	20"	2 lbs	Rocks
David	Shark	10 ft	580 lbs	Reef

    I do not recall the last of the above entries, could it be that my son David, who was only 10 years old at the time dreamed up this fishy story?

    When my sister Phyllis and her husband Bob came out to stay with us we took them out in a boat fishing. Bob was an expert fisherman and in those days spent many hours and nights in Weymouth Bay or along the Chesil Bank fishing, usually for mackerel. We all sat in the boat with our lines out and we all caught several snappers and other common fish, some times two at a time, except Bob. He did not catch a thing!

Our social life was good. We, that is, the 8 Officers at HMS MALABAR, were made up of:

1 Commodore, Senior Naval Officer West Indies (SNOWI)
1 Colonel (Royal Irish Rangers),
1 Major (Army Intelligence),
1 Major (Royal Marines),
1 Lieutenant Commander, Staff Officer Operations (SOO)
1 Lieutenant Commander Secretary to SNOWI
1 Lieutenant Commander, Resident Naval Officer and Aide to the Governor of the Island and Commanding Officer of HMS MALABAR.
1 Lieutenant, First Lieutenant and Manager of the Dockyard and Officer in Charge of the Communications centre (myself).

Additionally, there were eight Senior Ratings and twenty four Junior Ratings. All personnel were married and accompanied by their families. This was a prerequisite for being drafted to HMS MALABAR.

After I had settled in and calmed the previously rather tense social atmosphere left by my predecessor, we all got on well together and had frequent parties. As we all got to know local Bermudan friends our combined circle was quite wide. One of my tasks was to organise social and sporting events for visiting ships such as Cocktail Parties, Soccer, Tennis, Shooting and Cricket or Rugby matches against local teams such as the Police. This provided me with even more contacts.

Leading my small band on Remembrance Day 1976

We received many visits from Royal Naval ships, submarines, Royal Fleet Auxiliaries and also from Dutch and Canadian naval ships. The U.S. Navy ships berthed at their own Naval Base a few miles from us. When a ship was due to visit, it was my task to arrange berthing and fuelling as well as provision of stores. This was no real problem once I had gained a little experience but I had several 'hairy' moments whilst learning the ropes. Here are a few examples:

The Royal Yacht, HMY BRITANNIA was due to come to Bermuda and would require fuel. She was one of the last vessels in the RN to burn Furnace Fuel Oil (FFO) as opposed to Diesel fuel oil. The Dockyard Fuel Depot was owned by the RN but managed by SHELL. The manager was a friend of mine and when I asked him whether he could supply the required amount he said; "*Yes. No problem*", however when I spoke to the Captain of the Cable and Wireless Cable Laying ship which also burned FFO, he told me that the SHELL FFO was too thick and his fires went out! I quickly had to learn a lot about the viscosity of fuels and about terms such as 'Redwood Seconds' of which I had never before heard. It soon became evident to me that I could not chance giving HMY Britannia bad fuel. Just imagine the Queen being adrift at sea in the Royal Yacht, all because an inexperienced Lieutenant didn't know anything about fuel!

I explained my problem to my colleague, the Staff Officer Operations and he managed to get a Royal Fleet Auxiliary Oil Tanker to be diverted to Bermuda from the Jamaica area to get some decent fuel put in the Shell tanks. Saved!

Another problem with the Royal Yacht's visit was the catamarans needed to be placed between the ship and the jetty. The very large tomb of paper containing the visit instructions received in advance of the Royal Yacht's visit specified that the catamarans must be of a certain size and length in order not to damage the ship side paint work. I measured the catamarans I had in the Dockyard and found they were too high out of the water and that I would need to sink them by about ten inches to comply. As this was a specialist task and they were old and rusty I decided to have two of them completely refurbished for the Queen.

They were accordingly given to a contractor who had them towed round to the other side of the Island to be refurbished. The job was done on time but the weather blew up and the contractor could not get them towed back to the Dockyard before HMY Britannia came in. Panic. I had to put two of my old catamarans in place which were old, rusty and of the wrong height out of the water. On the day the Royal Yacht came in I was on tenterhooks, would I get into trouble? I went on board and sought out the Second Lieutenant who acted as the 'bosun' of the Yacht and apologised for the wrong type of catamarans. He looked at them and said; *"Don't worry Len. These are perfect, much better than we have when at our normal berth at Whale Island! (Portsmouth)"*.

Another Royal Yacht problem was the gangway. The wordy instructions specified that the gangway should be of such a length that the angle between the ship and jetty for the Queen's descent/ascent should be not more than so many degrees. (I forget how many). I didn't have a long enough gangway to ensure this was complied with. As always, I had made friends, and I turned to the Director of the Port of Hamilton and his Port Manager. They had large gangways which were for use by the large cruise ships and they would lend me one. Saved again!

Another story regarding fuel. HMS BULLDOG and HMS BEAGLE, two Coastal Survey vessels which had been surveying the coastline somewhere off the South American coast, had called in to Bermuda on their way home to the UK. They had sent a signal requesting 40 tons of diesel fuel each. This I arranged with the Esso Fuelling Company to be provided at a certain time. The evening before the ships were due to sail from Bermuda for UK, the Commanding Officer of HMS BULLDOG, the senior officer, rang me and asked if I could arrange for his fuel to be provided by the Shell Company in the Dockyard where they were berthed instead of the ships having to sail to the other side of the Island to the Esso Depot. This would save them about four hours. The reason for his request was that the Atlantic weather forecast was not good and they were likely to be late in arriving at Plymouth. This would upset the Christmas leave plans for the crews.

Always helpful I rang my friend, Stan, the manager of the Shell Depot. His first reaction was that he was not supposed to supply the RN with Diesel fuel as his tanks were being refurbished. That is why the ships had been booked into the Esso Depot. I explained that the ships only needed 40 tons each and that I knew that he did have some diesel available. This because he had many contracts to supply other small vessels and also the hotels and public buildings which relied on diesel for power to run fridges, lifts, air conditioning etc.

He gave in. I rang the ships and told them the fuel lines would be connected at 0730 the next morning and that they could take their fuel and sail on time. The COs of both ships thanked me profusely and the next morning I was on the jetty, saw them properly fuelled and then at 0900 waved them good-bye. About an hour later my friend Stan from Shell rang. He was very upset. "*You told me the ships only wanted 40 tons each Len.". "That's right Stan. That is what they asked for in their signal."* I replied. *"Well one ship took 70 tons and the other 65"*, he said. I realised then what had happened. The ships had sent their original requirements a week or more before arrival and had been in Bermuda 5 days during which time they had been using fuel, and also that they wanted to make absolutely sure they had enough to cross the Atlantic in bad weather so they topped up to the limit. Stan said he was now so low in diesel fuel that he would have trouble fulfilling his Hotel contracts. I apologised to Stan, went to see the Staff Officer Operations, and once again he managed to divert an RFA Oiler to Bermuda to provide Stan with his Diesel fuel. We were then friends again.

Submarine visits always tested my organisation as it is the normal procedure for submarine crews to live ashore when in harbour. We had no hotel in the vicinity of the Dockyard large enough to accommodate the seventy officers and men from a diesel submarine and therefore the submarines were usually berthed at St. George's, a small town and port at the other end of the Island. There I booked them in to a large Holiday Inn situated only about a half a mile from the berth where they could all be together and enjoy themselves.

This meant travelling to and from the other end of the island for myself and my staff for administrative purposes, at least once a day. No real problem, but as the speed limits were about 20 mph, it took over an hour each way. My Stores Chief Petty Officer was an excellent Chief. But. He usually drove the 10 ton lorry with stores and on arrival at the submarine tended to accept the gratitude of the submariners with one too many drinks. On more than one occasion he returned with a damaged lorry for which he incurred my wrath. I always forgave him because he was always so efficient and willing in other ways.

On one occasion, a submarine had a defect which required it to come to the dockyard. I then had to find accommodation for the crew in small packages at local hotels. Four men here, six men here, ten men there etc. An amusing incident occurred when, unbeknown to me, I had billeted a particular submarine rating who was known for his love of a drink, at an hotel which was a Temperance Religious Retreat. Everyone was most amused, but the lads there were quite happy. The submarine sailed after a couple of days but unfortunately broke down again and had to return. I had a special request from the Coxswain of the submarine to make sure that this particular rating and his chums were again put up in this Temperance hotel! Why? They had made friends with a group of rich Americans who were not adverse to secreting a few bottles of whisky in their rooms and having late night parties!

One other departure from the norm was when the Royal Naval ships in the Western Caribbean off Belize were having difficulty communicating with our own army units in Belize. I hitched a lift in an RAF Hercules carrying Puma helicopter parts and spent two days in Belize resolving the problems. It was my first and only visit to Belize. I felt for the troops stationed in that tropical jungle of a country. I have no wish to return to it. The most impressive memory I have is sitting on boxes of spare parts in the body of the plane and looking out over the Florida Keys as we passed over at about 18000 feet. It was a wonderful sight.

Another story I must tell. This was to be another most memorable day in my life. The Queen, accompanied by Prince Philip, was to visit and open the Maritime Museum which was situated near to HMS MALABAR. A centre piece of the museum displays were to be the Tucker Treasure, which were some priceless items discovered in the wreck of a Spanish Galleon some few years before by a local character named Tommy Tucker. He had either willingly or unwillingly, I cannot recall which, given the treasure to the State. The centre piece of the treasure comprised a large gold cross encrusted with emeralds and diamonds and was undoubtedly of very great value. Security was therefore the order of the day, not only with regard the treasure but also that of our Queen and Prince Philip.

The local Chief Inspector of Police, another friend of mine, was in charge of Traffic and Security. I had previously arranged with him to provide a few sailors to assist his own men with car parking and directing traffic, and I was to retain the rest of my men, seven sailors! to fall in at the side of the road and salute the Royal couple as their motorcade passed. On the morning of the great day, my policeman friend rang to say he was short of men and could I provide two more to guard the Museum entrance? I had no one left and had to refuse his request. The Queen came and left, I had put on a brand new suit for the occasion and gave the appropriate sword salute to her as she and Prince Philip passed in an open car.

All went well for me. But: After the Royal Party and the other dignitaries had left, the police came buzzing around in force. The Tucker treasures had been stolen and replaced by replicas! How glad I was that I had declined to send my sailors to guard the museum entrance. I have no idea what happened to the treasure, although my policeman friend told me they reckoned it was a very professional job and that the treasure was on a plane within hours and on its way to Switzerland.

My day was not over yet. Whilst still wearing my best suit, the Stores Chief arrived at the Dockyard from the Airport with two large electrical generators or some such equipment, each of which weighed about two tons and were to be taken to an RFA which was anchored in the Sound. They were very urgently required. Snag. There was a strike of the civilian tugboat men. The Director of the Port of Hamilton Harbour and the Port Manager, plus one other person agreed to pilot and help man the tug. I together with my one Able Seaman, were to be crew. We had our own dockyard ten ton Coles Crane which was operated by my one Mechanical Engineering Mechanic. He slung the large crates on to the tug and off we went.

The weather was 'choppy'. When we arrived at the RFA, slings, which we had previously put round the crates were attached to the ship's crane and the first crate was successfully transferred. The second crate, perhaps because of our combined inexperience, was not steadied properly and when it had been raised about 20 feet above the tug, it began to spin. Try to visualise a tug in choppy seas with a two ton crate spinning above it and likely to crash on to it and probably go right through it at any moment. I was at the stern of the tug and knew that I would be under the crate if it fell. I looked into the water, thought about my best suit and decided that to jump was the only solution. Fortunately the RFA crane operator managed to lower the crate back on to the tug to stop the spin, but not without some damage to the tug furniture and to the crate. We secured additional guiding lines to it and it was then successfully hauled up. My suit was saved!

In general, many people regard Bermuda as a tropical paradise, indeed even UK travel brochures and newspaper statements lead one to think so. This is not correct,

Bermuda is nowhere near the tropics or even sub tropical as are the West Indies. The weather can be very warm in the summer and mild in the winter, but the wind blows often and suddenly and it rains. I heard many American tourists complain that they had wasted a weeks holiday in Bermuda when it rained every day, even in the summer.

My main concern with regard to the weather was the boats. I was responsible for them and if they were in the water when the wind blew they got damaged. My mind was therefore only at rest when they were out of the water and safely stowed. This state of mind was not compatible with everyone's wish, including my own, to get out in a boat to fish off the reefs or for whatever recreational activity one wished.

As previously stated, the major industry of Bermuda is tourism and the great majority of tourists are American. The island's economy is based on its 'offshore' financial institutions and its economic links with the USA. Most goods and particularly food, are all imported from the USA, similarly the Television and Radio programmes are largely American. Here are two amusing examples of how the Americans regarded Bermuda.

I overheard the following conversation between an American tourist couple at a Trooping of the Colour ceremony at which the Governor and of course we, his troops, were participating:

> *"Gee honey, What tune are they playing?"*
> *"That is 'God Save the Queen' "*
> *"Why are they playing 'God save the Queen'? "*
> *"Because Bermuda belongs to Britain"*
> *"Gee, I thought it belonged to the USA"*

Another incident occurred one Sunday morning when I was down at a nearby beach with my son when I stopped and spoke to a middle aged American tourist. He asked me where I came from and I explained that I was from England. He replied that he had heard of England and he knew it was on the West coast of Europe and that he had met a minister who had actually been there and who had told him that it was very cold in the north, (we established he meant Yorkshire), but warm in the south where palm trees grew. I acknowledged that there may be a few palm trees in the Torquay area but it was not that warm. I first thought he was pulling my leg but after further conversation I realised that he was quite genuine in his 'ignorance' of England. He was from a small town in Iowa in the mid west and was a businessman who had flown out to Bermuda for the weekend so he must have been reasonably well off.

When one considers that he probably lived and was brought up in a mid west city with only local radio, television and newspapers and in a country where world geography is not generally taught in schools to the extent that it is (or used to be?), taught in England, one can understand that the incidents related above were not overly unusual.

Living in Bermuda was idyllic, but our daughter Linda who was then 19 years of age, could not get a job and was bored. Also she had left behind her boyfriend in England and was missing him. We therefore, most reluctantly, allowed her to return home. This was no problem as we had left the house ready for re-occupation, so she just flew home walked in doors and was happily settled. She then got a job and was able to see her loved one. They came out to visit us together later in the year (1975) and thoroughly enjoyed their visit. They married in

1977 and we now have a lovely granddaughter. My sister Phyllis and her husband Bob also came out to stay with us for two weeks and we greatly enjoyed showing them around.

All good things come to an end. Defence re-organisation, or cut backs?, determined that the post of SNOWI was to be abolished from 1st April 1976 and all his staff were to be withdrawn. HMS MALABAR was to remain as a much reduced base for ships passing to and from the West Indies station but with only one officer and ten men. My Communications Centre was to close and my own job as well as that of thirty of my ratings were also to be abolished.

Our last days in Bermuda included many rounds of farewells, even the Governor, Sir Edwin (Ted) Leather threw a dinner party for us. One last and most pleasant surprise for me was that on the day we were to fly home, and when we were waiting in our hotel before going to catch the plane, the Commodore's Secretary arrived at our hotel with a bottle of champagne and the news that I had been promoted to Lieutenant Commander. This was my ultimate aim and I was walking on air, or rather, flying on air, as we were to fly home in a few hours.

CHAPTER TWENTY FOUR

MANAGING A COMMUNICATIONS TRAINING DEPARTMENT

HMS MERCURY

(1976 TO 1978)

Experience is one thing you cannot get for nothing.

Oscar Wilde (1854-1900)

Before leaving Bermuda, my appointing officer had written to me stating that I was to be appointed to HMS MERCURY to start up a new Submarine section at the User Requirement and Trials Section (URTS). This suited me very well. However, whilst on leave during April 1976, he rang me to say that plans had changed and that I was now to go to Training Section of HMS MERCURY and take up the post of 'G1' in place of the previous incumbent who had died suddenly. He sweetened the change by saying that now that I had been promoted to Lieutenant Commander the URTS job was too lowly for me. I was happy in any event as it meant I could still live at home with my family.

The job consisted of heading the Training Section which trained ratings and WRNS for advancement to Leading Radio Operator and Radio Supervisor. In addition it ran the Pre Joining Training (PJT) courses for ratings about to go to new posts, both ashore and afloat. To assist me, I had a relatively large staff. Four Lieutenants and one Third Officer WRNS in charge of sub sections, plus an Instructor Lieutenant to teach Radio Theory. They all had Warrant Officers and Chief and Petty Officer Instructors to do the instructing and administration of their sub sections.

This splendid team of experienced communications personnel carried out the day to day instructing and I did not have to teach, but sit at the top of the tree and do the paper work. I enjoyed teaching and I soon found that I was sitting in on classes, partly to ensure that the students were getting the right form of instruction, that is, that the syllabi from which they were being taught reflected what they ought to know, and also to ensure that the instructors were doing their job properly.

I soon found that things had changed since I was last teaching ten years previously. In the early 1970s, the 'Schoolies' or Instructor Branch Officers had reviewed training throughout the navy and had come to the conclusion that all training should be 'rationalised' and 'brought up to date'. There were very good reasons for this as there is no doubt that some aspects of naval procedures, customs and methodology were not up to date. To implement this new teaching approach, a series of large documents called 'Nine Part Documentation' were produced for every sub specialisation in the navy. Much work was put into these, and in addition, administrative sections, headed by Instructor Officers, were set up to assess training and set and mark examination papers.

All this in theory was a good thing. But it was not as I knew it and I soon found many anomalies which made me unhappy with many aspects. I found ratings were being taught too much by rote, and not enough emphasis being placed on what to do in a ship 'at war'. This led to me have many battles with the Instructor Officers who were producing the syllabi and setting and marking the examination papers. If I was to be head of the Training Section I wanted a say in what was taught and what examination questions were set and how they were marked at the end of the day, I had to make the decision on whether a student passed or failed his advancement examinations, not them. Most differences were resolved in the end and I got most, but not all of my way.

A particularly pleasurable part of my job was to sit in on and assess lectures given by students to their own class and instructors. These lectures were normally about thirty minutes and each advancement class student was required to give two lectures. One on a technical communications subject and one on anything he or she wished. The object was to give the student confidence in speaking in front of others as well as to enable his general performance to be assessed. Many students gave super lectures, in particular the WRNS ratings. The WRNS communications ratings were, in general, of a higher educational standard than most of their male counterparts. Most had passed five or six good 'O' Levels before joining. Many of their lectures were of particularly high standard. I recall one by a Leading WRNS Radio Operator on the subject of TAROT Card reading that had every one in the audience completely hooked and so interested that I think the lecture overran by an hour.

During this period our daughter Linda married and our son David was then 12 years old and of an adventurous nature so we often went out to the woods or visits to places of interest. I was also able to visit my mother at Wincanton every six weeks or so. She looked forward to our visits, which were usually on a Sunday and she always had a roast lunch ready for us.

I also took the opportunity of redecorating our modest home and having the roof re-tiled, the walls re-pointed and an extension built. It was about that time that we decided that we were not going to move to 'a nice little cottage in the country', but to stay where we were. It was that long ago experience of mine when my parents moved every year which has influenced my determination not to move and have a settled home. I have achieved this and do not intend to move - ever!

Perhaps the only less than satisfactory aspect of my two years in the Training Section was that it was a time of change in the navy generally and whereas previously the Captain and the Executive Commander of HMS MERCURY had always been communications officers and usually persons who I had known over the years, the Captain and Commander were then non communicators. This should have made no difference at all and I am sure that had they, or I, been of different character there wouldn't have been. But over about a twelve month period I did not get on with either of them. Why? I do not really know. Except that they both seemed to me to be over ambitious and too ready to prove themselves. Perhaps I had become a staid and stubborn communicator and did not want change. That is how they probably saw me but I do not really think this was entirely so and my career and actions in later years certainly did not show this.

This short period was the only time in my 49 years service in the Royal Navy that I felt that I did not respect my Captain and Commander. Despite this I had no problems with my own direct bosses, the Training Commander and others on the Training Staff to whom I was directly responsible and we all got on well and I received a very good report from him and I was well respected by my colleagues. As I headed a training section which taught communications ratings and a close colleague headed one which taught officers I invented a phrase to tease him. This was that *"My Section taught 'Communications' and his Section taught 'Officers'"*.

At the end of my two years in the Training Section, I only had two years to go before retirement at the age of 50 so I did not want to be sent to any far away or high profile job. I was by then over age limit for promotion to full Commander. This step had never been on for me anyway as I had been too late going through for my commission in 1961/2, at the age of 32 to have a real chance of this promotion. Therefore when my Appointing Officer offered me the Submarine Desk job in the User Requirements and Trials Section (URTS), which I had originally been going to in 1976, I accepted it eagerly. I did not bother to ask him why I had been too senior to take the job in 1976 but was eligible to take it in 1978. I knew that Appointers use many words and make many promises to persuade their charges to accept appointments.

CHAPTER TWENTY FIVE

BACK TO THE USER REQUIREMENTS AND TRIALS SECTION (URTS)

HMS MERCURY

(1978 TO 1981)

In nature there are neither rewards nor punishments - there are consequences.

Robert G Ingersoll (1833-1899)

This new job did not require me to move home so my settled family life continued. The difference was that I was now required to establish and represent the submarine communications user requirements to the procurement agencies, dockyards and shipbuilders. I had already some background with submarines and I had made many submarine personnel contacts during my Singapore days in HMS FORTH. Further experience was gained whilst in my previous job in the training department as I there had a Submarine sub-section which taught submarine communications ratings advancement courses.

The User Requirements and Trials Section Staff - 1979

I needed to know much more and I set about this task by visiting as many submarines as possible, taking a couple of submarine passage trips to get the feel of the user requirements, and talking to everyone who knew anything about submarine communications. It was a pleasant job. I started doing inspections of submarines completing refits and building, attending meetings and generally representing the submarine communications user. I soon became a 'wheel' and gained much respect for the practical manner with which I managed my desk. A part of the job I enjoyed was going off on visits and attending meetings. This took me away from my desk and so relieved the monotony of the 'nine to five' desk job syndrome. I frequently visited the MoD in London, Devonport Dockyard, Vickers Shipbuilders at Barrow-in Furness and of course the MoD Procurement agencies at Bath and Portsdown.

I also began to visit and advise the commercial radio companies which produced the submarine communications equipments, such as Marconi, Redifon and British Aerospace. This was a most important aspect as many of the firms had extremely good development engineers from who I learnt much. Similarly I was often able to advise them and ensure that they did not go down the wrong path during initial development. My continual cry to them all was "*Make it smaller*". Space in a submarine is at even more of a premium than in a surface ship and it was essential that the radio companies appreciated this point. My other plea to them all was to make it simple to operate. I reminded them that many communications users did not have degrees in engineering as many of them had, but were young 17 or 18 year old lads who had only a couple of 'O' Levels. They had to operate equipments, often in darkened conditions, often under pressure and perhaps at times whilst they were very frightened.

In order push home the space problems, I produced some small scale Lego models of submarine communications offices. These I took to meetings to prove or disprove the drawings which had been produced by the engineering draughtsmen. A three dimension Lego model made more impact than the two dimension drawings and I won several space concessions using this method. And it was fun to play with Lego! Sometimes my son, David, used to help me construct the models at home in the evenings.

When travelling to meetings and inspections at Barrow-in Furness, I usually took the sleeper train. I left Fareham at 2030 of an evening got to Waterloo at 2200, then to Kings Cross by 2230 and then got on the Sleeper about 2300. The attendant would then bring me a next day's paper and a miniature bottle of whisky and I was usually asleep by the train left at 2330. The sleeper got to Barrow about 0630 and the first time I did this trip I went across the road from the station to an hotel called the Duke of Edinburgh. I enquired if I could have breakfast and was directed to the dining room on the first floor. I felt I needed a better wash than I had had on the train so I asked where the toilet was and when I went in I found that it was a typical old fashioned toilet come bathroom. I promptly ran myself a lovely hot bath and really freshened myself up for the day ahead. I then had breakfast and was picked up and taken to the shipyard by a colleague at 0830. This became a usual routine for me from then on. They were pleasant days.

During this period I was not always fully occupied with submarine communications and so I used to help out my colleagues working on surface ship projects, that is, doing very similar jobs to those I had done previously when in the section from 1971 to 1973. This continued to broaden my experience in communications generally and I also had the opportunity to teach or lecture to both officers and ratings classes occasionally. I have always enjoyed teaching and would always put myself out to take a class if I could find the time. Teaching, or instructing or lecturing, as it was usually termed, also gave one the opportunity to talk to and get views from others. This was most important in a job where I was representing their user requirements.

During the first year in this job we continued to visit my mother at Wincanton and indeed, I often combined a duty trip to Bath with a detour to Wincanton to see her. The last time I did this was in January 1979, just a week before she died. After that we still regularly visited relatives at Wincanton, Taunton, Dorchester and Verwood so we continued to enjoy that part of the county. Dorset in particular, being my birthplace has always been my favourite county and I still visit it often to this day.

My time in the navy was due to expire on my 50th Birthday in April 1980. I liked my job, was successful at it and had been well recommended for my work. I did not want to go. I therefore applied for an extension for three more years. It was during a period when extensions were difficult to get but I got it and so was delighted that my career was to be extended for 3 more years. However, a few months later, in the autumn of 1980, the head of my Section, who was a Lieutenant Commander in the post as a Retired Officer and therefore really a civil servant as opposed to being on the active list, died suddenly from a heart attack.

As I was the most experienced officer in the section and had a good knowledge of the running of the surface ship communications requirements as well as the submarine aspects, I stepped in to fill the gap until a successor for him could be found. I continued doing both jobs for many months and decided that I would like to take on this Retired Officer's post permanently. There were pros and cons to this. The big advantage was that I would continue to do a job I liked with colleagues I liked and the job would be secure as a civil servant until I was 65. The disadvantage was that the pay was not as good as that of a serving Lieutenant Commander. But, if I took the job as a Retired Officer I would still get my Naval pension, albeit somewhat abated. I decided to apply for the job and then apply to leave the Navy to take it up. I went before an interview board and was selected.

The next hurdle was to persuade the navy that I did not now want to complete my three year extension but to leave as soon as possible in order to take up my new job. This should have been simple as from everyone's point of view I was already doing the job and would continue to do the job whether I was serving or a Retired Officer. There was much humming and haa-ing up in the MoD, but I had many friends among senior officers who all wanted me to take the job and thereby retain my experience. My immediate superior, the Officer in Charge of the section was also most supportive and pressed my case most forcibly. He is a valued friend to this day, indeed he has assisted me with the proof reading of this book.

Eventually I won. I received a telephone call from my appointing officer on 20th June 1981 to say that my active naval service would expire on 26th June, which was a Saturday. I could therefore take up my new post on Monday 28th June. I was delighted, so were my superiors as continuity was extremely important in the work which we were doing. But, I had not had any of my 28 days entitlement of terminal leave, neither had I done any of the

Vocational training courses to which personnel leaving the service were eligible. I did not need any vocational training course as I was not in need of a new career in civilian life but I would have liked to have taken the leave. But I was too busy! I was still doing my old submarine job as well as that as head of the section and we were also one other officer short in the section. There was no way I could get away. I asked whether I could have a month's pay in lieu of leave but was told that this was not possible. Apparently I was *'eligible'* but not *'entitled'*!

On the Friday I was to leave the navy after 35 years service I rang the Captain's Secretary to remind her that I was leaving the navy on that day and therefore I supposed the Captain would like to see me and say Good-bye. She spoke to the Captain and then rang back to say that I could go to see him at 1500 if I wished. I went down at the appointed time and the Captain, a nice man, (but not a communicator!) said he was sorry I could not have pay in lieu of terminal leave and that he hoped I would be happy as a Retired Officer, and that was it. He did not appear to have my personal papers with him or know enough about me to say much. I went back to my section.

My immediate boss and nearly everyone else were away on various official meetings, I was duty 'locker up', so I put away my papers, checked the building for security, locked it up and returned the keys. I felt most deflated. Here was I leaving the navy after 35 years service and no one was there to say good bye or extend a kind word. I went home. On Monday morning 28th June, I went to work as usual, wearing my uniform as usual, and carried on running the section and doing three jobs at the same time. Nothing had changed since Friday! I did not have time to reflect any further!

CHAPTER TWENTY SIX

MUCH MORE OF THE SAME BUT AS A RETIRED OFFICER

HMS MERCURY

(1981 TO 1995)

The secret of being a bore ... is to tell everything.

Voltaire c. 1737

My new job was very demanding and I worked harder than at any time in my career, much of this was probably my own fault as my character is such that I have always been willing to help others out and take on tasks and responsibilities which were over and above those I needed to do. My colleagues often grumbled at me for doing this, especially as it often meant more work for them as well.

Nevertheless I thoroughly enjoyed the challenge. I made it my job to visit not only every class of warship but nearly every warship in the navy. Also I visited most Royal Fleet Auxiliary (RFA) vessels and all the larger Royal Maritime Auxiliary Service (RMAS) vessels. I visited Merchant ships to get ideas and even RNLI Lifeboats. I made myself conversant with the communications equipments in all these ships and with their operational requirements. Within a year I was able to quote from memory the communications fits, capabilities and shortcomings of nearly all these ships. This stood me in good stead when I attended meetings in the MoD and with shipbuilders and Procurement Executive authorities.

Once again I had built a rod for my own back as I became known as *'Len Foot, the chap who knows and will solve the problem'.* My telephone was always ringing, the calls were not only from naval colleagues but from civilian firms and shipbuilders who wanted to know some detail and they knew that I would either know or would find out for them much more quickly than any other means. I developed an interest in Commercial Satellite communications for maritime use and did much to get this system introduced into some ships. When funds were not available I 'borrowed' terminals from manufacturers to get them fitted for 'trial' in several ships and these were very successful. I fought a long hard battle to get these commercial satellite communications terminals fitted in all warships and RFAs. The big break thought came at the time of the Falklands war when Satellite communications were virtually the only method of communications over the large distances involved. The comprehensive world wide High Frequency (H/F) radio communications networks based at Ceylon, Mauritius, South Africa and Singapore on which the navy had relied on during the 1950s and 1960s and even the early 1970s were by then long gone.

The Navy bought a number of satellite terminals with the special Falklands war funds and these were afterwards fitted into and then transferred between ships deployed on remote deployments.

User Requirements and Trials Section Staff - 1981

I managed these commercial satellite resources on behalf of the Fleet for a number of years. Once again it was not really part of my job but I was interested in pushing these systems and willingly took on the additional work to pursue my aim. It meant that I was, on more than one occasion, rung at home in the middle of the night to ask me to organise the fitting of a terminal in a ship the next day. I recall spending the whole of one evening at home ringing the Harbour Master at Portland and other authorities, both naval and civil, in order for them to arrange for a certain ship to be moved to a berth with a crane early the next morning, it was a Saturday, so that we could fit the satellite aerial dish. The ship was due to sail on the Saturday evening. Every difficulty was thrown in my way, such as overtime for the crane driver and for the civilian berthing party, but I won in the end. *"Serve you right"* said my colleagues. *"You shouldn't have got involved!"*

My aim was to get these commercial satellite terminals fitted in all ships. My masters in the MoD smiled condescendingly and said that they were not really needed and in any case they could not afford them. I persisted (stubborn old Len Foot), and helped by the requirements of Gulf War in 1989 I won my point and it eventually became Naval Staff Policy to fit Commercial Satellite terminals, as well as Military Satellite terminals, in all major warships just before I left the Navy in 1995. It was my view then, and it still is, that the military satellite system was over complex and far too expensive for what it provided. It cost about £2,000,000 per ship installation and required a full time qualified senior electrical engineering rating to maintain it. It was inflexible in it's operational functions and prone to faults, particularly with it's cumbersome aerial system, whereas the commercial satellite systems cost about £30.000, or less, required virtually no maintenance and provided a much more flexible and 'user friendly' service, albeit limited with respect to fulfilling some of the more complex naval requirements.

This comment of course is not the full story as the military system met the standard requirements of a 'hardened' system capable of withstanding shock, jamming and many other sophisticated methods of electronic attack which were essential. That is what my superiors and the Defence Procurement boffins told me so they must be right - but I believed that many of the Defence Procurement personnel, and indeed some of our own senior officers, lacked what in my view was 'commercial awareness'! The electronics firms knew this and tended to take advantage, after all they were in the business of making money so one cannot blame them.

Other aspects of communications I became involved with were Maritime Distress affairs and liaison with the RNLI. These provided me with more contacts and meetings with interesting people outside the purely Naval environment and we all learned much from each other. In particular, I attended meetings with the Department of Trade and Industry, Home Office Regulatory bodies and also with Confederation of British Shipbuilders representatives. All were most enlightening.

All these tasks involved travelling to visit equipment manufacturers, shipbuilders and ships and also attending innumerable meetings. I continued to enjoy this aspect, but when away from the office the paperwork piled up and I then had to work late to get it all done. My colleagues continued to say: *"Serve you right Len for getting involved",* but I didn't mind as I enjoyed it.

. *Our Ruby Wedding Anniversary - 1991*

Audrey and me - 1991

Another enjoyable aspect of working in the User Requirements and Trials Section was the people. We were a small unit of only ten officers plus a couple of civilian clerical support staff. We all got on well together. We all knew our jobs and got on with them. Our work was much appreciated by our masters in the MoD to whom we were responsible and our advice much sought after.

I do not intend to bore the reader with any more details of my work during this period. Suffice to say that I was successful at my job, perhaps I was considered to be stubborn by some, particularly when I was fighting for an enhancement in the face of rapidly dwindling funds. I lost some battles but won many more.

As I was known to very many communications equipment manufacturers, I always received diaries and calendars from them at the end of each year. These I dished out to my colleagues. In some years I received as many as twenty diaries and calendars. I sometimes made it clear to some of the firms that if they expected my help with their innumerable questions then I expected a diary. Corruption? My chums used to tease me over this matter. The number fell off in the latter years as more and more firms cut back on expenses.

During the early 1990s, the Personal Computer became the 'in' thing and we were all given one to put on our desks. I was not happy at first and my colleagues teased me as being "*Too old to get the handle of these new fangled devices*". It was not long before I became hooked and was soon able to produce letters, papers and documents with even greater speed than before. My boss use to express amazement that after I had been away on visits for a couple of days I would return to the office, tackle my 'IN' tray and produce seven or eight complex letters on highly technical aspects of communications for him to sign within a couple of hours.

I made a separate personal file on which I used to record jokes. I built up a large store of a couple of hundred jokes, many of them rude or smutty. These I used to pull out for use on special occasions. One day I discovered that my colleague as well as the lady typist in the Section Registry also had these jokes on their files. They had 'knobbled' my floppy disc whilst I was away and copied it for themselves! I still have those jokes today but cannot print many of them in this family book!

In August 1991 Audrey and I celebrated our Ruby Wedding Anniversary. Our daughter, Linda and her husband Martyn, assisted by our son David, put on a party for us and had a marquee erected on their lawn and we invited all our friends and relatives. It was a lovely party, a lovely day and will always be remembered by both of us. David made a speech and proposed the toast. All was well with us.

Time marches on and in April 1995 I was due to retire at the age of 65. My superiors in the MoD in London and my boss were keen that I should stay on for another year, this was possible but I politely refused. My reasons for

The Communications Requirements and Trials Section - Staff Photograph - 1994

wanting to leave were several. In 1993 I had been feeling slightly under the weather for some time and went to the doctor. (Like my father it has never been my habit to visit doctors very much!). He diagnosed 'maturity onset diabetes' and ordered that I should lose weight. I was then fifteen and a half stone. I cut out sugar and fats and lost over a stone in six weeks. I have tried to reduce to under fourteen stone many times but cannot yet manage it. I am now steady at a constant fourteen and a half stone. This is rather more than it should be but I feel OK. I do not have to take any drugs or insulin. Just watch my diet. The only noticeable effect was that I felt that I tended to get tired more quickly. But then at the age of over 60 I suppose that I should have expected it but I still tried to work as hard as ever.

Another reason for wanting to leave was that the navy was changing. The very severe cuts in both personnel and materials were making life very difficult. I was seeing projects on which I had worked for several years being cancelled from lack of funds. Worse still, some projects were so reduced in funds that the end product did not meet the original requirement and was in many aspects worse than nothing. In my own opinion money was being wasted and not being of a nature to keep silent when I had an opinion, I voiced it on many occasions. *"Why not give all the money to me and let me run the navy ? "*

The last two months before I left the navy were memorable for the number of farewell parties I attended. I was much privileged to be dined out by my brother officers in my own mess at Leydene. (HMS MERCURY had by then closed). I was then hugely privileged to be 'dined out of the navy' by my superiors and colleagues in the communications branch as a whole. Over 80 communications officers, ranging from Admirals, Commodores, Captains down to my own colleagues gave me a wonderful and most memorable send off. There were many speeches of farewell. Not least my own which I tried to make amusing and will reproduce below. In addition, the many friends I had made in industry were all sorry to see me go and I was lunched out many times by different firms with whom I had worked for so long. Many of them made tentative offers of a job for me on retirement but I made it clear that 'I was going to retire'. Several offers were quite attractive, being consultancy jobs for perhaps two or three days a week. I was tempted but turned them down. Today I have no regrets at this decision.

An amusing incident was that during the last few days of work I was due to attend a meeting in London together with my successor. I made plans that we would attend the meeting which was with MoD Procurement, shipbuilders, Royal Marine and Army authorities, in the morning and that in the afternoon I would take my successor round to meet the various MoD desk officers with whom he was to work. I rang them all up previously and said I would be there in the afternoon. Unfortunately at the end of the meeting, about 1300, the Chairman, who was a ship Platform manager from MoD Bath decided that as this was my last meeting we should go to a pub to celebrate. Off we all went and had a lovely time, I recall that about 1530 I was going to the toilet and the Chairman said "*You are not going are you Len?*" I said "*No*", and on my return he had bought a half a dozen bottles of champagne which we then had to consume. It was a lovely impromptu party put on by colleagues from Bath, the Royal Marines and the Army. Fortunately I had come to London by train so did not have to drive after so long a session. I believe we left the pub about 1700. The next day I had several phone calls from the Commanders at the various desks at the MoD asking why I had not been to visit them. I replied that my morning meeting had overrun! They all laughed as word had got around as to why and where I had been all the afternoon.

My successor, an old friend and colleague and a great lover of parties and socialising, very much enjoyed this period when I was taking him round to introduce him to work contacts, and I had to keep reminding him to 'stop enjoying himself' as these were my farewell parties!

During the last hectic days before I retired, as well as being informally lunched out many times by groups of colleagues, I was officially dined out twice and therefore had to make a speech on each occasion. I will record them verbatim here as they sum up my thoughts at that time and perhaps give a view of the amusing side of my life in the navy and latterly at HMS MERCURY.

AFTER DINNER SPEECH GIVEN AT MY DINING OUT AT LEYDENE ON 23rd MARCH 1995

"Mr President, Admiral Rankin, Commander Stenning, Ladies and Gentlemen.

Thank you all very much for dining me out and for the very kind words you have said and for my gifts. I do very much appreciate them and indeed the support of everyone in the mess. Don't you all think that this Leydene mess has turned out well, it is the right size and in spite of it being rather out of the way for many, it has become one of the most pleasant messes that I have served in. And much credit goes to you Rob, (Rob was the First Lieutenant and President of the mess), *for the way you run it, and for your relaxed speeches and pleasantries.*

Yes I am going at last and have many memories of people and places - but I will not bore you with too many.

It may, however, be appropriate to remind some of the younger members here of the HMS MERCURY I have known over the past near half century.

I first came to MERCURY in December 1949 after two years at sea. The only brick building was the Main House. We all lived in Nissen huts, about twenty to a hut, although there were a few large ones for Senior and Junior Rates messes and for wash houses and bathrooms. There were no flush toilets, the duty watch or special parties emptied the buckets. Not a popular duty watch task.

I recall it was very cold that winter and the only heating was a coke burning stove in each hut for which we had a plentiful supply of coke, but to light it one needed coal. Coal was rationed to one shovel full per hut per day. If your fire went out after being lit you were in trouble. This often happened when everyone was at instructional classes and no one remembered to nip back to stoke up the fire in mid morning or afternoon. The answer was to steal a shovel of hot coke embers from an adjoining hut, this often did not work and then resulted in two huts being without fires.

Entertainment was a film two nights a week in the Main Cinema. There was a dance once a month when the WRNS were bussed over from Soberton, but there was never enough of them and so we danced with each other. It was quite comical to see sailors doing the waltz and foxtrot - but it never did me any harm - I hope! The main problem was that the floor, being a cinema floor, had a considerable slope to it, so we danced fast downhill and laboured slowly up the other side.

In the 1950s, National Service required everyone to do 18 months military service, most of the university graduates who joined the communications branch of the navy were Russian Linguists and were employed as Coder Educationalists - nicknamed 'Cod Eds', Crypto was then a time consuming business, converting text into 4 figure groups and then double subtraction from other basic groups to provide security. It was subtraction without carrying which I had no problem with after several years of practice but the Cod Eds couldn't get used to it. Though they could easily work out that the chances of the code being broken was 10 to power 18 ! The ones I had were all nice guys but most had problems with the simple things of life such as scrubbing out. One had to explain to them that first they had to put hot water into a bucket, then the soap, then rub the soap on the scrubbing brush, then rub the scrubbing brush on the deck. It was a painful business. I wonder if your present day linguists have the same problem?

I remember the Cod-Ed in MERCURY who had given his station card as security for a broom - this was normal procedure as even brooms were in short supply. As the Buffer's store was locked when he went to reclaim it, he fell in for Libertymen's inspection and tried to hand in his broom in lieu of station card. Much mirth from the Crushers. He did not get ashore on weekend.

I spent some time as Petty Officer of the Guard in the mid 1950s. We used to have foot patrol and a bicycle patrol. One night, when the bicycle patrol rating had failed to return after nearly an hour when his patrol should only have taken him 15 minutes, I sent out a search party and he was found pushing his bike around the perimeter of the establishment. He had been afraid to tell anyone that he could not ride a bike when he was detailed for this duty.

The bicycles use were nicknamed 'red devils' and, as they were ridden by robust young duty watch lads from 1700 to 0700 every night, their life span was about 28 days. The Chief 'Jack Dusty' reckoned that by then they were beyond repair.

I was Divisional Officer for a large number of Electronic Warfare ratings when I was here teaching in the mid 1960s and was quite pleased when I found a group of lads were regularly drawing camping gear from the 'Exped' Store at weekends. My illusions were shattered one Monday morning when the Master at Arms rang to tell me that they always camped in a field at Soberton, adjacent to the WRNS quarters, and half of them were on defaulters that morning for disturbing the peace at the Pink E. (Elephant), which was the local pub at Soberton, properly named the White Lion, and for breaking into, or rather, being found inside, the WRNS quarters. We had to put a stop to that as sex was not allowed in those days !

I shall miss the navy after so many years, everyone asks me what I am going to do. My present intention is to retire, start re-decorating the house and do gardening. I am running four gardens at the moment, And to visit places and people and very much please myself. Whether I will be allowed to do these things we will have to see.

I had better tell just one story:

A Naval Officer - he was an SD - came home from work early and when he went upstairs found his wife in bed with another man. He pulled back the bed clothes and there was this man - starkers, except for his socks of course. He was so angry that he dragged the man out of bed and threw him down the stairs, knocking him unconscious. When the man awoke he was in the garden shed with his private parts fixed in the vice and the irate husband was standing over him with a carving knife. "You are not going to cut it off are you?" he cried. "No. You are" said the husband. "I am just going to set fire to the shed".

Thank you all once more for dining me out - and for my gift - I hope to keep in touch."

AFTER DINNER SPEECH GIVEN ON BEING DINED OUT OF THE ROYAL NAVY AT HMS COLLINGWOOD ON 7 APRIL 1995.

"Captain Mike, (Captain Mike Caswell was at that time the Chief Naval Signals Officer and had organised my dining out), *Admiral Sanders, Commodore Wyatt, Ladies and Gentlemen, Old Friends and New Friends and Colleagues.*

Thank you very much for the many kind words. Thank you all for coming and for dining me out so splendidly and for a really tremendous evening, and for my gifts. I have always wanted a "Jimmy" and have attended many presentations to others over the years and always been secretly jealous that I never had one. Now I have one of my very own. Thank you all.

As many of you will know. I did not volunteer for any of this. I would have been happy to slip quietly away, before the clamour of "It's all Len Foot's fault" gets too loud. I reckon I am going to get blamed for at least the next ten years - so I shall be going into hiding on 23rd April.

Your kind words have tended to make me feel guilty as many of you will be aware that I have been known, on very very rare occasions of course, to make disparaging remarks about my superiors, particularly those in the MoD when their communications policy decisions did not entirely fit in with mine !

(All were very well aware that I made these remarks at least once an hour !).

In fact, I must admit that the words "Those TURKEYS up in the MoD", have been known to fall from my lips -

(Again, all were aware that I always referred to them as Turkeys !)

- when I have failed to get my way or a decision had been made with which I did not agree.

This brings to mind an article you may have seen in the Daily Telegraph a few weeks ago which stated that the Government were planning to sell of some of the Whitehall Governmental buildings to private ownership and then lease them back. The Treasury building was quoted as being the first of these. This leads to speculation as to whether that well known Norfolk entrepreneur - Mr Bernard Matthew's - might not try to buy up MoD Main Building. I am sure this rumour is untrue!

Having gathered you all together as a captive audience, I cannot let you go away until I've given you some of my views and opinions on past and future communications.

The subject of this lecture is 'Communications Control and Management Systems'. It's security classification is Restricted. It's all right I haven't brought my Vu-foils !

I would like to reminisce for a few moments. My first ship after HMS GANGES was HMS DUKE OF YORK which I joined in 1947. She carried Commander- in-Chief Home Fleet - Admiral 'Tich' McGrigor, who was only about 5 feet tall, but he frightened me. The Fleet Communications Officer was Commander McCrum, who later became Director of Naval Signals and the Fleet Communications Assistant was Lieutenant Paterson who later became Training Commander at HMS MERCURY - then he retired and entered the church as a vicar. (Most appropriate !).

I cannot remember the full communications fit but I recall that we had a Type 57 transmitter which had a power output of 3kW and Type 59s which had a power output of 1 or 2 kW plus an American navy transmitter called 'Janie', I never knew its proper name. This had a power output of about 8kW and had been used to Broadcast news bulletins to the British Pacific Fleet during the 1944/5 operations against the Japanese.

The reason I mention these is that the Communications Control System to manage and bring the communications assets to the operators was called the 'Comprehensive Wireless System (CWS)' My memories of this system probably explain why I have always been so insistent, and difficult, and stubborn, in pressing the need for us to get our Communications Control and Management Systems right in present and future ships.

The CWS units were 'plug in' modules, rather like a VCS unit box in use today but a little taller and they contained a loudspeaker, a Morse key, a headset socket and a telephone type dial. By dialling we could call up a transmitter on a pre-set frequency, and select high, medium or low power. There was also a 'W/T Silence' switch. The

Morse key and speaker were also used for Internal Communications, which was by Morse only. Nevertheless it was an internal/external communications system. All communications offices, including the FCO, FCA and Warrant Tel's cabins were connected by this system. All users appeared to me to transmit at 40 words per minute plus and as a young lad I spent half my time sending IMI (repeat). The FCO, FCA and Warrant Tel also had radio receivers in their cabins so they could monitor the W/T circuits - and they did - Big brother really was watching us.

The general description of the CWS states;
Primary Object   -   Simplicity of Operation.
Secondary Object   -   Efficiency of operation.
Third object   -'   Reliability.

It is of interest that we have never since had a system with all these capabilities and even the ship at present dearest to my heart - the Landing Platform Dock Replacement (LPD(R), which will be my best effort to provide state of the art management and control in the year 2000 will not enable selection of power by the operators. (Maybe we do not need it?), or to fully control the VHF, UHF and SHF bands. These capabilities were lost during the cost cutting reductions some eighteen months ago.

There is no glamour in a Communications Control Exchange system, it doesn't in itself transmit or have a high visibility to Senior Officers. It has, in my view, in the past been much neglected and it is only now that its importance is being appreciated to enable less manpower to manage more complex systems and attempts are now being made to improve matters. I plead guilty to forcing this issue over the past ten years or so. My complaints about present systems have been never ending. In fact, Captain Mike, there will be a particularly difficult problem arriving on your desk, or at least your desk officer's desk, next week with regard to HMS ARK ROYAL's control system problems. I timed it especially to make sure I was out of the way before it hit your desks!

Since 1947 we have had many control systems, in HMS BOXER (the four masted one!), we had a system called 'KNOBBLY' it had no other name, and was called such in the Handbook. I was the only one who understood it and was regarded as a 'wheel' by the Operations Room and Air Direction Room staffs. I used to permanently walk around with a headset round my neck, a screwdriver in one hand and a soldering iron in the other. This was before the 'Greenies' came and stopped us fixing our own kit!

We moved to 'Integrated Communications' in the 1960s when ICS1 was introduced, which is still at sea in HMS FEARLESS and HMS INTREPID. But these systems were never truly 'integrated'. Even the latest systems at sea such as ICS4/6 with Outfit KMY only partially integrate HF and UHF. SHF and Automated Message Handling System connectivity is left out.

My own view is that we will never achieve a truly integrated communications system as long as the elements of the communications systems are split between different Procurement projects under different Assistant Directors who control separate 'pots' of money. But I must keep out of politics. As I said the LPD(R) will not achieve it as the integration of SHF SATCOMS and control of UHF Multicouplers has already been lost in the Cost Capping.

However, my very dear colleague Nick Humphrys, is working on a 'Fully Integrated Communications System' FICS, for the Future Nato Frigate. This started life as a 'Future Integrated System'. I think 'Future' is a better word as I do not know what 'Fully Integrated' means, as it is either 'Integrated' or it is not! Maybe you should call it a 'Truly Integrated System', Nick - TICS, or a 'More Integrated System' - MICS. I do not know the chances of achieving it, or whether it will finish up as the 'French Italian Communications System' Sorry about that Nick but I couldn't resist it.

Not all is lost however, and here is a thought and the point of this story. The CVSG(R) (New Aircraft Carrier), studies are just starting - and if we can get a FICS or TICS or MICS or CWS into this new ship which may go to sea in 20 years from now, and if it has a 30 year life, we could well have a ship at sea in the 2030s and 2040s, which may have a communications system which has caught up with that in HMS DUKE OF YORK - Just one century earlier!

Progress really will have been made !

I have here a 'General Description' of the CWS, written circa 1940, which I would like to bequeath to Nick Humphrys. If he adds about 200,000 extra words to it as padding and translates it into French and Italian it should do for his FICS User Requirement for the year 2004!

Gentlemen, I believe we around this table have all had the same aim - to do our best for Naval Communications in general and for Communications personnel in particular. We have fought our battles to the best of our ability. I do sincerely thank you, especially my Senior Officers, for your support and for putting up with my stubbornness in trying to improve our communications systems. I think we have won more battles than we have lost.

I have often complained, together with others, about the MoD Procurement Executive not producing the goods. But I would like to pay a special tribute to one person who is here this evening and who, in spite of being in the PE, is serving we communicators well. He is Lionel Baker, Project Manager for the LPD(R) Communications Systems. He has the most difficult Project Manager's task of any project I know and throughout he has been wholly supportive of our requirements - even when I kept changing them!, and he and his team have fought our case so well that I have every confidence that the LPD(R) will 'work' in five years time. They haven't finished yet though, there is much work ahead - I shall be gone. Thank you Lionel for your support.

Another emotive topic of mine is Training. I believe we must pay more attention to it. We have the best men we have ever had, but training, in my view, is getting worse - Sorry 'C' School - But I visit many ships and I see CRSs in CVSGs who do not know their systems, or even what kit they have on board and RSs in Frigates who do not know the full capabilities of their systems. We are now moving to even more complex systems, with far fewer men, and I have fears that unless we do better, there will be big problems ahead with future systems. The Chief Software Engineer for BAeSema actually told me a couple of weeks ago that the Security Officer in the LPD(R) will need a degree in Computer Science, and the CRS, RS and LROs managing the communications system must really know how to manage the very powerful facilities they will have available to them. This problem will of course apply to other computer based systems, particularly the Command Support System.

As an ex Radio Communications Instructor, I admit that I am biased, but I believe this is one aspect of communications which has deteriorated over the past twenty years. Was it about twenty years ago that we passed the responsibility for Training Planning to the 'Schoolies' (Instructor Branch)? I think it was about then that they invented the Nine Part Documentation.

End of Lecture

I have gone on again. I will conclude with another thank you to all, and to the Wardroom Staff here for a superb supper. I have enjoyed my near half century in the navy. It has been the people that matter, particularly you who have honoured me tonight and I will always have happy memories of places and people.

Everyone asks me what I am going to do now. Like the American General when asked by press reporters why his troops were retiring after they had been scattered by a North Korean advance. He said, "American soldiers never retire, they just advance in another direction". I will try to do just that.

They say that to make your fortune a young man should go west - so I am going to California for a holiday so may start a new career out there. What do they do in Hollywood ? Failing that I hope to see you all at the Signal Officer's Reunion in July.

Just one story. It is an old one but it is true !

The Admiral was inspecting the wards at Haslar hospital when he saw a man in the end bed rubbing his elbow and groaning loudly. He asked the Sister what was wrong with him. The Sister explained that he had just had a very painful operation for piles. "But why is he rubbing his elbow?" asked the Admiral. "Well", said the Sister. "He is a Weapon Engineering Officer - He can't tell his ass from his elbow"!

One more ?

Another true story

A Naval Officer, I think he was an SD, while ashore in Gibraltar, went to the Rock Hotel and had a few whiskies, after which he went to the dinner dance. He espied an attractive figure across the dance floor, splendidly dressed in blue and purple and he went over and asked for a dance. He was politely refused and when he inquired why he was told there were three very good reasons;

1. *He was drunk.*
2. *The band was playing the Spanish National Anthem.*
3. *He was talking to the Bishop of Malta*

GOD BLESS AND THANK YOU ALL

I must apologise to the reader for the technical content of the above speeches inasmuch that they were aimed at fellow communications officers and some of the terms used and the nuances implied may not be readily understood by those with a non naval background. The reader will however gain an impression of my views and character during these last days in the navy.

I am proud to recall that I wrote the above words a couple of weeks before I was dined out and during a very busy time for me. Although I made notes of key points on a card to use during my speeches, on the evenings in question I did not once refer to my notes. My colleagues noting this were much impressed and my response to them was ***"I am not over the hill yet even if I am retiring!"***.

PART THREE

RETIREMENT - AND REFLECTIONS

CHAPTER TWENTY SEVEN

RETIREMENT - AT HOME (1995 TO NOW)

You can rise when you want,
Do as you please,
Work in the garden,
Or just sit at ease.
Your options are many,
Everyday will inspire,
For a new life begins
On the day you retire.

Phyllis Ellison (1994)

The first weeks of retirement seemed strange and I could not get out of the habit of rising by 6.30 a.m. and of the work ethic of **'It must be done now'**. I did much work in my garden, in my daughter's garden, in my son's garden and most of all in my sister's garden at Verwood in Dorset.

Her husband, Fred, had died in 1990 and I have been keeping her very large garden up to date ever since, even whilst working. I decorated at home, decorated at my son's house and generally kept myself busy. As a diabetic I have been advised to get plenty of exercise, so on any day that I have not been working over much I go for a walk. I walk for two or three miles every day and every now and then make it a four mile walk. I enjoy walking and have a 'thumbstick' with which I stride the Solent shoreline, the countryside and the streets of Fareham. I cut and made the stick myself from a yew sapling. What very few people realise is that during my walks I recite to myself, and to my walking stick, the ritual which I have to learn for my considerable Masonic duties. I expect some say *"Who is that old chap with a funny walking stick going along talking to himself?"* More of this aspect of my life later.

One last aspect of work. In April 1996, a year after my retirement, I was rung up by an ex colleague to ask if I would like a job for 6 months teaching radio theory at the engineering establishment HMS COLLINGWOOD. He said he thought I might be bored in retirement! I thanked him very much for thinking of me but said that I was far too busy to take a job and that in any case I would be 66 years of age in a few days and there must be some younger persons qualified to do the job. (I note in the local newspaper as I write this today, 4th January 1997, that the job is still being advertised!) The navy has lost so many experienced men that I fear that much past excellence is being lost. But perhaps this has been said many times by my predecessors!

We decided to have a retirement holiday and booked up a two week tour of California, Nevada and Arizona.

This was super and my wife and I thoroughly enjoyed it but were both glad to get home again. We love home and although we have the occasional holiday, we went to Cyprus with friends in 1996, also to Belgium for a few days, but we are always glad to get home again. My own preference is for short three or four day breaks rather than a week or more away.

I have still kept in touch with my old naval colleagues and they invite me to reunions and social get-togethers quite frequently. It is nice to see them and yarn about old times, but I would not like to go back to work now. As I tell everyone; *"I am too busy"!*

This book is naturally taking up much of my time and the research of my family history has been most enjoyable and enlightening.

We enjoy going out for pub lunches, sometimes on our own and sometimes with friends and have discovered many super country pubs. We often say *"We will go there again one day",* but seldom do as there are so many new places to explore.

The highlight of this year, 1997, was a visit to Ontario, Canada . My wife, our son David and myself went to Toronto on 3rd May. We spent four tourist type days in Toronto seeing the sights and two days at Niagara. Then we hired a car and went to an hotel in Aurora which is a township about thirty miles north of Toronto city.

Samuel David Foote of Aurora, Ontario, meeting and greeting the author, his second cousin Leonard George Foot, on 10th May 1997.

My Canadian cousins. The Foot/Foote/Cain family gathering of cousins in Aurora, Ontario on 10th May 1997
From Left to Right (seated): Joyce Cain, Audrey Foot, Mary Foote, Marie Foote (wife of Bruce), Myrtle Foote (widow of Walter, Sam's brother). Back Row: Edward Everett Peters Cain, Keith Foote son of Sam), Leonard George Foot, David George Foot, Samuel David Foote, Joel Foote, Robert Foote, Bruce Foote.

There we met for the first time, my second cousin Samuel Foote who had gathered in his apartment as many Foot/Foote relatives as he could and we all had a family reunion. It was a lovely gathering and I found all my cousins to be delightful people and all most interested in the work I was doing and in their Dorsetshire ancestry in general.

In addition to the 'get together', as several members had done research into the family history, they willingly supplied me with much information, some of it was new to me and some of which helped me to confirm the work which I had already done. I was delighted to be given many photographs of my ancestors plus many anecdotes and snippets of information, particularly about my own grandparents and great grandparents which I have now included in Part One. I even discovered that in 1902 when my father was 14 years old, he was away at boarding school! - and I had always suspected that he never went to school at all!

To round off the visit, Sam Foote took us on a tour of the farms on which our common ancestors settled from about 1835. We saw the remains of some old farm houses and many of the barns which were all constructed in a similar manner which was then, and still is, the optimum way of sheltering the cattle and storing the fodder.

It was great to visualise the forested countryside as it was over one hundred and fifty years ago and to imagine how my great grandparents and granduncles worked so hard to clear the trees and scrub and cultivate the land so as to make a living in what was then a remote area with only a few tracks leading down to the port of Toronto which is on Lake Ontario.

My son, David George Foot standing at the entrance to a barn similar to that on his great, great grandfather's farm. (This was at one of his great granduncles' farms). Note the wood on the supports and ladder was not machine turned but shaped with an adze.

In many cases the farmsteads are still intact and appear to be owned by quite prosperous farmers. In others, the urban spread from Toronto has caused houses, industrial units and golf courses to replace the farms in that once peaceful countryside.

Sam also took us on a tour of the townships of Uxbridge, Whitchurch, Newmarket, Stouffeville and many others. In each of which we stopped at the cemetery and he showed us the graves of many of our Foot, Foote and Cain ancestors. They are all there and still beautifully kept. My great, grandfather Samuel and his wife Elizabeth, plus nearly every child and relation which they and the other cousins who emigrated in the 1830s had throughout the last century and well into this. I took photographs of them all.

We visited second cousin Sam's son, Keith Foote who has a farm near a town called Orillia, some 100 miles north of Toronto. There he breeds horses and has many other business interests. The delightful thing to me was that he has named the farm *'Pallington Farm'*, after that of my father's, grandfather's and great grandfather's at Tincleton in Dorsetshire. I was also told that another cousin has a farm named *'Thirnwood Farm'*, named after the *'Thirnwood'* farm at Mappowder, Dorset, which was also the home of my Foot and Bennett ancestors

An amusing incident occurred on the morning we were due to fly home. Joel Foote, a cousin had promised my son David a pair of moose horns and he arrived at our hotel at 0620 in the morning to deliver them. David came into our room at about 0630 saying *"I shall never get these in my case!"* They were over four feet across and a good twenty inches high. My response was that was his problem, sort it out. David went over to a convenience store across the road, bought about $30 Can. worth of bubble wrap and sellotape, came back to the hotel and bandaged them up so much that the 'package' was then twice the size. We just managed to get them into the back seat of the car to drive to the airport, David was on tenterhooks wondering whether they would take them on the plane. They did, as fragile luggage, and they made the flight home safely. We had a similar problem in the taxi from Gatwick airport to home. We sat in the back seat with the horns across our knees for the sixty mile journey.

I felt *'at home'* in Ontario. After all it was the home of my great grandfather and grandfather and I am sure that I will return to explore and find out even more about my cousins one day.

Whilst studying a map of Ontario I spotted a place named *'Foot's Bay'*, when I looked it up I found the following description:

"Foot's Bay is sited on the west side of Lake Joseph in the municipal township of Muskoka Lakes, district Municipality of Muskoka, 33 km south east of Parry Sound, this place was named 'Footes Bay' in 1890 after William Edward Foot, who had settled there in 1871. Its post office was called Staney Brae in 1903, but was renamed Foote's Bay in 1912. It was officially spelled that way until 1975, when it was changed to reflect the founder's name."

I want to believe that the above William Edward Foot was one of my great grandfather's children, that is. one of my granduncles, as both William Foot and Edward Foot would have been about 30 years old in 1871 and could have explored that area. Alternatively he could have been a descendant of one of the other cousins who emigrated in the 1830s. I am unable to confirm this and cousin Sam is of the opinion it was not one of us, but may have been a Foot of Irish descent. What a pity!

On Friday 16th May we said our farewells to Sam and his wife and to Anita Johnstone who also helped to look after us during our stay. She has recently had a baby daughter named Lydia and is the wife of Robert who is my third cousin once removed. Her daughter is a tenth generation of our clan which is therefore assured to continue well into the middle of the 21st century. My own grand daughter, Charlotte Louise Abery, is also of the tenth generation as is Richard Foot's son, Robert Mark and, I am sure, many others both in Britain and in Canada.

My priority task now is to update my book with all the information given to me by my cousins and then get it in print.

CHAPTER TWENTY EIGHT

REFLECTIONS

THE EFFECT OF MY BACKGROUND ON MY OWN CHARACTER AND ACTIONS THROUGH LIFE

"Those who obey their conscience are of my religion and I am of the religion of all those who are brave and good"

Henry IV of France

This chapter is going to be the most difficult for me to write as it is intended to describe me as I think I now am and this may not be as others see me. I have no doubt that my wife, my children and my sisters and my colleagues will disagree with some aspects. Anyway here goes.

My family moved 18 times between 1922 and mother's death in 1979. All the moves which I can remember were worrying and unsettling times, both for reasons of starting a new school and also of having to make new friends. This has influenced my life inasmuch that when I could afford to buy a house for my family in 1960 I determined I would never move again. Thirty six years later I am still in the same house, albeit it is not a very imposing one and I could probably, and still could, have afforded better, but, circumstances permitting, I hope to die in it.

The above paragraph may be seen to reflect a little stubbornness. This must be true and I have no doubt I inherited this from my father, and he from his ancestors. I still retain the principle of always trying to tell the truth, without of course telling the truth to the extent that one hurts others' feelings.

When writing about my stubbornness and that of my ancestors, I am reminded of Rudyard Kipling's lines in which a Norman baron advises his son on how to handle the Englishman's Saxon ancestors:

"When he stands like an ox in the furrow
With his sullen eyes set on your own.
And grumbles, 'This isn't fair dealing'.
My son leave the Saxon alone".

Having said this, although myself and my ancestors are generally fair haired and blue eyed, I cannot really be sure whether we are descended from Saxons or came over with the Normans.

Religion. I was brought up to believe in God and as a member of the Church of England and went regularly to church with my mother and sisters as a child. My father only attended church once a year, for the Harvest Festival service. On joining the Royal Navy I continued to go to church and was confirmed whilst at HMS GANGES. During the 1950s, 1960s and 1970s I continued to attend church as regularly as I could together with my wife and family.

However, by the end of the 1970s and early 1980s, I became disillusioned with the Church of England for what appeared to me to be their activities in creating trouble and supporting unrest in African countries, in particular with their blind policy of support for rights for the blacks to the detriment of all other considerations. Similarly in England, the Church was ever critical of the elected Government of the land and condemned the government for not giving more aid to Black Africa and to the poor and needy. I noted the Church did not spend much of its own resources in these areas. This coupled with the Church's support for homosexuals, the proliferation of cases where church officials were found to be either homosexual or perverted caused me to stop attending church on a regular basis. I still do go to church on special occasions such as harvest festivals, weddings, christenings and funerals.

I believe that if I now lived in the country, in a small village where the church was the centre of the community, as I did when I was growing up and as my parents and as my ancestors did throughout their lives, then I would still be attending church regularly. Perhaps, like my ancestors, I would have become a Church Warden! But church in town is an impersonal place and does not engender the same sense of belonging.

This is not to mean that I no longer believe in God, I do, it is merely that I no longer wish to be associated with an organisation which I deem to be corrupt at many levels and which does not seem to be over interested in putting its own house in order but is still prepared to criticise the Government and other very worthy organisations which are generally doing their best to do the right thing.

By pure chance in the mid 1980s I found an organisation, or society, which gave me a comradeship, friendship and loyalty which much better suited my ideals and gave me the opportunity to practice that need to help others which is within us all. Additionally it has largely replaced and provided me with a continuity of the cameradie and friendships which I had in the Royal Navy, of which many leaving the service very much miss when in retirement.

It is Freemasonry. Freemasonry is not a religion, although freemasons are expected to believe in a God or in a Supreme Being. It accepts all races and creeds, from Christian to Moslem, Buddhism or whatever. Freemasons never talk about religion or politics during Masonic meetings, in fact both are discouraged as a topics of discussion at all times during our assemblies.

The ideals of Freemasonry are: …'*Brotherly Love, Relief and Truth…*' and Freemasons are expected to be '*…just, upright and true men of mature age, sound judgement and strict morals…*'. Very considerable sums of money are raised by the Freemasons and given to both Masonic charities and to non Masonic charities, the Samaritans in particular benefit very largely from donations from freemasons. Much money is also donated to hospices for both the elderly and for children. The charity work is done quietly without much publicity and few people realise just how much good is done by freemasons. Unfortunately as our rites and ceremonies are private this upsets the media, the established church, press and many organisations who want to know more about us and we therefore tend to get a bad press. Much is often made of *'the secrets of Freemasonry'* but really there are none.

Those who criticise Freemasonry are of the same mind and usually the same people who want to destroy the Monarchy, to destroy the House of Lords, to discontinue Public and Grammar Schools and generally destroy excellence in life. It is very sad. Every element of society has the occasional *'bad egg'* but I am very confident that there are far, far less *'bad eggs'* in Freemasonry than in any other group of persons. Whether they be a group of Politicians, Clergy, Doctors, Lawyers, members of a Rotary or Golf Club, or Choral Society or whoever. Any freemason who has been found guilty of a crime in the courts or who commits a misdemeanour relating to his Masonic duties is invited to leave very quickly. This is not done by many of the above named groups as we all are well aware.

When one considers that many of the great men of history were freemasons it cannot be that bad: George Washington, (and indeed a very goodly number of US Presidents since that time, including Presidents Roosevelt and Trueman), Davy Crockett, Sir Winston Churchill, King Edward VII, King Edward VIII, King George V, King George VI and many others. Princes and poets have long been among our number. Our present leader is HRH The Duke of Kent and our numbers are made up of many notable people from all walks of life. Included in our numbers are Judges, and many members of the legal profession, doctors and theatrical personalities as well as policemen, firemen, servicemen, engineers and postmen. Many senior churchmen were once freemasons and there are still quite a few but not so many now due to pressure from above. And I don't mean from God! All are welcome provided they meet and embrace our ideals of believing in a Supreme Being of whatever creed and are prepared to support and give to charitable causes.

I have found that Freemasonry is unsurpassed in character forming and in giving confidence to those who, perhaps unlike myself, did not have the benefit of many years of training in the Royal Navy. I only wish I had become a freemason at the age of 26 and not at the age of 56. I have seen many others; mature men who have never had the opportunity to speak in front of others, who have been virtually tongue tied when first asked to make a small speech or recite a piece of ritual. Within a very short time these persons develop a confidence and show qualities which they were wholly unaware they had in them.

The Government set up a House of Commons Home Affairs Select Committee in 1994/5 to inquire into Freemasonry in the Police and the Judiciary.

Here are some extracts of evidence given to the committee:

The Lord Chancellor: stated that: *"he knew of no evidence of 'any substantial kind' that Freemasonry had any adverse effect on the conduct of magistrates or judges".*

The Magistrates Association: declared that: *"they saw no problem with Masonic involvement in magistracy. They did not believe that Freemasonry had a malign influence".*

The Association of Police Officers: admitted that: *"they had no evidence of any impropriety resulting from Masonic influence".*

The Police Superintendents Association: stated that *"they had no evidence that Freemasonry caused any problems in the police force".*

The Police Federation: stated that *"they had no evidence that Freemasonry was an undesirable activity, or that it led to any conflict of obligations for a Masonic police officer."*

The Law Society: *"could recall no occasions of Masonic influence on either the judiciary or cn a solicitor."*

The Bar Council: *"had no evidence that there was any substantial problem in respect of Freemasonry and in the administration of justice."*

Here are some of the **conclusions** which the committee reached:

"We have given careful consideration to each of submissions received and note that many of them are devoid of real evidence, or are anecdotal in nature, or where there is evidence it has been largely circumstantial".

"We have received no evidence to suggest that we should doubt that the only element of freemasonry that is intrinsically secret is the 'formal means of proving that someone is a freemason'."

"We do not believe that there is anything sinister about freemasonry, properly observed, and are confident that freemasonry itself does not encourage malpractice."

In spite of the above statements and many others in a similar vein, the amended conclusion adopted by the Home Affairs Committee was disappointing to us freemasons. It reads as follows:

"It is obvious that there is a great deal of unjustified paranoia about freemasonry and we have no wish to add to it. We believe that there would be practical difficulties in requiring a register of freemasons in all areas of the Criminal Justice system, but it would certainly be possible to establish one. We also note that the Prime Minister himself has said that he was in favour of a requirement for public officials to declare whether they are freemasons or not and that the Shadow Home Secretary believes that membership of the freemasons should be a declarable and registrable interest".

"We note the claim by United Grand Lodge that freemasons are not a secret society but a society with secrets. We believe, however, that this distinction is lost on most non-masons. The solution is not bans or proscriptions or any form of intolerance. We acknowledge that a lot of honest people derive innocent social pleasure from membership of freemasonry and we have no wish to deprive them of that pleasure. The solution is disclosure. We recommend that police officers, magistrates, judges and crown prosecutors should be required to register membership of any secret society and that the record should be available publicly".

As I mentioned earlier, this conclusion was disappointing to us freemasons as we do not believe or accept that we are a secret society and therefore the conclusion was flawed. Will members of Round Table, Lions International, The Ancient Order of Foresters or Rotary be similarly investigated and also be obliged to declare their memberships? I will let better men than I argue over this matter. I am content that all masons I know are genuine and upright men from whom I derive loyalty and friendship.

My years of service in the Royal Navy have taught me to believe very strongly in law and order and proper punishment for those who commit crimes. As previously recounted in Chapter Fourteen, I learnt from my own experiences that if minor offences are swiftly and properly punished, then more serious crimes are less likely to follow. I have no time for those who say that petty thieving is not a crime and should be overlooked, or for those who consider that 'non violent' crime such as shop lifting, burglary or larceny need not be punished with a custodial sentence. Any person who has had their home violated by burglary will, I am sure, agree with me that they have had violence committed against them. I believe the death penalty should be re-introduced, together with a method of ensuring it is carried out swiftly and without being allowed to be dragged out by interminable appeals as happens in the United States of America.

I read recently that the average time actually spent in prison by men who were sentenced to 'life' imprisonment in Britain is 9·5 years, and for women the figure is 7·8 years. This is not justice. My Member of Parliament, Sir Peter Lloyd, unfortunately does not support the death penalty and has, in my own opinion, also shown himself to be 'soft' on the need to expel illegal immigrants. For this reason I wrote to him in 1996 and informed him that, although I am a Conservative and would not vote for the Labour or Liberal candidates, neither would I vote for him or the then present government of John Major, which I believed to be indecisive and too liberal with promises which were not kept.

Whilst writing the above words I recalled the words of my father, who was also a Tory. His reaction to lawbreakers was *"Shoot the buggers"*. It would appear that his uneducated reaction of 50 or 60 years ago is little different from my own 'educated?' reaction of today!

The love of my life always has and always will be my family. My retirement years are now wholly taken up with helping them and I enjoy every moment of it. I am always busy and am forever pottering about in my own garden, and in my daughter's and my sister's gardens. I love the countryside and am sad to see so much beautiful countryside being taken up by roads and houses. I do not understand why the government continues to permit the influx of African and Asian immigration into our lovely country? What is their motive? We are over populated already and we cannot solve the problems of the world.

I believe that different races and cultures should respect each other, I do not believe white is better than yellow, or yellow is better than brown or black, merely that we are *different* and all of us have different strengths and weaknesses. I am convinced that the present policy of the government to force different cultures to integrate will eventually lead to dreadful trouble. The present situation in Bosnia, Croatia and Serbia is a good example of the trouble one gets in when different cultures or religions are forced together.

Do the above reflections make me a racist? What is a racist? If it is one who is proud to be English, (albeit part Canadian!), proud of one's country, its history and its achievements, proud of my own achievements and proud of the beautiful countryside, particularly in the areas of Dorset where I and my ancestors lived and grew up, then I must be a racist. This is a great sadness to me as I hold no animosity to any race, religion or culture. Perhaps I am a Nationalist ? But the *'do good'* Liberals will interpret this as my having Fascist tendencies. Why are Scottish Nationalists and Welsh Nationalists treated with respect and given a forum to express their views while English Nationalists are derided for their aspirations?

What will become of our country? I suspect the problems now occurring in Bosnia, caused by the Christians trying, far too late, to halt the flood of Mohammadism, will be a microcosm of the problems we in England shall face in 30 or 40 years hence. I thank God that I shall not be here to witness the chaos for which my generation has laid the foundations.

Another bee in my bonnet is the way the media manipulates public thinking and thereby our governments. A recent case of media *'hype'* was after the dreadful massacre of the children at Dunblane in Scotland. The media supported the vociferous minority groups in calling for a ban on all hand guns of whatever kind, the Labour and Liberal parties naturally climbed on the bandwagon and over reacted as always. The consequence was that our weak government succumbed and banned all but small calibre handguns. I am sure that passing laws in haste will not solve such problems and that even if the law had been in place before the Dunblane shooting, it would not have prevented the tragedy.

I believe the media, particularly the BBC, has much to answer for in respect to creating hype over minor issues and causing them to be treated totally out of proportion to their true worth. Time and time again the vociferous minorities, and indeed lawbreakers, are searched out and paraded and lauded on Television with a consequence that they win their case or cause, often to the detriment of the quality of life of the silent majority.

The above is how I see myself today in July 1997. Perhaps my views will change and mellow before I die. Perhaps the reader may not agree with my views. They are views which have been formed by my own background and experiences. I regret they do not follow those of the successive governments or the *Liberal Establishment*, but of one thing I am very sure; they are views also held by many, many of my friends, acquaintances and former colleagues in the Royal Navy. My concern is that if so many people share these opinions, why is there no significant movement which has the courage to state them and is willing to address them?

I know I cannot solve the problems of the world, but I will continue to support my family, friends and worthy causes to the best of my ability and I hope this record will be of interest to my descendants and to others in generations to come.

CHAPTER TWENTY NINE
CONCLUSION
(1997)

Memories, images, and precious thoughts,
That shall not die and cannot be destroyed.

William Wordsworth (1770 - 1850)

I am told that all good books should have a conclusion. Well this the end of **my** story. If I continue I shall be accused of 'waffling'. I doubt if anything too exciting is going to happen to me from now on as I am very happily retired and now 67 years old. I expect it will take me some time to get these words into a fit state to publish. Will a publisher produce my book for me? Will I make a fortune? I doubt it as the market will be too limited, therefore I will have to do it all myself. I shall therefore apply myself to this task and become my own 'Publisher' and if you the reader get to read this far then you will know that I have succeeded. I have no illusions that I have written a literary best seller. I do not really want to make a profit, but neither can I afford to spend too much money on producing copies so I shall have to find a compromise somehow.

If I am bored in 1998 and this book is successful, will I try to do more research into my family history? Will I try to trace my maternal family tree? (That task looks much too difficult!). Shall I try to trace the Australian connections? Will I find more **FOOTSTEPS**? Will I leave more **FOOTSTEPS**? I do not know, but I know that I must do something, or at least try, as I am not made of the stuff to sit about doing nothing.

The satisfaction to me is that I shall leave behind me a record of my ancestors, my family and an account of my own life and opinions for others to read in the 21st century.

I leave it to you, dear reader, to judge the character of my ancestors and that of myself, for better or for worse.

THE END ?

APPENDIX 1
A SYNOPSIS OF IMPORTANT DATES
"THROUGH TEN GENERATIONS"

I know that I should include an Index to this book but I find it too difficult to compile, and do not really think it necessary. I have therefore included a comprehensive Contents of Chapters, an Index of Photographs and this Appendix instead.

The following dates summarise important events in history related to **FOOTSTEPS** and those dates of significance through the ten generations of my family history. The reader may find them a helpful reference.

DATE	EVENT
1680 (c.)	My great, great, great, great, great grandfather William Foot born.
1713 or 1717	My great, great, great, great grandfather William born 19th October.
1727	King George I died.

DATE	EVENT
1747	My great, great, great grandfather John born 17th March.
1749	Quebec taken by the British.
1751	My great, great, great grandfather George Foot born 1st August.
1760	King George II died.
1773	The 'Boston Tea Party'.
1775	My great great grandfather Samuel born 4th September.
1776	Declaration of Independence - USA.
1777	My great great grandfather Cave Bennett born.
1783	William Pitt, the younger, only 24 years of age, accepted office - Prime Minister for 17 years.
1783	Boundaries of Canada fixed.
1784	My great, great grandmother, Betty Foot born.
1789	Start of the French Revolution.
1792	The beginning of Parliamentary government in Canada.
1800	August 2nd Act of Union. The Union Jack came into being.
1803	My great grandfather Samuel born 6th November.
1805	The Battle of Trafalgar.
1806	William Pitt died.
1812	My great grandmother Elizabeth Bennett born.
1815	The Battle of Waterloo.
1820	George III died.
1820	Failure of crops in Ireland brought many immigrants to Canada.
1830s	My great grandfather Samuel together with several cousins emigrated to Canada.

DATE	EVENT
1830	King George IV died.
1833	Abolition of Slavery.
1833	Susannah Hooper, **beloved** wife of George Bennett died in Canada, age 31.
1834	The Tolpuddle Martyrs deported to Australia.
1836	The first railroad in Canada was opened between La Prairie and St John's.
1837	William IV died. Princess Victoria acceded to the throne.
1837	Rebellion in Canada. Elizabeth Bennett was entrusted with important documents and jewellery belonging to the Governor of Upper Canada - Sir Francis Bond Head.
1838	Ships operated entirely by steam crossed the Atlantic carrying coal enough for the entire journey.
1839	The Tolpuddle Martyrs settled in Ontario.
1839	My great grandfather Samuel married his cousin Elizabeth Bennett in Toronto.
1839	Penny postage introduced all over the United Kingdom.
1840	Queen Victoria married her cousin Prince Albert of Saxe-Coberg.
1843	My grandfather George Leonard Foot born in Ontario 5th July.
1845	Harvest failure in England and Ireland.
1845	Samuel Foot had a sale and moved from the 4th concession to the 6th concession near the township of Whitchurch, Ontario.
1846	My granduncle, Walter James Foote born 22nd August.
1847	My paternal grandmother Emily Bennett born.
1849	Gold discovered in California.

DATE	EVENT
1851	Gold discovered in Australia.
1851	Emigrants poured into the colonies.
1851	The year of the Great Exhibition in London planned by Prince Albert.
1854	The Charge of the Light Brigade, October 25th.
1857	My maternal grandmother Emily Parks born 14th November.
1857	My maternal grandfather Joseph Thorne born.
1858	Ottawa chosen by Queen Victoria as the site of Canadian Parliament.
1858	Decimal currency introduced in Canada.
1860	Betty, wife of Cave Bennett died.
1861 to 1865	Civil war in the United States between the northern and southern states.
1866	Reciprocity Treaty expired and the U.SA. refused to renew it. The Fenian Raids.
1867	The British North American Act passed and came into force. Confederation. The Dominion of Canada. The name chosen from the bible - *"He shall have dominion from sea to sea"*.
1867	My great great grandfather Cave Bennett died.
1868	My great grandfather John Bennett took over the tenancy of Pallington Farm.
1869	The Red River rebellion.
1876 (approx.)	My grandfather, George Leonard Foot took passage on a cattle boat from Ontario to England. He stayed with his uncle, John Bennett at Pallington Farm.
1877	George Leonard married Emily Bennett 26th June.
1877	George Leonard returned to Canada with his new wife.

DATE	EVENT
1879	Joseph Thorne married Emily Parks.
1879	My great grandfather Samuel Foot died.
1880	My uncle Garnet born to George Leonard and Emily in Ontario.
1880	Reginald Ernest Bennett born.
1880	My Aunt Amelia (Millie) born.
1882	My grandfather George Leonard Foot and his wife Emily and son Garnet returned to England because Emily was homesick for her parents and her mother Sarah, was very ill.
1882	My grandmother Sarah Bennett died 9th October.
1883	Leonard Bruce Foot (Uncle Bruce) born 17th February.
1884	My great grandmother Elizabeth died.
1884	George Leonard Foot took over the tenancy of Pallington Farm.
1885	My Aunt Ciss (Sarah Ann Cordelia) born.
1885	The North West Rebellion.
1886	Canadian Pacific railroad completed.
1887	My Aunt Annie born.
1887	My father. George Arthur Foot born 3rd September at Pallington.
1889	My uncle, George Thorne born.
1889	Richard Wallace Foot (Uncle Wallace) born 3rd May.
1890	My great grandfather John Bennett died.
1891	Barwell Bennett youngest, brother of my great grandmother, Elizabeth died and left money to nephews and nieces all over the world.

DATE	EVENT
1892	My mother, Alice Thorne, born 27th July.
1892	My granduncle, Walter James Foote came to England to visit relatives and collect for the Canadian nephews and nieces their share of the 'fortune' left by Barwell Bennett.
1893	Granduncle Walter Foot died.
1895	George Leonard Foot won a silver cup for the best acreage of swedes.
1897	Queen Victoria's Diamond Jubilee.
1899	Start of the Boer War.
1901	Queen Victoria died.
1902	My granduncle, Walter James Foote J.P. made his second visit to England.
1902	My paternal Grandfather George Leonard Foot died.
1902	End of the Boer War.
1903	Aunt Amelia married.
1904	Uncle George joined the Royal Navy.
1908	Aunt Amelia died.
1910	Edward VII died.
1914	Start of World War I.
1914	My second cousin Samuel D. Foote born in Ontario on 7th October.
1918	End of World War 1.
1919	Uncle George married Aunt Dora on 2nd October.
1921	My father George Arthur Foot took the tenancy of Northfield Farm at Cheselbourne.
1921	Maternal grandfather Joseph Thorne died.
1922	January 23rd. My mother and father were married by special licence in St. George's Church, Dorchester.
1924	My sister Phyllis born 13th September.

DATE	EVENT
1925	Walter James Foote J.P. made his third visit to England at the age of 80.
1926	My family moved to Chapel Farm at Farnham near Sixpenny Handley, Dorset.
1926	Father and his brother, my Uncle Garnet, went into a farming partnership.
1926	My sister Doris Alice born 27th May.
1927	Lindbergh flies the Atlantic alone.
1928	My granduncle Walter James Foote died in Ontario.
1929	Uncle Garnet emigrated to Canada.
1930	I was born 23rd April.
1930	My twin sister, Beryl Grace Foot died, 2nd May.
1930	Paternal grandmother Emily died 28th May.
1933	Family moved to East Luccombe Farm, Milton Abbas.
1936	King George V died. Accession of Edward VIII. Abdication of Edward VIII Accession of George VI.
1936	Richard Bruce Foot born 3rd June.
1937	Day trip to Weymouth. I went on board HMS ROYAL OAK.
1937	My family left East Luccombe Farm. Farm sale.
1937	My family moved to Winterbourne Whitchurch.
1938	My family moved to Charlton.
1938	My maternal grandmother Emily's cottage roof fell in on her whilst sleeping.
1938	My family moved to Tarrant Monkton (Field Barn).

DATE	EVENT
1939	My family moved to Manor Farm at Tarrant Monkton.
1939	September 3rd World War II started.
1939	HMS Royal Oak sunk at Scapa Flow, October.
1940	Uncle George rejoined the Royal Navy.
1940	The Fall of France.
1941	I passed my Scholarship and attended Blandford Grammar School.
1939	Start of World War Two on 3rd September.
1942	My family moved to Crichel. I attended Wimborne Grammar School.
1943	Uncle George lost a leg during the bombing at HMS VERNON in Portsmouth.
1943	My family moved to Morgan's Vale in Wiltshire. I attended Bishop Wordsworth's School at Salisbury.
1944	My family moved to Landford in Hampshire.
1944	D-Day 6th June.
1945	My sister Phyllis married Robert William Giblett on 15th August. V.J. Day.
1945	My family moved to Swallowcliffe in Wiltshire.
1946	I left Bishop Wordsworth's School in July.
1946	I joined the Royal Navy as a Boy Seaman on 10th September.
1946	My family moved to Lyndhurst in Hampshire.
1947	My family moved to Fonthill Bishop in Wiltshire.
1947	I joined HMS DUKE OF YORK.
1947	My sister Doris married Frederick William Wearn.

DATE	EVENT
1948	I joined HMS CADIZ.
1948	My family moved to Tisbury in Wiltshire.
1949	My family moved to Wincanton in Somerset.
1949	I joined HMS MERCURY.
1950	Uncle Garnet (J G A Foot) died.
1950	Start of the Korean War.
1950	I joined HMS SCORPION.
1950	My family moved to Yarlington.
1951	My maternal grandmother Emily Thorne (nee Parks) died in January.
1951	I joined HMS MERCURY.
1951	I married Gladys Audrey Oaten on 2nd August.
1952	King George VI died. Accession of Queen Elizabeth II.
1952	I joined HMS HIGHFLYER.
1952	Uncle Bruce died.
1954	Richard Wallace Foot (Uncle Wallace) retired and sold up at Pallington farm.
1954	I joined HMS BOXER.
1955	Our daughter, Linda Jean Foot, born on 3rd May.
1955	I joined HMS GLASGOW.
1956	I joined HMS MERCURY.
1957	I joined HMS AFRIKANDER.
1960	I joined HMS WAKEFUL.
1961	I joined HMS MERCURY.
1962	My second cousin Grace Foote-Powell started compiling a book on the Foot/Foote family history.
1962	June. I received my commission and was promoted to Sub Lieutenant (SD)(X)(C).

DATE	EVENT
1962	My cousin Joan died.
1962	I joined HMS NUBIAN.
1964	I joined HMS MERCURY.
1965	Our son, David George Foot, born on 4th October.
1967	I joined HMS ARGONAUT.
1968	My uncle George Thorne died.
1969	My father died 12th January.
1969	I sailed for the Far East on January 22nd. in HMS ARGONAUT.
1969	April. I joined HMS FORTH.
1969	My mother moved to Wincanton.
1971	I joined HMS MERCURY.
1973	I joined HMS WARRIOR.
1974	I joined HMS MALABAR.
1976	I joined HMS MERCURY.
1977	Our daughter Linda married Martyn Edwin Abery.
1979	My mother Alice Foot died 26th January.
1981	Robert Mark Foot, son of Richard Bruce Foot (my first cousin once removed) born 20th January.
1981	I retired from active service in the Royal Navy. and continued serving as a uniformed Retired Officer.
1982	April. Argentina invades the Falkland Islands.
1982	May. British troops retake the Falkland Islands.
1983	Our granddaughter Charlotte Louise Abery, born on 8th January. Tenth generation.
1990	My first cousin Peter Foot died in January.

DATE	EVENT
1991	Audrey and I celebrated our Ruby Wedding anniversary.
1990	The Gulf War.
1995	I retired as a Retired Officer from the Royal Navy on 23rd April.
1996	February. I started to write this story.
1996	I made first contact with and met Ann Foot, the wife of my late first cousin Peter Foot, in July.
1996	I made first contact with and met my first cousin once removed, Richard Foot in December.
1997	I made contact with and visited Mary Bertram (nee Bennett) in March.
1997	Lydia Johnstone born 28th March. The latest addition to the Canadian Foote clan and of the tenth generation. She is my second cousin 3 times removed.
1997	I visited my second cousin Samuel D. Foote in Aurora, Ontario in May..
1997	June. I met my first cousin Pamela Spark (nee Foot) daughter of Uncle Bruce.
1997	August. **'*FOOTSTEPS*'** goes to print

APPENDIX 2

COUNTRIES WHICH I HAVE VISITED DURING MY NAVAL CAREER

Whilst musing over this final part of my life story I came recall all the countries which I have had the good fortune to visit during my naval career. These I have listed below as the experiences of these visits must of necessity have influenced me with regard to my present views and general outlook on life. I doubt if anyone joining the Royal Navy today will get the opportunity of visiting so many countries during their career.

Abu Dhabi	Ethiopia
Anguila	France
Australia	Gan
Bahrain	Germany
Barbados	Gibraltar
Barbuda	Holland
Belgium	Hong Kong
Belize	India
Bermuda	Iran
Ceylon (Sri Lanka)	Israel
Cyprus	Jamaica
Denmark	Jordan
Egypt	Kenya

Kuwait	South Africa
Lebanon	Spain
Leeward Islands	Sweden
Libya	Syria
Malaysia	Tanzania
Malta	Thailand
Morocco	Tobago
Norway	Trinidad
Oman	Trucial Oman Emirates
Pakistan	Tunisia
Portugal	United States of America
Sierra Leone	Virgin Islands (various)
Singapore	Windward Islands
Somalia	Yemen

To the above of course must be added Canada which I visited in search of my Canadian cousins in May 1997.

Two important European countries which I have never visited are Italy and mainland Greece. I will try to put this right over the next few years.

Map extract on dust jacket
© Ordnance Survey
Reproduced by kind permission of
Ordnance Survey, Southampton